About the author

ROBERT G. WILLIAMS is Voehringer Professor of Economics at Guilford College, where he has taught courses on globalization, finance, trade, and development for more than twenty years. With a B.A. in economics from Princeton University in 1971, he received a Ph.D. in economics from Stanford University in 1978, serving an interim period as research economist at the Brookings Institution from 1973 to 1975. Author of *Export Agriculture and the Crisis in Central America* (UNC Press, 1986) and *Coffee and the Rise of National Governments in Central America* (UNC Press, 1994), in 1995 Williams turned his attention to world currency markets, taking with him the research methods of ethnography, history, economics, geography, and political economy that made his Central America scholarship accessible, widely read, and highly regarded by professionals. *The Money Changers* makes extensive use of ethnographic footage taken in interviews with currency market participants from 1996 to 2005, a period of rapid change in world financial markets.

The Money Changers

A guided tour through global currency markets

ROBERT G. WILLIAMS

HONG KONG UNIVERSITY PRESS
Hong Kong

FERNWOOD PUBLISHING
Nova Scotia

SIRD
Kuala Lumpur

ZED BOOKS
London & New York

The Money Changers was published in 2006

Published in Mainland China, Hong Kong, Macau, Taiwan and Japan by
Hong Kong University Press, 14/F Hing Wai Centre, 7 Tin Wan Praya Road,
Aberdeen, Hong Kong, hkupress@hku.hk

Published in Canada by Fernwood Publishing Ltd, 8422 St Margaret's Bay Road
(Hwy 3) Site 2a, Box 5, Black Point, Nova Scotia, B0J 1B0

Published in Malaysia by Strategic Information Research Development (SIRD),
No. 11/4E, Petaling Jaya, 46200 Selangor

Published in the rest of the world by Zed Books Ltd, 7 Cynthia Street, London
N1 9JF, UK, and Room 400, 175 Fifth Avenue, New York, NY 10010, USA
www.zedbooks.co.uk

Copyright © Robert G. Williams 2006

Designed and typeset in Monotype Garamond
by illuminati, Grosmont, www.illuminatibooks.co.uk
Cover designed by Andrew Corbett
Printed and bound in Malta by Gutenberg Press Ltd

Distributed in the USA exclusively by Palgrave Macmillan, a division of
St Martin's Press, LLC, 175 Fifth Avenue, New York, NY 10010

A catalogue record for this book is available from the British Library
Library of Congress Cataloging-in-Publication Data available
Library and Archives Canada Cataloguing in Publication

    Williams, Robert G. (Robert Gregory), 1948–
      The money changers : a guided tour through global currency markets / Robert G.
    Williams.
    ISBN 1-55266-200-4
      1. Foreign exchange market. 2. International finance. I. Title.
    HG3851.W54 2006   332.4'5
    C2006-900914-7

ISBN 1-55266-200-4 (Canada)

ISBN 962 209 816 9 (Hong Kong)
ISBN 978 962 209 816 9

ISBN 983 2535 824 (Malaysia)

ISBN 1 84277 694 0 Hb (Zed Books)
ISBN 1 84277 695 9 Pb
ISBN 978 1 84277 694 0 Hb
ISBN 978 1 84277 695 7 Pb

Contents

Acknowledgments

Some of the most significant contributors to this book may not have been adequately acknowledged in the text and endnotes. Reflecting back on the strongest influences on my early thinking about monetary theory and international finance, I acknowledge intellectual debts to several professors in graduate school, especially Duncan Foley, Ronald McKinnon, and Tibor Scitovsky. For more recent influences, I give special thanks to Paul Davidson, whose scholarship on uncertainty and the liquidity preference theory of money and financial markets[1] convinced me to go back and read closely, with fresh eyes, the works of Keynes.[2] For those who have contributed over the years to my appreciation of ethnography, I thank my undergraduate professor, Hildred Geertz, housemates at Stanford University, Shelly and Renato Rosaldo, and colleagues in the field of anthropology, most notably Carol Smith, Jeff Boyer, Philippe Bourgois, and Marc Edelman.

In researching this book, I have been fortunate to have met financial market practitioners who were willing to share with me insights they have gained from years of direct experience and thought. For practitioners who have contributed to breakthroughs in my thinking about global finance, I wish to acknowledge Avinash Persaud, Eugene Rossitch, Jennifer Calari, George Thomas, Graham Bishop, and Franco Passacantando. Among the colleagues and former students in the financial services industry who have made connections for me or given me clarity in their areas of expertise,

I express special thanks to Ed Gross, John Lipskey, Alica Stubnova Sparling, Paul Grube, and Roger Lifson, who contributed importantly at key moments in the discovery process. For setting up the London interviews, I thank Signor Luigi Marini, and for accompanying me in the euro fieldwork, Walter Blass.

I am grateful for the many students and colleagues who have read sections of the manuscript and given me suggestions. I wish to recognize specially Tom Huey, Marna Williams, Vlad Gilevsky and Ellen Yutzy, who paid careful attention to the manuscript and made valuable stylistic critiques. Editors Peter Dougherty and Ken Macleod encouraged me in earlier phases of the project, and Zed editor Robert Molteno's keen interest in the project drove me to take it to completion.

Material support has come from many sources along the way. Guilford College's sabbatical program, faculty development grants, and academic dean's research funds have sustained the research and paid for several field trips to London and New York, where friends have offered the hospitality of their homes.

One final word of thanks goes to my wife and to my son, who encouraged me all along the way but may not have seen as much of me as they would have liked, especially in the project's final stage.

Responsibility for any factual errors in the final text and possible misinterpretations of the evidence belongs to me.

Preface

At almost $2 trillion per day in trades, currency markets vitally connect the world together. Yet few people know what goes on behind the scenes to make them work and why they are prone to instability and bouts of panic. This book is not a technical manual for business professionals or a tract on how to get rich betting on currencies. Rather, it is a guided tour of the places, the machines, the circuitry, and the people involved in moving world money. For the tourist with no background in economics, the mundane act of changing money should take on new meaning. For the curious observer seeking clarity on a dimension of globalization poorly understood by almost everyone, discussions of global finance will be demystified. For the student tired of dull textbooks, this reading should surprise, awaken, and make globalization more comprehensible.

The tour begins with a traveler removing foreign currency from an ATM machine in Istanbul. Back home from the trip, the traveler tries to find answers to basic questions by examining currency issues covered in the newspaper. At the bank where the traveler's account was debited, the head of the foreign exchange department answers some basic questions and introduces the currency traders at work in the trading room. Step by step, the tour proceeds from the simple to the complex and from the periphery of the market to its neural centers in financial hubs like London and New York. Currency traders, market analysts, money managers, and payments systems architects show their workplaces and reveal their day-to-day experiences in this unpredictable and rapidly evolving world.

The tour retraces the actual steps I took in coming to grips with how the world's largest – and perhaps most complex – market really works. Before October 1996, I had never entered a trading room or spoken with a currency trader. For more than two decades I had watched currency markets from the sidelines, in the 1970s as a graduate student in economics with a field of concentration in international trade and finance, and in the 1980s and early 1990s as a professor who taught the subject to undergraduates. It took a direct encounter with currency markets in 1995 to drag me from the sidelines and launch me on the quest to discover the market's inner workings.

From January through May of 1995, I was faculty leader for my college's study abroad program in the Italian Alps. In December 1994, before we left for Europe, news broke of a financial crisis in Mexico, but the US dollar was trading at 1,648 Italian lire, right at the 1,650 lire exchange rate budgeted for the program. At that time, there was no reason to believe that the 'tequila effect,' as analysts later dubbed the aftermath of the peso crisis, would cross the Atlantic and get us. Over the course of the semester, fourteen students and I watched the dollar lose 20 per cent of its value against the German mark, the Austrian schilling, and the Dutch guilder, a hazard encountered when students ventured north on weekends. As program director and the payer of bills, my nightmare was the Italian lira, which gyrated wildly against the dollar.

The banking arrangement was quaint. Instead of wiring funds to a program account in Italy, the business manager handed me several weeks' worth of travelers' checks and four large cashiers' checks in my name, all denominated in dollars. My primary concern was misplacing the checks, but when I arrived at the bank to unload my burden I discovered I had more to worry about. The dollar had slipped below 1,620 lire. As I waited in the lobby to speak with the branch manager, I calculated where expenses could be trimmed without sacrificing the educational mission of the program. The banker, whom I will call Herr Schmidt, seemed delighted to see me and ushered me into his office. 'So,' he began, 'I hear you are an economist,' which in this case was a good thing, because he wanted someone to converse with about the Mexican crisis. 'I see the peso is rising some today with a rumor of a bail-out by your country.' Fortunately, I had read the previous week's London-based *Economist* on the airplane so I wasn't at a complete loss during this first of several debates with Herr Schmidt.

I got around to business by dismantling the wad and spreading its contents on the desk. 'What exchange rate can you give me for these?' I enquired. Herr Schmidt said he would be happy to exchange any amount of travelers' checks at today's rates, but he could not guarantee any particular rate on the cashiers' checks. Sensing my discomfort, Herr Schmidt launched into a routing story I found hard to follow at the time: something like the checks would take ten days to two weeks to 'clear,' at which time they would be exchanged for lire at another bank and the proceeds would be wired into my account, after a transaction fee was deducted. 'But at what exchange rate?' I pressed. He said that was not up to him but rather to the currency markets. The lire I would get would depend on the 'spot rate' whenever the checks cleared.

'But, Herr Schmidt (I pointed out the window) exchange rates are beginning to look like your skyline here. What if the dollar drops to 1,400 lire within the next two weeks?' I confessed that I would be forced to cut out scheduled trips, reduce student allowances, and face a possible rebellion.

Herr Schmidt was amused by the scenario but sympathetic to my case. 'Would it be possible for me,' I began thinking aloud, 'to open a dollar account *and* a lira account at your bank? After the dollar checks clear, I could then change smaller amounts and know what rate I'm getting.' Herr Schmidt began working the idea in his mind. 'This has not been done here... but it might be legal now.' He would look into it and would know by Wednesday.

I endorsed a thousand dollars' worth of travelers' checks for the students' first weekly food stipend. As the teller counted out stacks of five, ten, and twenty thousand lira notes, I pictured in my mind what would happen if this pile of loot – amounting to more than 1.5 million lire – slipped from my clutches on the way down the mountain.

When I returned in two days, Herr Schmidt proudly showed me the legal documents to set up a lira account *and* a dollar account in my name. The dollar was up a bit from Monday, so I endorsed enough travelers' checks to start up the lira account, and I endorsed all of the cashiers' checks for deposit in the dollar account. I asked him if it would be possible to call someone at the bank to change money for me over the telephone. This could save me a hike up the mountain and might be useful later when we would travel to Venice and Florence. Herr Schmidt pulled out a business card and underlined a number. 'You may call me during the week at this number, and I will give you our best rates, but you must change a thousand dollars or more at a time.' We shook on the deal.

The Monday the checks cleared, the dollar had dropped to 1,577 lire. As I changed a minimal amount into lira, Herr Schmidt peeked out of his office. 'Professor Williams,' he pointed to the rates posted on the wall, 'look what would have happened if all your dollars had changed into lira today.' I groaned, 'Yes, we dodged a bullet, but I pray it doesn't keep dropping.'

The dismal forecast of 1,400 did not come true, though the dollar bounced around between the 1,580s and 1,610s for another month, painfully below my budgeted 1,650. This meant cutting out little extras – like group meals at restaurants – that had been recorded in last year's program. This was not a problem, but I worried that if the dollar didn't strengthen, treats advertised in the brochure might have to be removed from the table.

As an economist, I found the most agonizing part was being cut off from my customary sources of market information. The Italian newspapers available at the general store in the village sensationalized how politicians in Italy were moving global markets, while the German accounts I could read lamely using a dictionary for a crutch. If I hiked for forty-five minutes down the mountain to the train station, I could buy the previous week's *Economist*, good stories that were helpful in fielding students' questions and prepping me for encounters with Herr Schmidt. But the news was so old by the time I got it, the information was practically useless in making currency decisions. With feelings of insecurity at first, I had to put aside my formal training in international economics, stop worrying about causes, and just settle for effects. I came to rely almost exclusively on the electronic billboard outside a tourist bureau in the village, where rates changed throughout the day. I made a habit of passing it on the way to the general store, and students, who knew their fate was tied to my currency dealings, would report back what they saw on the billboard in case I had not climbed to the village that day. The rates quoted were for small transactions and were always poorer than the rates I could get from Herr Schmidt, but they moved in tandem with his quotes, so it was a bit like using an oven that heats at ten degrees higher than the reading on the knob. My strategy was to wait for a more favorable rate to appear and then change enough dollars for the upcoming lira payments. If I was lucky, I could hit a little local peak and exercise damage control with the budget.

It wasn't until the last days of February that the dollar shot up above 1,650 for the first time. The previous Monday, the billboard had read 1,588 and that Monday it hit 1,665. Students alerted me to the move at lunchtime and bombarded me with questions about what they should do with their dollars. I shuffled around their questions, not really knowing what *I* was going to do. Secretly, I faced the same dilemma: I needed help from someone who understood these markets better than I did.

I called a friend from graduate school days, a central banker who had dealt with speculative episodes like this. I remembered the story he had told me three years earlier about his experience during the summer and early fall of 1992, when he attended 'swat team' meetings every morning to decide on his central bank's strategy for the day. 'The speculators started small,' he had told me. 'First they took out the Bank of Finland, forcing the markka [the Finnish currency] out of the exchange rate band. With their stockpile of winnings from Finland, they began betting against us.' He described it like a cross between a poker game and a war. 'Some days we lost hundreds of millions of dollars in reserves. Our losses only made the monster grow, feeding it more chips to bet with. The day we lost $4 billion, we finally saw we could not win.' He had turned remorseful at that point in the story, almost blaming himself, 'In just a few weeks, we blew what had taken us *fifteen years* of reserve management to save.' All of this he viewed as a futile attempt to defend the European Exchange Rate Mechanism against George Soros and the other funds. He said that after the speculators defeated the Bank of Italy, they went for the Bank of Spain for even higher stakes. Finally, they took on the Bank of England, which lost $20 billion before caving in to the speculators in September 1992.

Being involved in normal times and in extreme episodes like this, my friend had developed intuition and wisdom about a world I had only read and theorized about. Fortunately, my friend had returned from lunch. After he briefed me on the play of forces and his view of the intensity of speculative pressures, I asked: 'If you had $50,000 and needed to change it into lire over the next few months, would you do it all now or would you wait?'

'I think... I would...' (he paused for an eternity) 'I think I would wait.'

Immediately I called Herr Schmidt and got a quote, a very good one, and made the largest transaction so far, enough to pay for mid-term program bills, three weeks of stipends and the forthcoming trip to Florence. But I took my friend's advice to heart and held onto a sizeable reserve of dollars for later.

With all the tourist traffic and exchange booths in Florence, it was easy to check on rates. A run on the lira was underway, and rates zoomed higher than we had seen all semester. By midday on Thursday, banks were offering 1,685 for retail transactions, so I called Herr Schmidt from the hotel, and he changed enough for me at 1,694 to last another three weeks. On Friday, students returned for the evening meal excitedly reporting that the dollar had risen to 1,730 late in the afternoon. Unfortunately, I was in the Uffizi gallery and didn't get out until dark. I looked at my watch and saw it was too late: Herr Schmidt was at home for the weekend. On the Sunday train back to the castle, I read the Italian papers, which described a political scandal in detail, calling the market sell-off 'Black Friday for the Lira.'

Sunday evening I discussed the situation with our host at the castle, who told me that doctors and other wealthy people from the town below had been transferring funds to Austria and Germany. In a month, the lira had lost more than twenty per cent of its value against the Austrian schilling and German mark, and people were edgy. Our host asked how I was managing the situation. I told him about my setup at the bank, and he accurately summarized it, 'The dollar and the lira are two dive bombers, and you catch the lira when it dives past you.'

I rushed to the bank early the next morning, hoping to get in on Friday's rates. I had never seen such a crowd there. The grocer, the baker, the butcher, the pharmacist, the postman, waitresses, policemen, farmers, teachers, faces familiar and unfamiliar mulled about like livestock, our breath smoking the icy air. The grocer approached me, seeking advice about the schilling. I told him I was not the best person to get advice from in such a time of panic, and he asked, 'but what will *you* do?' When I said I was thinking about buying a lot of lire, he looked at me as if I were crazy. The heavy doors squeaked and the mass lunged for the opening, though once inside no one broke line. Herr Schmidt stood calmly next to the vault ready to replenish the stacks of prepackaged notes laid out neatly on a table behind the cashiers. I was nowhere near the front of my line, and three lines trailed out into the courtyard. Villagers were leaving with schillings and marks.

When it came my turn, Herr Schmidt approached and I asked what he could give me for dollars. He wrote down on a piece of paper 1,736 lire, which looked like it was based on Friday's price reported in the papers. I asked him what the minimum balance was to keep the dollar account open, and he said one hundred dollars. I instructed the teller to transfer all but a hundred dollars' worth into the lira account.

My stock with the students rose. We were so flush with lire that any idea with a decent rationale could get funded. When the weather warmed up we had barbecues for our faculty hosts, who, in turn, worked in extra field trips for the students. In April, we were able to afford an unplanned field trip to Verona for the weekend. Students' questions about currency markets deepened. How does it work when I use my credit card, get instant lira, and then it shows up later as a dollar charge on my Visa bill? What are the electronic connections that allow this? Where is the center of the market? Who controls it? Can economists predict exchange rates? Why are the currency markets going haywire? What will happen when European currencies merge into the euro? All of these were worthy questions that an intelligent beginner would ask, and as you will see, their questions later became the main chapter topics of this book. At the time, I had no idea how to answer the more practical 'how does it work?' questions, though I could field the ones that fell within the confines of international economics, and we had good discussions.

Unfortunately, I began to be plagued with forecasting questions in the village. Would there be another run on the lira? Will the German mark keep rising? I couldn't buy a loaf of bread without getting pestered. Soon thereafter, word got back to the castle of a rumor circulating in the village that the American professor was holding séances down at the castle, channeling the spirits of the currency markets.

A few weeks after I had made the large transfer, I was withdrawing lira for the week, and Herr Schmidt asked to speak with me in his office. This began as one of our typical discussions, basically me pumping him for recent news about global financial markets. Toward the end, however, he turned more serious, asking me in different ways how I knew when the lira had bottomed out. The more I denied knowing, the more suspicious he became. Finally, I told him that for me it was like playing a dice game, where I could see results of lots of rolls, but I only chose the ones I wanted. I had lucked out and had some good rolls to choose from.

The last roll of the dice must have confirmed Herr Schmidt's suspicions that I had insider information about the lira. I just happened to close out the accounts for the program the second Monday in May. That day the dollar hit its lowest point since February, a day that turned out to be a six-month high for the lira. When I transferred the remaining lire back into dollars, I inadvertently made a windfall gain for the program, and Herr Schmidt wired back to the college a sizeable sum of dollars.

The lucky rolls encouraged me, giving me subliminal delusions of becoming a forecasting guru, but the lucky rolls didn't pull me into this project. On our balcony in April, a student told about her trip to Spain over the spring break. She observed how much cheaper things were there compared to Italy. Another commented that Prague was amazingly inexpensive, while a third complained he had to sleep in the park in Amsterdam because rooms were so expensive. This naturally led to a discussion of exchange rates.

An English major asked me, 'Could you recommend a book on global currency markets for someone like me, who will never want to open an economics text?'

'Have you seen the comic books put out by the Federal Reserve? They're not a bad introduction,' I recommended.

'Come on,' she complained, 'just because I don't want to work through the jargon doesn't mean I want to read something that talks down to me.'

I must have looked stunned. She softened a bit, 'What I mean is, I've felt exchange rates this semester. I'd like to hear about the people who run the show, but in language I can understand.'

Her request resonated with me. Globalization was in full swing: free-trade areas, the global assembly line, people crossing borders to travel, to study and to work, the breakdown of the Soviet empire and the integration of the remnants into the West, the information technology revolution, the erosion of barriers to financial flows, and the extension of Wall Street finance to 'emerging markets.' All of these processes have a monetary dimension. All get channeled – one way or another – through currency markets. Yet, with a stream of books coming out on globalization, there was no exposé of the central conduit that I could recommend for someone like her: a curious, intelligent reader who lacked training in economics and exposure to the business world.

My friend in Rome was later appointed to a high-level position in Washington, where he mentored me on payments systems – how banks settle up with each other to enable transfers of money. Whatever data I needed, my friend would score for me, and because of his professional contacts and position, he could open doors that are otherwise locked to ordinary mortals.

A sabbatical beginning in the summer of 1996 allowed me to begin research in earnest. I started by thoroughly reading the economics literature on the subject and closely studying statistical evidence relating to the actual market structure: who sells what and how much of it to whom, and where and how they are doing it. The most comprehensive survey of currency dealers is administered by central banks around the world every third year in April. When I began the basic research, I had the final results of the April 1995 *Central Bank Survey of Foreign Exchange and Derivatives Market Activity* to work with, and I could look back in three-year intervals all the way to April 1986 when the first such snapshot was taken.[1]

The picture I found was far more complex than I had imagined. The economics literature had some major gaps in terms of crucial areas not covered, and one of the areas best covered – exchange rate forecasting

– while fascinating on a theoretical level,[2] yielded disappointing forecasts, a problem that persists to this day. The surveys of market structure were a helpful starting place and have provided valuable benchmarks for charting the evolution of the market since then, but without direct knowledge of the various players in the market – their positions, motivations, and constraints – I had great difficulty reading and interpreting the data in the surveys. Even some of the commonly traded currency contracts, which had their definitions clearly spelled out in an appendix, only made abstract sense to me, without knowing how those contracts were useful for various actors engaged in the market. I needed more than theory, statistics, and press reports could offer. I needed to meet the money changers.

I sought out strategic insiders, people with direct experience in various facets of the money-changing business.[3] A number of former students had risen to positions of responsibility in the financial world, as had several classmates from graduate school. These and other contacts arranged for me tours of trading rooms and scheduled for me interviews with currency experts. Sometimes after a tour, I would end up on the back row of the trading room with the rookies, where I could watch the commotion and eavesdrop on conversations. Other times a seasoned veteran would pull me aside and spend time answering my questions and explaining how things worked from his or her life experience.[4] Instead of tape-recording, I scribbled notes on a legal pad. Following the advice of my anthropology professor in college, I set aside a block of time as soon after the interview as possible to flush details from my memory while they were still fresh, drawing maps and diagrams of the structures observed, and filling in the gaps in my shorthand notes. Unanswered questions could sometimes be obtained from a follow-up email or a telephone call to an informant. I kept hard copy of these notes and then I transcribed them into fuller, more comprehensible form, saving them in fieldwork files on my computer. The live footage taken between October 1996 and May 2005 fed back into my ongoing data analysis of the moving structure, and it provided narrative material for most of the chapters.

In several chapters I have chosen to use ethnographic footage in a direct way, placing the interview in real historical time and geographical space, revealing the actual names of the experts interviewed and their positions at that time. In cases where an expert named is the central figure of a chapter, I sent a draft copy for the expert to check for accuracy and to be certain security features and/or proprietary information were not compromised. In chapters where the specific historical moment is essential to the message, an appendix is sometimes attached to update the subject matter for the current edition. Two informants with extraordinary insights into the workings of the foreign exchange market inspired the partially fictionalized characters – Mr Roberts, who runs a foreign exchange department of a regional bank on the periphery of the market, and Genevieve, a working mother with graduate training in economics who trades Tokyo at night for a large financial institution. The principles these two informants taught me are fundamental and just as applicable today as they were on the days of the interviews. While these two informants and their co-workers may recognize aspects of their character, the trading rooms they worked in, and the conversations we had, they will quickly see the literary license I have taken to disguise their identities and that of their institutions, and to apply the essence of their instruction to more recent history. The reader should quickly recognize that Professor Smith in Tokyo in a later chapter and the traveler in Istanbul in the pages that immediately follow are completely made up with no connection to any real persons whatsoever.

A tour guide has to make difficult choices. Include too many excursions, and the travelers grow weary. Exclude too much, and the tour is woefully incomplete. In selecting the itinerary, I have tried to strike a balance. In the beginning, the excursions stay within the world directly inhabited by the money changers, allowing the traveler a glimpse into where and how they work, what they trade, how they arrange deals, how currencies are delivered, and how their philosophies and actions, taken together, move the market. Later chapters venture outside the workplace to view storms that periodically sweep through and evolutionary changes in the system as a whole. What the money changers do and how they respond to shocks feed back on the broader world, affecting other financial markets and real economies, sometimes in profound ways.[5]

The experts interviewed may use unfamiliar terms, but the logical progression of the chapters and the participants' stories told in workplace settings bring abstract concepts down to earth. After finishing the tour, the reader should have a mental picture of the geographical and structural organization of global currency markets and the people who move them. This vision of a volatile, evolving structure should provide a useful framework for deciphering the complex causes of yet unforeseen financial events.

Encounter with a money changer

You get off the plane in Istanbul, have your passport stamped, and proceed through customs, where you declare the amount of currency and travelers' checks you're carrying. Then you proceed to the exchange window, where an electronic billboard lists a dozen or so currencies. Next to the listing for the United States, the 'we sell' column reads 1,455,000 TL and the 'we buy' column reads 1,317,000 TL. So, as any business, they buy low and sell high. They'll give you about 1.3 million lira for each dollar, so at this exchange rate, a million lira is worth about 75 cents, but for every million lira you don't spend they'll give you less than 70 cents back when you come through on your way home. Then you notice another problem. At the bottom of the billboard is a message that reads 'Travelers Cheques – 2,000,000 TL charge per cheque.' It's easy enough to figure that changing a bunch of $20 travelers' checks is out of the question if they're charging you more than a dollar a check.

As you debate how much you should change at the airport, a gentleman in a business suit sees your dilemma and whispers, 'If you have dollar bills you might save them for a *doviz* in Istanbul. They'll give you a better rate. If you have a card, the best bet is over there.' He points to an Automated Teller Machine (ATM).

After you put in your card, the screen reads, 'This ATM charges 2.0m TL per transaction. Do you wish to continue?' You think, that's about $1.50 – about what they charge at home. You agree and enter your PIN number, and the screen reads 'Verification... please wait...' After entering

the amount of Turkish lira you want, the screen reads 'Processing...
Please wait' and starts clicking. In less than a minute, the machine starts
vibrating, your card pops out, a receipt slides from another slot, and the
cash compartment opens to reveal a stack of brightly colored bills. You
grab your card, then the money, and finally the receipt. A buzzer rings
and the clear plastic shield slides down.

You inspect the cash advance receipt. Turkish Bank, SA, the correct date
and time of the transaction, the last four digits of your VISA number,
and 200 m TL Cash Advance. Nowhere on the slip does it say how many
dollars you were charged. A streak of paranoia runs through your mind.
You think to yourself, what did they really charge me? Is my bank account
in the United States now at the mercy of Turkish Bank, SA?

By getting foreign currency from a teller machine, it is difficult to
know how many dollars you will be charged two or more days later when
your bank bills your Visa account. Exchange rates for the Turkish lira
and many other currencies fluctuate, sometimes suddenly and by large
amounts, depending on how currency traders in major financial centers
respond to news that feeds across their computer screens. From these
changing wholesale rates, Visa somewhat mysteriously selects a single
daily rate for each of the currencies used in its 150-country service area.
The exchange rate Visa charges your bank is Visa's rate for Turkish lira
for the day that the bank in Turkey posts the charge in the Visa system.
For a teller machine in a large city like Istanbul, the machine is likely
to enter the charge automatically into the Visanet settlement system, so
you'll get an exchange rate based on that day's currency conversion rate
adopted by Visa.[1] However, if you purchase from a merchant who puts
your card through an old washboard device and the merchant does not
deposit the charge for two weeks, your rate will be based on the exchange
rate two weeks after you made the purchase, which would benefit you
if the value of the currency has fallen, but harm you if it has risen in
value on world currency markets.

In addition to the daily Visa exchange rate, Visa charges your bank a
1% 'international service assessment' that is not a currency conversion
charge but an access charge for using Visa's global payments network.[2]
Your bank pays Visa the international assessment fee and the amount in
dollars to cover your currency advance at the Visa exchange rate. The
bank charges your account this amount plus a percentage markup ranging
from 0 per cent to 5 per cent, depending on your card agreement with
your bank. So, if you travel a lot, it's a good idea to get a card from a
bank that offers a low markup fee, and you will beat the money changer
at the booth, where mark-ups over wholesale rates can range from 4

per cent to upwards of 10 per cent depending on circumstances, plus additional fees for traveler's checks.

What happens behind the scenes that makes the card work, and how does the system do its job so fast? Look on the back of your credit card and you'll see a black stripe, which has your account information encoded magnetically. Inside the automated teller machine is an electronic card-reading device that verifies if the number you punch in at the prompt matches your PIN on the strip. If it doesn't, the machine says 'Wrong PIN Number... try again,' and if this fails, the machine aborts the transaction and spits out your card. After your PIN is verified and you have entered the amount of local currency you wish to withdraw, the screen says 'Processing... please wait.'

What happens during this brief lapse? The card-reading device inside the ATM instantly pumps the account information along with the amount requested into the fiberoptic network it is licensed with. The card network automatically routes the request in the most direct manner to your card-issuing institution. This may include being bounced off a satellite and entered into a second fiberoptic network through a central transmission center on your continent, where it will be relayed to your region. The receiving terminal at your institution electronically checks if your account has an adequate balance or credit line to support the requested withdrawal, in which case it relays back through the network a 'Yes' or 'No' answer to the ATM machine requesting the authorization. If 'No' is the answer, you walk over with your travelers' checks and get ripped off by the money changer. If you've called in to report a stolen card, the terminal at your bank relays back the message for the ATM machine: 'Eat that card.'

If 'Yes' is the authorization answer, it will take longer for the machine to deal out your pile of foreign currency than it did for the network to tell the machine to start counting. The authorization requires a journey over thousands of miles from where you're standing in a foreign land to your bank and back. On a normal day, the round-trip takes between six and twenty seconds, and with annual increases in transactions volume, card companies are constantly finding faster ways to do the job.

Clearing and settlement of accounts happens after you've walked away and are spending the strange money. At a certain time every day, the ATM transactions pending for the day will be closed out. For each transaction an electronic message will be sent into the appropriate clearing and settlement network: 'Send us the money you owe.' Along with the account information of the cardholder, the authorization code, the amount of the cash advance, and the account number to which funds should be delivered, the message will contain a unique tag. If the machine short-changed you and you dispute the transaction when you get home, the card company uses the tag to retrieve the details of the transaction throughout its life cycle. When you pay for something or get a cash advance with your card inside the United States, your account is cleared and funds are delivered for settlement usually the next business day. When you make payments abroad, processing must be arranged through at least two banking systems and settlement involves currency conversion, requiring at least an additional day.

The instructions for clearing and settlement of accounts will involve the card company's global netting system, which may use more than one settlement bank in addition to your bank at home and the bank that owns the teller machine where the foreign currency was withdrawn. The general principle of the card network is to find the least expensive, most rapid and secure way to accomplish the movement of funds. With cross-border transactions growing rapidly and global payments systems evolving at an alarming pace, by the time this book comes to press, old Turkish lira will be out of circulation and procedures used by the card companies may have changed. A computer chip may have replaced the magnetic strip on your card or you may be able to withdraw foreign currency using a micro-card on your key chain.

More than 50 million Americans travel abroad each year, spending on average $1,400 apiece, perhaps changing money or getting cash advances a half-dozen times per trip. This is the largest single group that gets a direct taste of how currency markets can suddenly change one's lifestyle. After returning home, the traveler may not realize the number of currency transactions that facilitate day-to-day life. However, the labels on light manufactures should give it away. The shirt reads 'Made in Thailand,' the tennis shoes 'Made in China,' and the tennis racquet 'Bangladesh.' Even fresh vegetables have stickers reading 'Grown in Honduras' or 'Product of Guatemala.' Manufacturers of more complex products like cars may boast the item was 'made in our factory in Kentucky,' but the public relations team does not disclose that components were shipped in from Mexico, Brazil, Korea, Taiwan or Japan. Remove the panel on your computer and you'll see a veritable map of Southern Asia and Latin America.

The people who add value in the global assembly line are almost invariably paid in local currency, so that one or possibly several foreign exchange market transactions are required to get a product to the US consumer. The number of currency transactions depends on the home base of vendors and subcontractors in the supply chain. For a hypothetical example, Wal-Mart may pay US dollars to a tennis shoe vendor in Hong Kong, who pays a subcontractor in Hong Kong dollars, who in turn pays workers on the mainland in Chinese yuan. The subcontractor, in turn, may be buying laces, soles, and canvas from a Hong Kong vendor in Hong Kong dollars, who paid US dollars to subcontractors, who paid local currency to workers in the Philippines, Indonesia, or Sri Lanka.

United States imports of goods and services in 2004 amounted to approximately $1.8 trillion, but those purchases could have generated several times that amount in foreign currency transactions due to the global dispersion of the workforce and the complexity of supply chains. Some of those imports may be processed further in the United States for re-export to foreign markets, whereby additional currency transactions must take place to sell to consumers in their local currencies. In 2004, US exports of goods and services amounted to approximately $1.2 trillion, though the currency transactions required to reach the ultimate buyers could have been higher, depending on value added by workers along the way and payments to vendors or transporters operating in other currency zones.[3]

With free trade agreements, improvements in transport and communications technology, and pressure on corporations to find the least expensive sources of supply and the most lucrative markets, world trade in real goods and services has tripled in the past two decades.[4] Nevertheless, globalization of real economic activity cannot begin to explain the high turnover in currency markets. In April 2004, world currency transactions averaged $1.88 trillion *per day*, an amount exceeding US imports of real goods and services *for the entire year*.[5] Seven days of foreign exchange market activity could have more than paid for everything that was produced for sale in the United States for an entire year. Six days' of foreign exchange market transactions could pay for all the world's trade in real goods and services for a year.[6] Twenty days of foreign exchange market transactions could pay for everything produced in the world for a year.[7]

More mysterious than trade in real goods and services and far more influential on currency markets are global flows of financial capital. Movement of real goods is constrained by complex logistics of transferring goods from points of production to points of sale and by relatively slow to change contracts that bind together the multiple links of the physical supply chain. When ownership claims to stocks, bonds, money, and other forms of financial wealth were recorded on pieces of paper, their movement was restricted much like the transfer of physical merchandise. In today's world of electronic book-keeping, secure and rapid communications networks, and ever-enhanced processing capacity, the lapses between receiving financial market information, executing trades and transferring financial property to new owners are dramatically shortened and undaunted by distance, enabling faster financial market turnover and global connectivity in real time.

Emboldened by technology's conquest of geography, large financial firms used free-market ideology and political muscle to break down regulatory barriers to their movement. Commercial banks merged across state and national boundaries and formed international holding companies, collecting investment banks, brokerage houses, and insurance companies under the same logo. With their managers seeking ever-higher returns and greater diversification, financial portfolios became more global, and 'emerging financial markets' were created where once there was none. Now when the Tokyo market swoons, portfolios become unbalanced, and in Sydney, Hong Kong, Singapore, Mumbai, Frankfurt, Paris, London, and New York, financial institutions react as if connected by a seamless web. That web is foreign exchange. For a sale of stock in Tokyo to build up one's holdings in Sydney, one must first take the yen proceeds and convert them to Australian dollars in order to acquire stock on the Sydney Exchange.

At the time of writing, peak turnover on the world's largest stock market occurred on 18 March 2005, when 2.8 billion shares traded on the New York Stock Exchange for a total of $102 billion.[8] Currency market turnover on an average day in April 2004 was eighteen times this peak amount, and thirty-six times the New York Stock Exchange's average daily turnover for that same month. Turnover in bonds and other fixed income securities exceeds that of stocks, and the world's most actively traded fixed income market is for United States Treasury securities, also headquartered in New York. At the beginning of April 2004, out of the $3.5 trillion in US Treasury debt held by the public, foreigners owned almost half of that, or about $1.7 trillion.[9] Daily turnover of US Treasury securities is enormous, on the order of $520 billion per day in April 2004,[10] but daily turnover in the foreign exchange market, which links the world's financial markets *and* the world's markets for real goods and services, was more than three times that amount.

The traveler may not realize it, but the bank that issued the credit card and arranged for the cash advance in Turkish lira has a trading room that not only handles customers' currency needs but also has 'proprietary traders' who bet the bank's capital on short-term currency movements. Similar activity is going on at the insurance company where the traveler has a policy and at the brokerage house where the traveler has mutual funds and retirement accounts.

When you withdrew the funny-looking money from the machine you may not have known it, but you had just participated in the largest market in the world.

Back in the States:
a glance at foreign exchange

The radio blares from the kitchen: 'The dollar fell against the yen in heavy Tokyo trading today, closing at 105.75 yen, down two yen from Friday's close. In early European trading, the dollar is mixed against the euro and the pound.'

I look at the *Wall Street Journal*'s website (online.wsj.com) and select 'currencies' to pull up a table that lists about sixty foreign currencies from the Argentine peso to the Venezuelan bolivar. I select about a dozen currencies and download them to see what can be learned from this listing (see figure 1.1). I underline the first thing that catches my eye at the top. These must be the wholesale market rates in New York, because these quotes are for trades 'among banks in amounts of $1 million and more'; the fine print warns 'retail transactions provide fewer units of foreign currency per dollar.' So, as the trip to Turkey taught, the money-changing business is like any other. The middleman collects a profit.

The next thing that catches my eye is that for every currency they show two ways of quoting the exchange rate, one they call the 'US$ Equivalent' and the other 'Currency per US$.' To compute the difference I go down to the Japanese yen, and see that a yen was worth less than a penny on Friday, or about nine-tenths of a cent. So, if I were in Japan and was charged a thousand yen for this breakfast, I would know that the bagel and coffee were costing me a little over 9 bucks. The second way they're quoting it is from a Japanese point of view, the price of the

1.1 / Foreign Exchange Rates

Friday, 3 June 2005 NEW YORK (Dow Jones) – The New York foreign exchange mid-range rates below apply to trading among banks in amounts of $1 million and more, as quoted at 4 p.m. Eastern time by Reuters and other sources. Retail transactions provide fewer units of foreign currency per dollar.

	US perspective (*what that currency costs in $*)		Foreign perspective (*price of $ in that currency*)	
	US$ equiv.		Currency per US$	
	Friday	Thursday	Friday	Thursday
Argentina (Peso)	0.3459	0.3468	2.8910	2.8835
Australia (Dollar) *went up a bit*	0.7563	0.7547	1.3222	1.3250
Canada (Dollar)	0.8016	0.8011	1.2475	1.2483
1 Month Forward *expecting*	0.8019	0.8015	1.2470	1.2477
3 Months Forward *strengthening?*	0.8031	0.8026	1.2452	1.2460
6 Months Forward	0.8050	0.8045	1.2422	1.2430
China (Renminbi) *fixed rate?*	0.1208	0.1208	8.2764	8.2764
Ecuador (US Dollar)*	1.0000	1.0000	1.0000	1.0000
Hong Kong (Dollar) *fixed or pegged?*	0.1285	0.1285	7.7821	7.7821
Japan (Yen) *2 ways to quote exch. rates*	0.009282	0.009237	107.74	108.26
1 Month Forward *expecting*	0.009306	0.009262	107.46	107.97
3 Months Forward *yen to*	0.009361	0.009316	106.83	107.34
6 Months Forward *strengthen?*	0.009446	0.009400	105.86	106.38
Mexico (Peso)	0.09212	0.09251	10.855	10.810
Turkish (Lira) *fell some*	0.7318	0.7427	1.3665	1.3465
UK (Pound)	1.8130	1.8157	0.5516	0.5508
1 Month Forward *expecting*	1.8105	1.8132	0.5523	0.5515
3 Months Forward *pound to*	1.8064	1.8091	0.5536	0.5528
6 Months Forward *get cheaper?*	1.8021	1.8047	0.5549	0.5541
Euro *fell some*	1.2225	1.2277	0.8180	0.8145

* Adopted U.S. dollar as of 9/11/00.

Source: Reuters, as reported in *Wall Street Journal*, 6 June 2005.

dollar or how many yen it takes to buy a dollar. From Friday to today, the dollar fell in value from 107.74 yen to 105.75 yen. So for a Japanese tourist visiting New York, a $9 breakfast would have gotten a little less expensive over the weekend, since $9 would convert back into fewer yen on Monday than on Friday.

I see that the yen is like the UK pound and most of the other currencies listed; their values fluctuate from one day to the next. Two exceptions appear to be the Hong Kong dollar and the Chinese renminbi, which at this time look like they might be pegged to the US dollar since they traded at the same values on Thursday and Friday, both of them valued at more than twelve cents. Also, it looks as though on 11 September 2000, Ecuador eliminated its currency and adopted the US dollar.

Also I see the banks are quoting 1-month, 3-month and 6-months forward rates for the Canadian dollar, the British pound, and the Japanese yen, in addition to the rates for the day. I highlight these and note that the pound looks slightly less expensive to buy forward, while the Canadian dollar and the yen look more expensive forward. Are the currency traders predicting the pound will fall a bit, and the yen and Canadian dollar will strengthen against the dollar?

I note the euro fell slightly against the dollar and the Australian dollar rose from Thursday to Friday, so they are floating currencies. And then there's the Turkish lira, which appears to be falling.

This is about all that can be seen just looking at the table from the *Wall Street Journal*. There are two ways to express the same exchange rate. Some currencies float against each other; some are fixed. Some move more quickly than others. Some have developed forward markets, others maybe not. Banks are at the center of the currency markets, and there's a wholesale market for large blocks at a time in New York. Trades between banks are for sizeable amounts, but retail amounts to customers would cost more. But this little snapshot of two days' worth of foreign exchange trading raises more questions than it answers.

What exactly is being exchanged on the currency markets? Who are the major banks involved in this business? Who are their customers, and how much are they charged? How do customers buy currencies from the banks? How do the banks buy and sell currencies with each other? What makes some currencies float and others stay fixed? What are forward rates about, and why are they higher or lower than current rates?

I thumb through the telephone book and find a nearby bank that has a listing for foreign exchange. I need an introduction, so I call a former student who works there. Alice tells me she'll call the head of the department. She says the small group of traders are known at the bank for working hard and having a good time. In ten minutes, Alice calls back and gives me the go-ahead to contact the head of the foreign exchange (FX) department.

Mr Roberts says his schedule is filled for the rest of the week, but if I could get there in an hour he'll be able to work me in for about forty-five minutes. 'If you're interested, I'll introduce you to my people in the trading room, who'll show you what they do. Bring a photo ID You'll need it to sign in at the lobby.'

A visit to a local bank:
what do money changers buy and sell?

Mr Roberts tilts back in a leather chair behind a large desk.

'Have you always had all the security check-points?' I ask.

'No, they were put in after September 11th.' He describes some of the other changes at the bank, which was for most of its history a town bank but in the 1950s expanded to other towns and cities in the state. Then in the 1990s the bank began acquiring banks and opening branches in other states. These acquisitions were done cautiously and turned out to be profitable. 'Now we're a target for a takeover, if we don't successfully negotiate this merger.'

A senior vice-president and head of the foreign exchange department, Mr Roberts has worked for the bank for more than thirty years, most of that time in foreign exchange. He describes what it was like under fixed exchange rates. 'Back when I started, foreign exchange was a no-brainer, but in 1972, when Bretton Woods[1] broke down,' Mr Roberts's blue eyes light up, 'we had to mobilize. There hasn't been a dull moment since.'

'How has your currency business evolved over this time?'

'Our foreign exchange operations have always been simply an extension of corporate banking services we offer customers.' Before the expansion into other states, he served the customer base with a staff of four; prior to that he and two women ran the show; and it began with him and one clerk. 'The entire time we had a very high profit-to-expenses ratio. Then we acquired a bank in another state that had a foreign exchange department with fifteen people. They did a larger volume business but with a much lower profit-to-expenses ratio.'

'Did the acquired bank keep its foreign exchange department after the merger?'

'No.' He explains that the costs of outfitting a state-of-the-art trading room are high, and to cut down on staffing and other duplications, they decided to centralize their operations at company headquarters here. 'We kept the "niche" business. We offer competitive rates and a highly personalized service to our corporate customers, and we've combined it with a moderate dealing business.' He says proudly, 'We're doing all this with a staff of only ten people, including me.'

'And with a merger in the works?' I ask.

'Depending on who gets us. The bidders are much larger than we are. One has a trading room with three hundred stations, sixty of them devoted to foreign exchange, the rest to stocks, fixed-income securities, and money market instruments. Our department – though highly profitable – will soon be dissolved. Of course, I'm retiring before that happens.' Melancholy crosses his face.

I decide to shift to a happier past. 'Why, for the last few decades, have companies chosen to do business with you instead of going through a big New York bank?'

He brightens. 'First, they know they won't get a better deal with the big guys. Second, most of our customers already use us for cash management and payrolls. We know them and their creditworthiness, and they know us. They realize our account executives will spend just as much time on a $20,000 transaction as they would for a $20 million one. That doesn't happen in New York. Several years ago, we were attracting accounts from some of the big New York banks.'

'How did you do that?'

'It became known that we separated our corporate service section, which carries out orders for customers, and our dealer section, which trades to make profits for the bank.' He says that back then the typical New York account executive also made money from dealing – a conflict of interest in his view. 'You'll see in the trading room that we keep the two positions – account executive and dealer – separate, so our account executives work for the customer and try to get as good a price as possible from our dealers. The big banks saw this and copied us.'

'Mr Roberts, you've worked in this business for more than thirty years and know it inside and out. I've got some beginner questions for you if you don't mind. First of all, when I think of currencies being traded, I picture myself in a foreign land, at the airport or train station, changing my $20 bills for their money.'

Mr Roberts smiles. 'That's the picture most people have.'

'How relevant is this picture for today's world?'

'It's just the retail fringe.' He says that direct exchange of notes happens in every country, especially around tourist attractions. In Eastern Europe and developing countries, where there is little faith in the banking system, it takes on a more important role. He recalls a customer who did business in Russia. 'Before leaving, he would come in and get stacks of $100 bills. His man in St Petersburg would use the money for investment deals.' He explains that the center of the currency markets, where wholesale rates are set, bank account money is traded, not physical units of currency. 'Everyone else who trades in those currencies, even the money changer at the airport, watches these wholesale rates and adjusts buy and sell rates according to the wholesale changes at the center of the currency market.'

'How might the image of physical currency changing hands be misleading about the actual workings of currency markets?' I ask.

'People get confused by this all the time.' He explains that when physical currency is traded, there is an exchange of money from one country to the next. When bank account money is traded, it doesn't cross a border. 'It just moves between accounts inside the two banking systems.'

'Can you give an example?'

'Well, let's say I buy Swiss francs with dollars. On delivery day, funds from my dollar account in the US are sent to their dollar account in the US, and they'll send Swiss francs from their account to ours at a correspondent bank in Switzerland. Then they can make dollar payments and we can make Swiss franc payments.'

'When you say "send," do you mean you write them a check?'

'No. The funds are wired – electronically sent. Only the tiniest fraction of foreign exchange involves the trade of physical currencies, and practically none of the delivery instructions are made through checks.'

'You mentioned "on delivery day." Is there a gap between when you agree to trade a currency and when the funds are finally delivered?'

'There are two gaps: When and *where*.'

I ask him to explain, and he says that only with physical currency are there no gaps. You show how many dollars you want to change, the money changer writes down an amount of local currency you will get, you pass your dollars through the window and the money changer passes the local currency back. 'The deal and the delivery are in the same place at the same time.'

'And when the deal involves account money?' 'Account money deals can be struck anywhere.' He gives the example of someone in Timbuktu agreeing to trade US dollars for British pounds with someone in Machu Picchu. All they need is a secure communications line and assurance that the other will actually deliver the funds. After the deal is made, they instruct their banks in the US and in the UK to send the amounts agreed on to the other's bank account. 'The delivery of dollars and pounds to the correct accounts may take a few days, depending on the settlement systems used by the banks to complete the transfers.'

'A few days – you mean two?'

'Yes, for most currencies, the standard contract is for delivery two days after the deal is struck.' He says that this standard convention is called a 'spot' contract, and the two days between the 'trade date' and the 'value date' is to give ample time for banks to arrange for the movement of funds.

'You said "for most currencies." Are there exceptions?'

'Yes, for trades involving the US dollar and the Canadian dollar, the standard 'spot' contract is for next-day delivery.' He explains that the time zones are the same and the settlement systems closely linked, so next-day delivery gives ample time.

'But hasn't information technology speeded up funds transfer between banks, so same-day delivery can happen?'

'True. Technology has supported innovations that speed funds transfers, so same-day delivery is more likely now than five years ago. (Mr Roberts gives the example of Continuous Linked Settlement Bank, whose entire purpose is to settle currency transactions quickly and safely. See appendix to Chapter 11 for more details on CLS Bank.) Also with banks consolidating across borders, "cash" or same-day delivery is happening more often.' Mr Roberts gives the example of JPMorgan Chase, with branches worldwide. If both parties use accounts at the same bank, the electronic funds transfer takes place on the internal payments system of the bank. The delivery can happen the same day, because banks don't have to settle up with each other. 'But, despite possibilities for faster delivery, the standard "spot" contract is pretty much like it was twenty years ago, a promise to deliver funds two days after a trade.'

'What about the listings for "one month", "three months," and "six months" forward?'

Mr Roberts explains that "outright forwards" are deals to deliver funds one or more days after the "spot" value date. A one-day outright forward would be for delivery within three business days after the trade date, or spot plus one. The one-month, three-months, and six-months forward contracts are commonly listed in newspapers because they correspond to the duration of typical loan contracts. Because credit markets in different countries are linked through foreign exchange, those dates are heavily traded. He says they call these 'straight dates.' 'So much action happens for these dates that the entire market uses them as benchmarks for valuing customized forwards.'

'Customized forwards?'

'Often our clients know exactly when they want to make a payment abroad or when they will be receiving payment in a foreign currency, and they'll want to convert it back into dollars, so we can tailor deliveries for specific dates that aren't traded much.'

I ask why his customers ask for forward contracts, when they could just wait and use a spot contract.

'It's insurance against currency markets moving against them.' He says that many of his customers are manufacturers. If they have to make foreign currency payments in six months for parts or raw materials they've ordered, they don't want to be surprised to find the cost in dollars to have risen because of the currency markets. 'So they call us – sometimes several days in a row – to check on forward rates. When they get a forward rate that's inexpensive enough to assure them of a profit, they'll enter into a forward contract with us for the delivery of the foreign currency close to the time they have to pay the supplier. They're buying insurance against the dollar declining in value, which might otherwise drive up their costs and squeeze their profits.'

'But what if the dollar rises in value over that time?'

'In that case, if our client had waited until two days before the payment is due, he could have entered a spot transaction that would have cost the company fewer dollars for the foreign currency needed. But the company is in the manufacturing business, not the business of currency speculation, so our client's eye is on locking in manufacturing profits. We provide a service that allows the company to do that.'

'So when the bank takes on a forward contract on behalf of a customer, does the bank then absorb the currency risk?'

Mr Roberts smiles, 'Not for long. This is where our dealers come in. If an action for a customer gets the bank's currency exposure out of balance, we'll quickly counteract it with a reverse deal. That neutralizes our foreign exchange risk.'

'So, how do you make money on this? Do you charge a commission?'

'No, we don't charge a commission. We make a profit through spreads.'

He says a 'spread' is the difference between the price a currency dealer is willing to 'offer' to sell a currency for and the price they'll 'bid' to buy it for. 'At the wholesale center of the market, deals are in large blocks, trading is brisk, and there's plenty of competition so bid/offer spreads are thin. We have good credit with major currency dealers, so we can trade with them at wholesale rates. If a customer calls and wants to buy a particular currency, we first find out how much we could buy the currency for on the wholesale market, and then we adjust the "spread," which translates into a retail markup over what we can buy it for. Then our dealer, who watches the wholesale market carefully, finds the best deal to cover our exposure.'

'What if the market goes against you before you can find a deal?'

'We might lose on the transaction if our markup was too small. But we have ways of limiting this sort of risk.'

'How do you do that?'

'One way is if we see there is lots of volatility, we widen the spreads. This provides the safety margin of a larger retail markup. Sometimes we lose business from this, but when things settle down, we can make our retail spread for our customers closer to the wholesale spreads we face.'

'By adjusting the retail spreads to be wider than the wholesale ones sounds like a pretty sure way to make money. Do you also make money by buying when the price of a currency is low and then waiting for the price to go up?'

'Only short term.'

'What do you mean, weeks?'

'Hours, I would say. Our traders specialize in certain currencies and get a feeling for how they move, so if they see an opportunity, we allow them some room to buy low on the speculation that they can sell higher.'

'And isn't this risky?'

'Yes, but we have ways to limit this risk.'

'How?'

'We set intra-day loss limits for each trader, and we don't carry over-night exposures for the department as a whole. So by the end of the day, our exposure to currency risk is neutralized through counter-trades with other dealers.'

'I've heard the term "derivative" thrown around a lot. What does it mean?'

'It's a contract with a value derived from a more basic asset.'

'What's the basic asset for foreign exchange derivatives?'

'Spot rates. They're the center of gravity of currency markets.'

'So is a six-month forward contract considered a derivative?'

'Yes it is.'

I make a stab at the connection. 'If the six-month forward price of a currency is higher than the spot price, does that mean actors in the market expect the spot price for that currency to rise over the next six months?'

'That's a logical guess, but expectations about future currency prices have little to do with the forward rates except in extreme circumstances.'

'What's the everyday connection, then?'

'As I've come to see it over the years,' Mr Roberts's eyes squint thoughtfully, 'the forward markets for currencies are the canals that link national lakes of credit. When interest rates are higher in one lake than another, the spillover goes through the foreign exchange markets, making spot rates and forward rates differ.'

'Can you give an example of how the foreign exchange canal works?'

'Sure. If interest rates in Japan are 1 per cent and interest rates in the US are 5 per cent, and the spot exchange rate is the same as the forward rate, how could you make money on this?' he throws the question back at me.

My adrenaline picks up. 'Let's see, I'd want to do my borrowing in Japan,' I think out loud, 'and I'd immediately switch into dollars at the spot rate. I'd invest in some safe money instrument in the US at 5 per cent and' – I consider what would happen if the dollar slides – 'I'd cover myself at the outset. I'd get a forward contract. I'd want to sell dollars forward to buy enough yen to pay off the loan from the Japanese bank. That way I'd be borrowing low and lending high and making a 4 per cent per year difference on the borrowed money. And I could care less about what happens to the yen/$ rate because I've locked in a profit through the forward contract.'

'You have the idea.' He looks as if he's making up another test for me. 'Now imagine big international banks, who are in the business of borrowing low and lending high. They have boats in every credit lake. They regularly borrow and lend to each other, and they're aware of the slightest changes in credit conditions in the lakes. They'll be quicker than you and better positioned to take advantage of the differences.'

'Right.'

'When they sell the yen for dollars on the spot market, and buy yen with dollars in the forward market, what's going to happen to the currency rates?' he asks.

'Well, I'd suppose it would just be supply and demand. Their moves should drive down the price of the yen on the spot market and make the yen sell at a premium in the forward market.' I respond.

'Good. That's exactly why currencies of countries whose interest rates are relatively low tend to sell at a premium over spot on the forward markets, and currencies of countries where interest rates are relatively high will tend to sell at a forward discount relative to spot.' He goes on to say that it's also the reason that the straight dates on forward contracts are in regular intervals of one-month, two-months, three-months, six-months.[2] Regularly traded money market instruments have maturities with those intervals. He explains that multiple forces move spot rates at the center of the market, and then forward rates quickly adjust to the spot rate, depending on interest rates in the different credit lakes. 'That's how forward rates are derived from spot rates.'

'I think I understand "outright forward" contracts. What are some of the other foreign exchange derivatives out there?'

'A heavily used one is the "foreign exchange swap",' he says.

'What's a swap?'

'Well, instead of doing two foreign exchange transactions, buying dollars with your borrowed yen on the spot market and selling them for yen on the forward market, you could have saved by doing a single foreign exchange transaction, a swap. The swap has two legs – in this case, a short leg, the spot transaction, and a long leg, the six-month forward. It's a round-trip ticket in and out of a currency, with the fare set in advance.'

'Why is it called a swap?'

'The two counter-parties are just swapping the currencies for a mutually agreed period of time. You're swapping yen for dollars for a six-month period; afterwards you'll get your yen back.'

'What are some other foreign exchange derivatives?'

'Swaps and outright forwards are common over-the-counter derivative contracts offered by financial houses, but some of the world's stock exchanges and commodity exchanges also allow trading in currency futures. These are contracts to deliver standard blocks of foreign currency for a certain price at a future date. The contracts are actively traded on organized exchanges and, just like commodity futures, they're almost always settled for net amounts owed before maturity, so they very rarely result in actual delivery.'

'So, it sounds like currency futures are there as a way to insure against exchange rate changes or to bet on exchange rates without having to actually deliver the currency.'

2.1 / Total average daily foreign exchange turnover (US$ billion, April 2004 exchange rates)

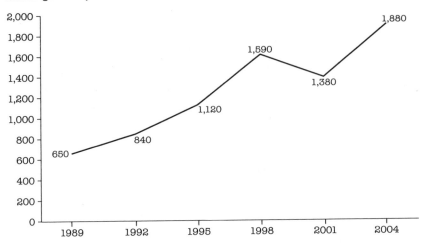

'Correct. And there are also foreign currency options offered by exchanges and banks. These allow someone to buy the right but not the obligation to purchase a block of foreign currency at a predesignated price for a limited time frame. Then they can choose whether to exercise the option or not. This is a relatively inexpensive form of insurance against currency risk.'

'Sounds like there are numerous ways to cover for currency risk. Are there any others?'

Mr Roberts smiles. 'Many, many more. Big banks have been creative at tailoring derivative combinations to meet the particular needs of their largest customers. Sometimes they'll combine foreign exchange derivatives with interest rate, commodity, or equity derivatives.'

'Has anybody tried to keep track of all this activity? I have heard that there are almost $2 trillion worth of currency trades per day. Where's this number coming from, and who's taking the pulse?'

Mr Roberts rolls his chair back from the desk and walks to the bookshelf. He pulls out a slick yellow volume and hands it to me. 'Have you seen this?' he asks.

The cover reads: Bank for International Settlements, *Triennial Central Bank Survey: Foreign Exchange and Derivatives Market Activity in 2004.* Inside is a description of the survey and its results. At the end is an appendix with about eighty pages of tables. I tell myself, if I can get this veteran's briefing on the contents, it will save me when I get around to decoding the hieroglyphics.

'Every third year in April for some time now,' Mr Roberts returns to his chair, 'central banks around the world survey foreign exchange market dealers and brokers operating in their countries. The Bank for International Settlements then compiles the national surveys into a single volume.'[3]

'Were you surveyed?'

'Yes, at the New York Federal Reserve's request. It took several hours a day of my account executive's time for an entire month to complete it. The results of the survey are worth it, but our business is so small compared with the major dealers, we could have opted out of it without affecting the results that much.'

'What are some of the results?'

'Well, the April 2004 survey showed daily turnover of traditional currency contracts was $1.88 trillion.'

'How does this compare with numbers from earlier surveys?'

Mr Roberts pulls out a manila folder with charts in it. 'I prepared some of this material for a presentation to other bank executives. The 1990s were incredible. Turnover more than doubled. It went from about $650 billion a day in 1989 to more than $1.5 trillion a day in 1998, but it dropped off to about $1.4 trillion a day in 2001.'

'Was the 2001 drop-off from the euro?' I ask.

'Partly.' He says the euro removed all the trades between the eleven currencies that merged, but 'possibly even more important was the reduction of trades due to bank mergers. When you have big dealers like Chase unite with other big dealers like Morgan, it eliminates a large portion of the inter-dealer market.'[4]

'And why the large increase in 2004?'

'That was a curious jump, because bank consolidation and electronic brokerage services continued to work to reduce inter-dealer orders.'

'How do you explain it, then?'

'That was a period of increased volatility of exchange rates, so some short-term traders were attracted into the market. Also financial houses and investment funds that were facing a low interest rate environment in the US and Japan borrowed in dollars and yen and invested the proceeds in higher interest rate locations like the United Kingdom, Australia, and New Zealand. Some decided not to completely cover themselves in the forward market, and found that they made money on this trade, because the high interest rate currencies tended to rise over this period while the dollar fell.'

'OK, so when the loan came due, dollars were less expensive to buy with the stronger currencies they owned, so they made a double profit, one on interest rate differences and the other on favorable movement of exchange rates.'

2.2 / Portion of daily foreign exchange turnover by type of transaction, April 2004

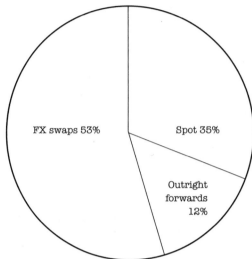

Mr Roberts says, 'People in the business call this a "carry trade." This trade and others that rely on momentum or trends in currency movements attracted speculative capital that in other settings would have been trading in stocks or bonds, so currency turnover increased.'

I ask, 'Did your bank get involved in this?'

'I can't disclose specifics. As I said, my department does not carry even overnight exposures, but there is some international cash management that involves currency transactions that we do for other departments of the bank. They tend to be very conservative, though I did notice some new developments at big banks in New York when I visited in 2004.'

'Where did you go?'

'I can't disclose which banks, but let's say they were major dealers who participated in the 2004 survey.'

'What did you see?'

'There were large sections in their trading rooms devoted to what they call "proprietary trading," which is essentially trading with the bank's own capital, and there were sections in the trading rooms where they actually allowed customers of the bank to trade. They referred to this as "prime brokerage." As it was explained to me, these were customers who had margin accounts at the bank and did large volumes of trades through the bank.'

'Who were these privileged customers?'

'When I asked that question, an example given was "hedge" funds, some of which use foreign exchange in their strategies.' Hedge funds are

2.3 / Foreign exchange daily turnover (traditional type of transaction, US$ billion)

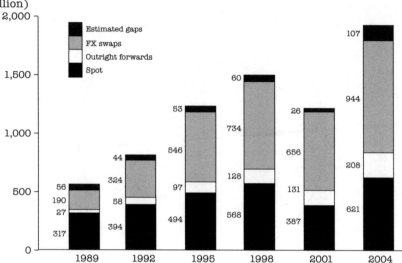

largely unregulated investment funds that come in a variety of shapes and sizes. After the collapse of Long Term Capital Management Hedge Fund in 1998, speculative capital moved out of these vehicles, but after the 2001 stock market crash and lackluster stock performance, high net worth individuals and institutions seeking higher returns began moving capital back into hedge funds. According to Mr Roberts, some of this capital was deployed in currency trades of various sorts. Mr Roberts recommended an article that contains these and other reasons for the surge.[5]

'What about the use of different instruments? Is the spot transaction, the basis from which the others are derived, the most widely used instrument in the market?' I ask.

'That used to be true, as you can see from the graphs; during the 1990s swaps and forwards became more popular than spot transactions. Spots fell from 60 per cent of the market in 1989 to only about a third of the market in 2001 and 2004. And swaps alone account for more than half the market now.'

'Why do you think swaps became so popular?' I ask.

Mr Roberts reflects for a moment. 'Global portfolio management took off in the 1990s and financial markets became more integrated. Swaps are a convenient way to manage money between the lakes without running the risk of currency fluctuations.'[6]

'What about the currencies traded? Which ones are the most important?'

2.4 / Top currencies traded (% of total, April 2004)

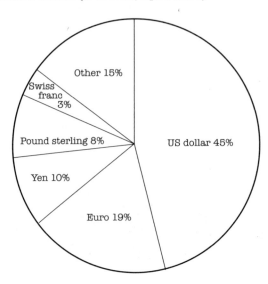

Mr Roberts slides another chart over his desk. 'The dollar is still king.' He reminds me that every currency trade involves two currencies, and the dollar is involved in one side of most currency transactions. In April 2004, the dollar participated in 90 per cent of the trades, or about 45 per cent of the value of total market activity. On an average day, the dollar was involved in more than $1 trillion worth of transactions. 'This was more than twice the involvement of the next most traded currency, the euro; four times the involvement of the Japanese yen; and nearly six times the portion of daily turnover involving the British pound.'

'Why is there such a concentration of trades through the dollar?'

'That could be a long answer.' Mr Roberts warns.

'How about a short version?'

He says that it makes trading faster and less confusing to have one currency that all the others are priced in. 'Imagine if there were zillions of currency pairs to keep up with. Also traders want to get business done fast and cheaply, so they'll go where there's lots of two-way traffic where spreads are thinner.'

'Can you give an example?'

He gives the example of someone wanting to transfer from Mexican pesos into yen. Instead of waiting around to find someone on the other side who wants to go directly from yen to pesos, the trader will sell the pesos for dollars, where there's lots of traffic and good competitive rates, and then sell the dollars for yen, which is also a quick and cheap route.

'It's like going on two stretches of super-highway instead of taking a country road. You get to the same place, but the highway route is faster and easier. For half a century now, the dollar has been the vehicle currency, or the central hub through which the super-highways pass.'

'What about the euro?'

He says the euro's share of total market turnover was higher than that of the German mark but lower than that of all the euro currencies combined in 1998. This was due to the elimination of trading amongst themselves after the merger. The most commonly traded currency pair was dollar/euro, which accounted for more than one-quarter of global market turnover.

Mr Roberts looks down at his watch. 'I must head upstairs for a meeting in a few minutes. I have some more on the market I'll show you later. You mentioned you'd like to visit the trading room?'

'It would be great to see first hand what you've been talking about.'

'I'll introduce you to our head trader and should be back by three.'

How do money changers
arrange deals?

The trading room buzzes with activity. 'We keep the currency dealers in the center here.' Mr Roberts motions to three traders with computer terminals and phone lines that form a workstation island in the middle of the room. 'Jean is our chief trader – I'll introduce you when she gets a breather. She trades European currencies, primarily euro, sterling, and Swiss francs, and she keeps an overview of the other trading activities done by Scott, who specializes in Canadian dollars, Mexican pesos, and South American currencies, and George, who trades Asian currencies, primarily yen and Australian, New Zealand, Singapore and Hong Kong dollars.'

Clustered in the center, the three traders have swivel chairs so they can communicate better with each other and with the executive salespersons stationed on the outer ring.

Mr Roberts points to four executive workstations on the left and two on the far right, all of them facing the central island. Talking with clients through telephone headsets, two sales executives are bending over, clicking a mouse, their eyes fixed on their screens. Farthest away on the right sits Karen, fielding questions on currency developments coming from branch banks. Mr Roberts explains that the sales executives have phone lines dedicated to corporate customers grouped by geographical region. Carlos takes accounts in Virginia and West Virginia; Taylor covers eastern North Carolina; Smith has South Carolina and western North Carolina;

John deals with Georgia, Florida, and the other Southern States; and Alice takes some of the big corporate accounts from New York, New Jersey, Connecticut, and Chicago.

Jean finalizes a transaction on her computer and looks up to make eye contact with Mr Roberts. We walk through the aisle behind the traders, who are busy at their terminals. 'Jean, this is Robert Williams, an economics professor at Guilford College, who wants to watch the action today. Can you make sure he sees what our different sections do?'

A no-nonsense woman in her forties, Jean says, 'Sure. When will you be back from your meeting?'

Mr Roberts glances at his watch, 'After three,' he says, 'and I'm a few minutes late, better be on my way.'

Jean says, 'Robert, I need to unwind a position in sterling, so I'm turning you over to Carlos, who'll show you what our account executives do.'

'Pull up a chair, professor. I seem to have a lull here. Got any questions?'

I point to a section of the screen on the top right that has quickly changing currency quotes. 'That one there that says EUR/USD, does that mean euros per US dollar?'

'No. Beginners get confused by that. When you see quotes, the slash doesn't mean divided by.' He explains that the 'base' currency, the one that's being traded, is always placed first; and the 'terms' currency, or the pricing currency, is placed next after the slash. He points to some small numbers that read 1.22 under EUR/USD. 'That's called the "big figure." It means a euro is worth about $1.22 right now.'

'And under 1.22, what are those numbers 55 and 57 in the blue boxes?'

'Those are the "pips," the small amounts that change fast. Combined with the big figure above, the numbers in the blue boxes give the best bid and offer prices for euro in the market. It means that if we could get the best deal that's out there, we could sell euro for $1.2255 or buy it for $1.2257. I usually just watch the big figures, so that when a customer calls and wants euro, I have a rough idea of what's happening in the market.'

I point to USD/JPY with a 'big' figure of 107 and the 'pips' showing 14 and 18. 'OK so let me see if I'm catching on. The currency being traded is the dollar, so a dollar is worth about 107 Japanese yen. If we could get the best deal, we could sell dollars to that buyer (bidder) for 107.14 and we could buy them from that seller (offerer) for 107.18 yen.' By the time I said that, the pips had changed.

The telephone rings and Carlos checks the caller identification. He pushes the connect button. 'Whatcha interested in today, Joe – Hong

Kong dollars?' Carlos clicks an icon on his computer, and the company's account appears on the screen. 'Swiss francs?'

'Your payment will be due on December 1st? Just a second, I'll see what we can do.'

Carlos shouts over to Jean, '2 dollars for Swissies shy of six months.' For my benefit he points to the USD/CHF 6M (6 months forward), which has a big figure of 1.23 and fast moving pips.

'All right,' Jean punches something on her terminal. 'OK tell him for $2 million, a week shy of six months forward, we can get them to him at twenty-three forty-five.'

Carlos tells his client, 'We can get you Swiss francs on November 30, 2005 at 1.2345 Swiss francs per dollar, so that comes to about 81 cents per Swiss franc.'

Carlos listens for a second, then says, 'Just a second Joe, I'll see what I can do.' He presses the hold button on the telephone.

'Jean, this is one of my best customers, can you do a little better for me?'

Jean looks again at her screen and waits, 'OK Carlos, tell him twenty-three fifty, but that's it. The market's squirrelly today.'

Carlos activates the telephone, 'Joe, the best I can do for you is 1.2350 Swiss francs per dollar and that comes to 80.97 cents per Swiss franc, but this won't last. You want to go with it or call back later?'

'All right, I'll arrange it, hold just a second.'

'Jean, 2 dollars for Swissies November 30th at twenty-three fifty.'

Jean looks Carlos in the eye and nods, then quickly moves to work on her terminal.

'Joe, we'll deliver 2,470,000 Swiss francs to your account on November 30th, and we'll debit your dollar account $2 million at that time. Give me your Swiss account number.'

Carlos writes on his pad, UBS–Zurich and a long series of numbers, which he reads back to Joe. 'OK Joe, done. We'll hear from you later about the rest. Take care.' Carlos punches the end call button.

I ask, 'Carlos, what is Joe going to do with the Swiss francs?'

Carlos says, 'He's the treasurer for a company, and they're ordering some specialty equipment from a manufacturer in Switzerland that won't be ready until early December. The actual amount he'll need to pay is close to 6 million Swiss francs.'

'So why did he just buy 2.5 million?' I ask.

'Well, he's been calling for about a week now, and I advised him not to do it all at once. He wanted to insure himself against a rise in the Swiss franc, so he made a move for about half the amount he'll need and then as the time approaches he'll probably get another forward contract for part or all the rest. He's probably costed the equipment in at about $4.5 million.'

'How did you know he was good for $2 million?' I ask.

Carlos clicks the mouse and blocks out the corporation's name so I can't see it. A nameless account appears on the screen. 'Well, I knew he was good from past transactions, but, as you can see, this company has substantial balances with us, and this shows an untapped line of credit for this company for $10 million. So the back office is giving me an automatic green light for this transaction.'

Carlos enters the details of the transaction on the screen and clicks the printer icon. He walks over to the printer and retrieves a sheet. He then enters a note in pencil on the sheet and explains. 'We have a verbal recording of the telephone conversation, an electronic recording that I entered, but I still do it the old way and write out details in long hand on hard copy as a triple check. The back office verifies the transaction and passes on the payment instructions.'

'And from there?'

'From there, it's all computers and straight-through processing. Nobody touches the message any more. It's set up so funds will go from our account in Switzerland to Joe's account on November 30th, so he'll have the funds to pay for his machinery on December 1st.'

'How do you know your Swiss account will cover this amount at that time?' I ask.

Carlos says, 'That's Jean's job. My guess is she has already bought Swiss francs 6 months forward from another bank at a slightly better rate than we sold them to Joe for. Did you notice her discomfort at the second rate she quoted?'

'I did. She didn't waste a second getting back on the computer. What was that about?'

Carlos explains, 'My hunch is her first quote would have given her plenty of time to wait for a better rate later in the day. The second rate didn't give her much room to maneuver, so she had to cover the bank's exposure fast, and sometimes that takes more moves. You should ask her about that later … Look, I've got a call on my email.'

On a partition at the top of the screen, Carlos sees a message that reads:

Carlos, I have 10 million pesos I want to transfer back. What can you do for me? Juan

Carlos calls across to the trading island, 'Scott, I need dollars for 10 Mexicans.'

'Hold on,' Scott checks his screen. 'I can give you nine nineteen US.'

Carlos replies:

Juan, 10 million pesos will transfer back as $919,000 U.S. I can have your dollars on Thursday. Are you on?

Si, andale pues. Con el problema con el gobierno, el peso cae.

Hasta pronto. Carlos.

As Carlos writes up the ticket, I ask. 'Do you get much Internet action?'

'Not so much yet. Most treasurers want to hear my voice. Juan's company does apparel across the border, and there's a lot of money transfers back and forth. He'd rather not sit on hold, and sometimes I have three or four waiting.' He points to the multiple-line telephone.

Jean calls over, 'Carlos taught you anything, professor?'

'You bet. Are you ready for me?' I ask.

She calls me over to her workstation and I pull up a swivel chair. 'How long have you been working at this, Jean?'

'I've been here for fifteen years now, first as a sales executive, then as a trader in some of the exotic currencies, and slowly I worked myself up to the European currencies.'

Alice calls over, 'Jean, I need 2 million pounds three months out.'

Jean punches her mouse and a scrolling list of bid/offer rates for GBP/USD forwards at various maturities appear on the screen. The offer quotes for 3M [3 months forward] are moving down a bit, the latest ones hovering around $1.8048. Jean calls back to Alice, 'I can give you 2 million pounds 3 months forward at $1.81.'

Alice relays the message to her client, waits a few seconds for a reply, and calls back to Jean, 'Done.'

Jean then looks at the scrolling list and punches on a 3-month forward quote from HSBC. 'We deal with them a lot. Let's see if they'll answer my call.'

'Good, we're in contact.' On the top right, a message appears. Need cable 3 months? Colin

Jean prints in. Want 2 cable. Still at 48? Jean

Colin replies. 2 cable's yours at 8048. Colin

Jean prints. We buy 2 cable 3 months forward at $1.8048. Jean

Done. Colin

A ticket appears on a partition, and Jean checks it over. 'This is one of the neat things about Reuters Direct Dealing. It has this artificial intelligence software that translates my direct communication with the other dealer, which is in dealer language, into a ticket, so 2 cable translates into £2 million. It has the rate we agreed upon (GBP = 1.8048 USD), and it automatically calculates the amount of dollars ($3,609,600) that we are to deliver in 90 days to HSBC Midland's account in New York, and it shows our account in London will receive £2 million.'

'Have you ever run into misinterpretation from the artificial intelligence?' I ask.

'You always have to check it. Sometimes if rates are moving fast and we're quoting the last two digits, it gets the big number on the left wrong, so in such a case it might have printed out $1.8148. That would have blasted our margin! Everything's right on this one, so I'm going to feed it in.'

'Feed it in?'

'Yes, once I check the ticket and enter it, a digital copy gets fed into the back office. They confirm the transaction with HSBC before passing on the dollar delivery message into the payments system. And it adjusts our back office book system. From his office computer, Mr Roberts can track our positions in different currencies as they change throughout the day. And I get a hard copy of the ticket that's being printed out over there.' She points to the printer with a sheet moving through.

'So you sold sterling to the customer at $1.81 and bought it from another bank at $1.8048?' I ask.

'Yes, that's the idea: sell high and buy low. I figure that's a gross of about $10,000, but we have to cover expenses. Also, if sterling had moved up, that margin could have been eaten up fast and we could have lost on the deal. So we get compensated for taking that risk.'

'Why didn't you hit on one of the dealers offering sterling at $1.8046?' I ask.

'None of them was a bank that I was sure we have credit relations with. I knew HSBC would accept our bid and our back office would accept them as counterparty. We have a strong relation with them, and I wanted to go ahead and cover our short position in sterling that was created when we sold sterling to Alice's customer.'

'How would you have done that deal before you had this direct dealing computer hookup?' I ask.

'When I first came to the bank, we did all our inter-bank deals over the telephone or using telex. Usually we'd call a big bank like HSBC that makes a market in sterling, or if it were a large order, we might call a broker in New York. Seven years ago when we upgraded our dealing room we bought into the Reuters direct dealing system, so, instead of just calling one bank, I can see what several dealers are offering and I click on the one I want to talk with. When one answers my call, I can have a secure direct conversation with that dealer, just as you saw over here on the right window. I can have up to four conversations going on at the same time, though I prefer no more than two at a time. Reuters came out with a Dealing 3000 product a couple of years ago that allows more than twenty conversations at the same time, something we haven't bought into.'

'What would you have done if you had seen the market changing in your favor while in the middle of a deal?' I ask.

'There's the interrupt button I can punch at anytime before confirming, and the counterparty has one too. The idea is you don't want to have long pauses when you're in direct conversation mode. You strike a deal and move on.'

On the screen she's been working on, she flips to Reuters 2000-2 Spot Matching, and explains how easy it is to make deals, especially for sterling, Swedish krona, and Australian and New Zealand dollars. She points to a screen on the left that looks like Carlos's slot machine line up. She explains that for euro and yen, the Electronic Brokerage Service (EBS) works better. 'It's easier nowadays with electronic brokers to see what's happening in the market.'

She points out the 'EBS Best.' 'That shows me the highest "bid" and lowest "offer" prices going through the EBS system, which is huge for euro/dollar and dollar/yen. See, it changes every second. All the dealers use that as a reference price for deciding what to offer customers. For sterling/dollar and Aussies, everybody uses Reuter's Spot Matching as a reference, because most of the market goes through them for those currencies. This electronic brokerage is so much easier to see what's happening in the market than what we used to have.'

'What was it like before?'

'We had a black box hooked into the voice brokers in New York. They would yell out over an intercom the highest "bid" and lowest "offer" prices and the actual deal sizes going through them. You could hear the urgency in their voices sometimes and that was a cue we don't get through the electronic brokers, but the electronic matching is much easier to see what's really happening. And with electronic brokers it only takes a second to act on a trade. We got rid of the squawk boxes years ago.'

'Jean, what would you have done a little while ago if you had thought sterling was going to fall further today?'

'I would have waited a while and watched the market, hoping to get sterling cheaper later on,' she says.

'Would you have waited overnight if you thought it would go down the next day?' I ask.

'No way. I have to close out open positions before the end of the day, though I can carry an intra-day exposure of up to $10 million. Scott gets up to $5 million, and George gets up to $3 million. Mr Roberts gets up to $30 million for the whole dealing room. If I see a good bet that will take me over, I call Mr Roberts and he usually approves it. George and Scott get approved through me, but our policy is for no overnight bets. Who knows what shock will hit in Tokyo, Singapore, or Europe while we're asleep.'

Taylor calls to George, 'I need 3 million dollars' worth of yen.'

Jane whispers, 'Go watch. George will go through EBS on this.'

As I walk to George's workstation, he calls to Taylor. 'One o six ninety.'

George is working off the EBS Spot screen, which has a price panel on the left with rows of large blue target boxes with yellow numbers inside them that flip every few seconds like Carlos's setup. A pair of boxes in the middle of each row gives bid and offer rates for that currency. The top row says USD/JPY, and shows in small black numbers 107, and the big target boxes in the middle read 32 bid and 35 offer in yellow. On the right side of the screen, George punches in a **SELL REQUEST** at 107.32 for 3 and looks up to Taylor, who nods that the deal is on. George punches the send button, and looks to see if the deal has gone through. When the confirmation appears, he says, 'Good, we made 1.26 million yen on that one.' I calculate if he were to use his yen profits and buy back dollars at 107.35 yen per dollar as quoted on the offer side, he'd have a profit of a little less than $12,000 on the deal.

'I don't see counterparties listed on the screen. How did you know the back office would approve?' I ask.

George says, 'With electronic brokerage, the yellow bids and offers in the big blue boxes are with counterparties that are pre-screened. They can trade with us for those amounts and we can trade with them. We can't see who the counterparty is. The broker electronically matches us up.'

'So, how is pre-approval done without knowing the counterparty?' I ask.

He explains that every morning the back office enters a counterparty list into the EBS and Reuters Spot Matching systems with credit amounts that each counterparty is good for. 'And they do the same for us.' George points out yellow and red warning panels across the top of the EBS screen. He says that those counterparties are approaching their credit limits, so a deal through them might not go to completion. He says the back office can increase or decrease counterparty credit at any time during the day.

I ask him whether he can tell if those are good prices.

He points to the small red numbers over his target boxes. 'These show the best deals on the whole market. See how the spreads are thinner than those of the target boxes.' The red numbers read 33 34 above the big blue boxes that read 32 35. 'Those red numbers are the highest bids and lowest offer rates coming through the entire EBS system, but apparently we don't have credit relations with those counterparties. The only ones I can hit on are the blue target boxes with the yellow numbers inside.'

'What if you saw the yellow numbers changing while you were preparing your sell request?'

He points to the 'Quit' button next to the 'Send' button. 'I would have punched that and the deal would have terminated.'

'Don't you have to pay a brokerage fee?' I ask.

'Yes, but Mr Roberts says it's small.' George explains that this saves time. You don't have to call around to find the best prices. What you see is what's really available to you, and the computer finds the best price available. He says he's noticed spreads have gotten thinner with electronic brokerage, so spot transactions are cheaper and quicker to execute.

'Can you get forward contracts electronically brokered?' I ask.

He says that spot markets are where electronic brokerage has worked best, but, in currency pairs that trade a lot, forwards are being done more and more through electronic brokers.

Jean has just finished a trade and motions for me to come back over.

'Jean, I'm curious about the moves you made after Carlos got the better deal from you on Swiss francs.'

'I had to move fast on that.' She puts the screen back on Swiss francs. 'I would have lost on it if I had to do the deal now. Look how the Swiss franc has strengthened.'

'What did you do, exactly?'

'First I tried to get a forward match through Reuters electronic broker- age, but the dollar wasn't crossing very fast with the Swiss franc at that moment.'

'Crossing fast?'

She explains that there wasn't much action that far forward between dollars and Swiss francs. Sometimes the Swiss franc crosses faster with euro than with the dollar, and the dollar crosses very fast with euro. 'Instead of waiting around to find a direct match with dollars to Swiss francs, I found a match from dollars to euro, then from euro to Swiss francs. And the two transactions got me to Swiss francs from dollars faster than going direct.'

'Jean, your job sounds more and more like that of a travel agent.'

Jean smiles, 'It's sort of like that, trying to find the least expensive and fastest route to a destination.'

I pull out my pocket calendar and look at it. 'But isn't 6-months forward going to end up on December 6th when you'll receive the Swiss francs? And wasn't Carlos's textile man promised the Swiss francs on November 30th?'

'You're catching on pretty fast... for an economist.' Jean says back-handedly.

I'm used to this treatment at family reunions, so I ignore it. 'So your Swiss francs don't arrive 'til December 6th. How will you get them into your account so they can be delivered to Joe on November 30th?'

'When the time approaches I'll enter a swap.'

'How will that work?'

'We'll see on our book that we're short Swiss francs on November 30th and long Swiss francs on December 6th. We'll do a one-week swap that will trade dollars for Swiss francs for delivery on the 30th of November, so we'll be able to pay Joe on time, and then reverse it back into dollars when our forward Swiss francs are delivered on December 6th.'

'Why didn't you just enter a forward contract for November 30th?' I ask.

'That wasn't a straight date, and the cheapest and quickest way to move is where there's a lot of two-way traffic.' She rattles off the straight dates, explaining that after three weeks forward, the standard contracts switch to one-month intervals up to one year, after which there's very little action. She flips to a 'Broken Dates' screen and points out how wide the best bid/offer spreads are for November 30th. Then she flips to the straight date window and shows the thinner spread on December 6th.

'So, let's see if I got this right. On the straight dates there is lots of trading, so you get more competitive pricing.'

'More competitive pricing and faster trades.' On the broken dates, she says, fewer deals go to completion.

'So when you started trying to cover your exposure from Carlos's deal, did you know you would have to go the route you took?'

'No. I just saw the direct route through the electronic broker wasn't crossing fast enough, so I tried the dollar to euro, euro to Swiss franc route, and it worked.'

'What would you have done if the forward matching proposals were slowed down by the back office?'

'I would have gone to the direct dealing window and traded forward with UBS or one of the other big banks we do a lot of business with.

I wouldn't have gotten as narrow a spread from them, but I would have been able to get the deal done.'

'What makes you so sure you'll find a good swap deal as December approaches?'

'That won't be a problem. There's lots of traffic in short-term swaps.'

'This amazes me. You did two forwards and then you'll do a swap, three transactions for the bank to cover one transaction on behalf of the company buying equipment.'

Jean says, 'Yes. The cheapest route in this business is not always the direct flight.' She looks up. 'There's Mr Roberts. I've got to check our overall positions. I think this afternoon may be busy.'

'Thanks for the FX lesson, Jean.' 'And thank you Carlos...' I catch Carlos's eye as he looks up from his screen. 'And George.' George is too deep in an Asia trade to hear me.

Who are the actors in the world's biggest market?

Mr Roberts welcomes me into his office. 'What did you see happening in there?'

I tell him about the order Carlos took from the manufacturer and how it led to three transactions by Jean to cover the bank's exposure. 'Is that typical?'

Mr Roberts passes me a chart over the desk.

4.1 / Customers of major currency dealers (April 2004)

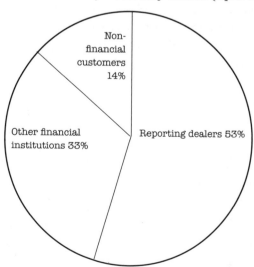

He points out that the deal Carlos made for the textile manufacturer would show up in the section labeled 'non-financial customers,' the smallest portion of daily market turnover. 'One transaction for a customer can lead to several transactions with other dealers as we find the cheapest and best way to adjust our books.' He points out that the largest piece of the pie represents the trades Jean made with other reporting dealers. 'The great bulk of the turnover in the market is not directly with outside customers but between currency dealers themselves.'

'Who are "other financial institutions"?'

'They're smaller banks that weren't being surveyed and the various fund managers I was speaking of this morning.' He gives examples of pension funds, mutual funds, and hedge funds that have globally diversified holdings of stocks, bonds, derivatives, and money market instruments. 'Most of *our* clients are manufacturers or export/import businesses. We don't do much business for fund managers, but the big guys do.' He points out that orders from other financial institutions were more than twice the orders from 'real economy' players like merchants and manufacturers. 'Before the 1990s, it was the reverse. The non-financial customers, like the manufacturers we serve, drove the market back then.'

I ask how the fund managers have altered the way the market works.

'The fireworks of the 1990s,' he says, 'were mostly set off by fund managers, who would move money into places that looked "hot." Later they'd get cold feet and rush for the exits. The stampede would pop asset-market bubbles and trigger currency crises.' He gives some examples including the Mexican peso crisis in 1994–95, the South Asian currency crisis in 1997, the Russian ruble crisis in 1998, and the Argentine default in 2001. 'Our manufacturing customers sought cover like everyone else, but their work didn't cause the fireworks.'

'The picture I'm getting is that the currency dealers react to orders from customers, maybe making several moves with other dealers to cover the exposures created by the outside customers, and they make money by charging higher spreads to their customers. You're implying that some of the fund managers speculate on the direction of exchange rates, but what about the currency dealers? Don't they bet on exchange rates?'

Mr Roberts considers for a moment. 'Most banks allow their traders room to speculate on the short-term movement of exchange rates and changes in interest rates. That's what Jean's doing now as our customer orders decline in the afternoon.' He explains how larger dealers in big money-centers allow their most experienced traders to speculate with much larger sums during the day, and, from his understanding of it, the most trusted ones might be allowed overnight positions. Those are the traders in 'the pit,' like those in the center in our trading room. 'Because this activity places the bank's own capital at risk, each trader is given time limits and loss limits and is allowed only so many chips to bet with.'

'What about the section of "proprietary traders" you mentioned you saw in New York? Are they given more freedom?'

'Specifics weren't disclosed to me, but I would imagine the proprietary traders have strict loss limits but are allowed more room to develop trading strategies than those in the pit. And their trades could involve stocks, bonds, money instruments, and commodities in addition to currencies.'

'What about the huge, multibillion dollar currency deals you hear about between banks? Are those bets?'

Mr Roberts emphatically shakes his head no. 'Those guys are hedging.' He says customers of banks, like so-called hedge funds and investment funds, speculate regularly, and taking their orders may require dealing banks to adjust their own exposures with some jumbo deals. He seriously doubts that the 'proprietary traders' at banks are making such orders. 'Of course there could be a rogue trader out there who somehow gets around the bank's betting limits.'

'How did the Barings collapse affect you?' I pick up on Mr Roberts's reference to Nick Leeson, a Singapore trader for the venerable 200-year-old British merchant bank, who got around the bank's internal control system with a secret trading account he numbered '8888.' Leeson's bets on the Tokyo, Singapore, and Osaka futures markets led to accumulated losses of £830 million, forcing Barings, where the queen herself banked, to fail on 27 February 1995.[1]

He reflects. 'After Barings, everybody in the business checked internal betting controls.'

'What about as middlemen? I mean, do a few big banks control it so they can price-gouge, or is there competition?'

Mr Roberts looks up for a second. 'There's both. Concentration *and* competition.'

'How concentrated is it at the top?'

'*Very*. And it's getting more so.' He passes me a chart and points out that the top twenty dealers in 2005 control 90 per cent of the market and the top three dealers control more than a third of the market. 'Our small business doesn't even rank us in the top forty.'

I ask him how accurate these surveys are.

He explains that the *Euromoney* surveys taken in May only poll outside customers, like corporate treasurers and assorted fund managers, who report how much currency business they did in the previous month with

4.2 / Share of foreign exchage turnover captured by top dealers (cumulative share of FX market turnover, %)

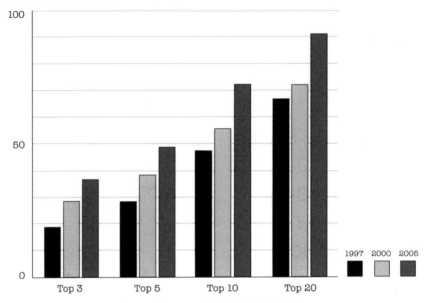

Source: *Euromoney* FX Polls, 1997–2005.

particular dealers. The *Euromoney* polls don't capture trades between dealers. But he notes that the more comprehensive central bank survey taken every three years shows the same trend of increasing concentration in the business. 'The New York Fed's survey that we participated in shows almost the same increases in concentration at the top that the *Euromoney* polls show.' He says that according to the New York Fed survey, the top ten dealers in the US had increased their share to more than 70 per cent of the US market in 2004, and the top five had increased their share to just under half the total reported turnover in the US.[2]

'Why has the currency business gotten so top-heavy?'

'Consolidation.' He says that mergers and acquisitions have relentlessly reduced the number of banks. 'Barriers of all sorts broke down in the 1990s, and there was a feeding frenzy.' He says that for the foreign exchange business this has meant fewer dealers. 'In 1992, there were 180 currency dealers in the New York Fed survey. In 2001, there were 79 of us. Last year, 2004, there were 43. By 2007, we will have opted out of the survey if we haven't been gobbled up by one of the big currency dealer banks.'

I ask him, 'So where's the competition?'

4.3 / FX overall market share (May 2005 *Euromoney* Survey)

2005 rank	FX Bank	2004 rank	Market share 2005 (%)	Cumulative share (%)
1	Deutsche Bank	2	16.72	16.72
2	UBS	1	12.47	29.19
3	Citigroup	3	7.50	36.69
4	HSBC	5	6.37	43.06
5	Barclays Capital	7	5.85	48.91
6	Merrill Lynch	10	5.69	54.60
7	JPMorgan	4	5.29	59.89
8	Goldman Sachs	6	4.39	64.28
9	ABN Amro	11	4.19	68.47
10	Morgan Stanley	13	3.92	72.39
11	Royal Bank of Scotland (RBS)	9	3.62	76.01
12	Lehman Brothers	14	2.46	78.47
13	Dresdner Kleinwort Wasserstein (DrKW)	12	2.37	80.84
14	Credit Suisse First Boston (CSFB)	8	2.36	83.20
15	Royal Bank of Canada	17	1.77	84.97
16	Bank of America	15	1.60	86.57
17	State Street	16	1.35	87.92
18	Caiyon	21	1.15	89.07
19	BNP Paribas	18	1.09	90.16
20	Société Générale	20	0.80	90.96
21	SEB	19	0.68	91.64
22	Mizuho Financial	31	0.49	92.13
23	Mitsubishi Tokyo Financial	26	0.48	92.61
24	Standard Chartered	24	0.43	93.04
25	Svenska Handelsbanken	30	0.39	93.43
26	Danske Bank	22	0.34	93.77
27	Zurich Cantonalbank	48	0.34	94.11
28	HVB Group	29	0.33	94.44
29	Westpac Banking	25	0.31	94.75
30	Nordea	27	0.28	95.03

Mr Roberts says, 'There's major jockeying for position from one year to the next. That keeps the ones on the top watching their hindquarters.'[3] Mr Roberts passes me a list of the top twenty currency dealers in the *Euromoney* May 2005 survey. He points out how Merrill Lynch went from tenth place to sixth place in one year, and how two newcomers (ABN Amro and Morgan Stanley) entered the ranks of the top ten, displacing the same number from the previous year's top dealers.

I look over the list. I notice that Merrill Lynch, Goldman Sachs, and Morgan Stanley are not commercial banks but are brokerage houses and/or investment banks, and they all ranked in the top ten currency traders in 2005. 'How did these become important in the money changing business when they're not commercial banks and don't issue account money[4] themselves?'

Mr Roberts's eyes sharpen. 'One doesn't have to issue account money to own it and trade it.' He explains that in the early 1990s, the top twenty dealers were all commercial banks, but as global investment in stocks and bonds exploded, investment banks and brokerage houses set up their own in-house dealing rooms to handle currency exchanges they had farmed out to commercial banks before. 'Once they tasted the profits from the currency trading business, they expanded their dealing rooms and became aggressive competitors with the commercial banks.' 'But,' he reflects, 'back then the lines were clearer between commercial banks, and investment banks and brokerage houses.'

'Weren't the lines drawn in the 1930s after the US banking system collapsed?' I refer to the Glass–Steagal Act, which kept commercial banks, which issue account money, from taking on risky investments like stocks.

'Yes, and then the firewall broke down in the 1990s.'

'How did that happen?'

He explains that big American banks – like Citibank – saw themselves losing out to international competitors like Deutsche Bank. In Germany, there were no restrictions on commercial banks holding stock and underwriting new issues. He points to the top of the list. 'Notice the dealer in third place in 2005 is *Citigroup*, which contains Citibank, Salomon/Smith Barney/Schroeder, an investment bank/brokerage house, and Travelers Insurance Company, among others.' He points down to seventh place JPMorgan, an investment bank, which in 2001 merged with Chase Manhattan, a big commercial bank. 'Not only are we seeing mergers of commercial banks, but banks are merging and forming holding companies with other types of financial service firms.' He points out that every currency dealer in the top ten on the 2005 list has a sizeable investment banking business. 'That's how important stocks and bonds have become for currency markets.'

I notice a black and white photograph on the wall behind Mr Roberts. 'Who's in the photograph?' I ask.

Mr Roberts gets up and takes down the picture. 'This is my first FX team.' He lays it down in front of me. It looks like an old Polaroid snapshot that was later enlarged. Sepia stains make it look older than it is.

'Is that you?'

He nods affirmative.

'You look like Neil Armstrong.'

He says, 'Yes. I felt like I could fly to the moon back then.'

'Just two of you ran the show?' Thirty years his elder, a woman peers out through black, pointy-rimmed glasses. She has a pencil in her hand, a ledger book and a calculating machine in front of her.

'That's how we started.'

'Three rotary phones, for two of you?'

'Yes, and sometimes we had all three going at once.' He explains that two lines were set up to receive calls from customers, but one was a dedicated toll-free line to the dealers in New York.

'Weren't there touchtone phones back then?'

'Yes, but we saw no reason to invest in them. But we did have an IBM selectric typewriter. She demanded it.' He points to the typewriter on the edge of the picture.

'I don't see a voice broker speaker box.'

'We didn't get that until the 1980s. We never jumped on the newest gadget.' He explains that from the very beginning his department was there not to build up a volume business but to serve the currency needs of the bank's customers. Only if a technology could be justified to serve the customer better at a cost advantage would they introduce it. 'That's one reason we've remained a reliable profit center for the bank.'

'How did the voice broker loudspeaker help?'

'We could hear the brokers shouting orders that were coming from big dealers at the center of the market. That gave me an edge when I'd call a dealer in New York to place an order. I would have a sense of the current market conditions that would help me negotiate with the dealer, and some of that benefit would be passed on to our customers.'

'And now I see you're using electronic brokers.'

'Electronic brokerage is terrific.' He says it's easy to see the best prices being offered in the market and to use this information to bargain with their regular currency providers. 'Electronic brokerage has narrowed spreads, and it has allowed us to pass on savings to our customers.'

'And for other deals I noticed your traders were using Reuters–Direct Dealing.'

'Yes, we added that ten years ago, and we've gone along with a few updates since. This system has served us well. The latest version is called Reuters–3000.' He says Reuters–3000 speeds things up and allows traders more room to tailor their screens to their needs, but that wasn't enough to justify the additional cost. 'Anyway, we'll be bought out before it would pay off.'

'Mr Roberts, I noticed your traders in the center island never picked up the telephone the entire time I was in there. All their connections with other banks were through computers. But your account executives on the outer rim were talking with customers through telephone headsets. I saw only one customer request come in through your website. Wouldn't it be easier for corporate treasurers to shop around for better rates if they used the Internet?'

'That's happening as we speak for the big users.' Mr Roberts explains that until very recently even the frequent foreign exchange customer used the telephone to connect with their currency providers, while the banks shifted long ago to computerized communication.

'But why has e-commerce been so slow to take off in foreign exchange, when it has zoomed in stocks and bonds?' I ask.

He answers wryly, 'Some might say it's because the foreign exchange providers have enjoyed profits by keeping their customers on single lines.' He explains that foreign exchange providers, 'just like us,' first set up electronic access for customers through their banks' individual websites. Customers who wanted quotes from several banks would have to log on to several different sites and enter passwords to establish contact. This was just as cumbersome as using the phone, but a person's voice was not on the other end. So most customers didn't go to the trouble. 'But this is changing fast at the center of the market.'

'What's happening?'

'The biggest dealers got together and set up multi-bank portals. With one logon and one password, customers can do business with several currency providers at once.' He gives the example of a multi-bank portal called FXall. 'All but one of the top twenty dealers on that list can be reached through the FXall website.'

'How does FXall work?'

He explains that once logged onto the website, a customer has access to all the liquidity providers on the system that the customer regularly does business with. This gives the customer access to the research products of those providers in addition to Reuters' market news, allowing quick briefings on market developments. The customer can watch market prices and volumes. When ready to move, the customer can request quotes from all its liquidity providers at one time. Then the customer clicks on the best quote. After the customer's credit is checked and both sides confirm the deal, it is entered electronically and delivered using straight-through processing, which is more accurate and saves on back-office costs.

'So, why haven't you offered this to *your* customers?'

'We would have to pay FXall for each deal, so we'd have to charge for this in the prices we quote.' He says that it's probably worth it for customers who do large volumes of trades to use FXall, but his clients haven't asked for the service.

I think to myself, how vulnerable Mr Roberts's operation is. Within three months Mr Roberts will have ended a distinguished career. Within six months his bank, a mainstay of this region, will have been absorbed by a much bigger bank. Jean and Carlos, I suspect, will keep their jobs if they're willing to move to a giant trading room in a money-center. The others in the trading room will be job hunting.

'Mr Roberts, I hope you're planning to write your memoirs. It could all take place from this building. A film noir angle on the world's largest market.'

He laughs, 'Yeah, it would be called "Dealing on the Edge."' He points to a color photograph of his wife, and his voice brightens, 'but before anything else, my wife and I are going to travel. Our first stop is the center of it all.'

'I guess you're going to New York?'

'That's what most people think. But the real center of it all,' he whispers as if telling a secret, 'is London.'

Where deals are made: historical geography of money changer enclaves

Packed into a tiny area of old London, dealers make more currency trades than anywhere else on earth. Nine months before the birth of the euro, London dealers reported more trades in French francs than were reported in all of France, and they traded more marks than were traded in all of Germany. The United Kingdom did not join the European Monetary Union, yet five years after the euro's birth London dealers were making more euro trades than all the dealers in the twelve-country Eurozone combined. Working out of trading rooms in a financial district slightly larger than 1 square mile, currency dealers in London reported more than one and a half times the value of US dollar trades than all the dealers surveyed in the 3.6 million square miles of the United States of America. The City of London transacts more than one and a half times the foreign exchange business of its closest rival, Manhattan, and almost four times that of Tokyo's financial district. Yet, when the April 2004 global foreign exchange survey was taken, Britain's own currency, the pound sterling, comprised 8 per cent of global foreign exchange turnover, tracking in fourth place behind the dollar, the euro, and the yen in world currency trading.

Bounded on the north by the Old Roman Wall and on the south by the River Thames, 'The City,' as it is popularly called, has its own government headed by the Lord Mayor, its own regulatory bodies to ensure the soundness of financial business and the exchanges, and its

5.1 / Foreign exchange hotspots (average daily turnover, April 2004, US$ billion)

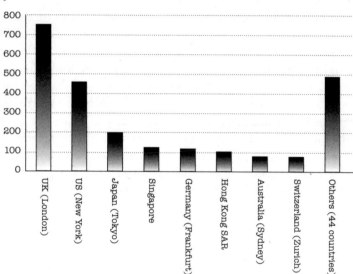

own courts for the settlement of disputes. Until recently, international financial houses had to be located within the strict boundaries of the City to receive the City's protections, but it was difficult to contain the construction boom within a 680-acre area, so the old law was relaxed to allow for building in other sections of Central London. International financial houses spilled over the wall, down Victoria Embankment and the Strand to Victoria Station, and they were allowed to operate under a City charter just as if they were inside the old boundaries. In effect, the City acquired another several hundred acres of London. So what is still referred to as 'the square mile' is really larger. 'The City' has grown to cover an area the size of a typical Midwestern corn farm.

On this plot along the Thames, more foreign banks have branches than in any other financial center in the world. In all, 287 foreign banks have branches and subsidiaries in London, 158 more than in Frankfurt, the official financial capital of the Eurozone, and 52 more than in New York, the actual financial capital of the United States.[1] In fact, more US banks have offices in London than they do in New York. Within earshot of the bells of St Paul's, 20 per cent of the world's cross-border lending originates, 43 per cent of the world's over-the-counter derivatives contracts are sold, 44 per cent of the world's trading of foreign stocks turns over,

6o per cent of its international bonds are underwritten, and 70 per cent of its international bonds are traded on secondary markets.[2] London is the largest center for international insurance and the hub of the world's gold and silver markets. Pension funds, insurance companies, mutual funds, hedge funds, and investment companies of all sorts manage their international portfolios out of London. While New York leads the world in investment banking and hedge fund management, about half of Europe's investment banking is conducted in the City of London and three-quarters of European-based hedge-fund assets are managed there.[3]

All of the international business in stocks, bonds, precious metals, oil, financial derivatives of all sorts, insurance, shipping, borrowing and lending, generates requests for changing money. On a typical day in April 2004, trading rooms in the City of London did about $750 billion worth of currency deals. This amounts to almost one-third of the world total, one and a half times the $460 billion daily turnover for the United States, almost four times Japan's $200 billion, and six times Singapore's $125 billion daily currency deals.[4]

The London foreign exchange market is remarkable not only for its daily volume but also for its depth and diversity. Dealers located in London have direct contacts with banks in every country of the world, including some that occasionally have been off limits to dealers operating out of the United States. Clients, like the former Soviet Union and certain Middle East oil states, who have wanted to avoid having enemies freeze their financial property, have chosen London over New York. Other clients, including some large US banks, who wish to escape costly and cumbersome regulatory requirements of central banks, raise funds or place them in the deep financial markets of London, which provides a smorgasbord of financial instruments of varying risk, maturity, and currency denomination. In terms of international financial expertise, London has the largest talent pool on earth, with some 300,000 professionals who enter and leave the City on a daily basis.[5] Savings from all over the world are channeled into London, processed by financial experts there, and sent to parts of the globe seeking the highest expected return – adjusted for perceived risk, of course. The City may be compact, but for global finance London is a giant money churn.

London-based money changers, however, are not that different from their counterparts elsewhere. Except for a few night-owl traders, who turn on their terminals to catch market developments where the sun still shines, London foreign exchange traders generally keep bankers' hours. They arrive in the City in the morning with everyone else, log on to their computers, commence trading, take a quick lunch break, work through the afternoon, and try to close out their positions before the closing bell. After shutting down their terminals and grabbing their jackets, they head for the pub to chat with their colleagues from other trading rooms. A London currency trader once told me, 'Really, old boy, all the City is is trading rooms and pubs. We just watch the clock in the afternoon and move to the next meeting place.' An extraordinary affinity for pub life aside, London foreign exchange traders are much the same as their trading partners in New York, Tokyo, Hong Kong, Singapore, Frankfurt, Sydney or Zurich. They speak English and are tolerant of other cultures. They prefer to sleep at night and stay away from their terminals on the weekends. I once walked through the City on Sunday. Dead. Not even a pub was open. Yet before the opening bell rang at the Royal Stock Exchange on Monday, the sidewalks and streets were bustling with pedestrians and taxis.

Because of the biological rhythms of its participants and the cultural legacy of keeping bankers' hours, the world currency market follows the sun's light around the globe. The trading week begins on Monday morning in Wellington, New Zealand, at 8 o'clock, when it is 9 o'clock Sunday night in London and 4 o'clock Sunday afternoon in New York. Without major financial centers open, trading is very thin until Tokyo opens three hours later at 8 o'clock Tokyo time. An hour after Tokyo opens there is a surge of trading volume, especially in dollar–yen and other Asian currency contracts, as the Hong Kong and Singapore markets open. This heightened activity of the Asian morning session lasts about two hours or until 12 noon Tokyo time, when trading drops off for a Japanese lunch break. Activity doesn't pick up to Asian morning intensities until 3 p.m. in Tokyo, when it is 8 a.m. in Frankfurt, Zurich, Paris and Milan. Peak trading for the Asian trading day – in Asian and European currencies – takes place between 4 and 5 p.m. Tokyo time, which corresponds to the opening hour of trading in London.

World trading volume steadily declines for the remainder of the morning session in London as Tokyo, Hong Kong, and Singapore close out. Volume does not pick up again until 1 p.m. in London, when traders have returned from lunch and it is 8 a.m. in New York. The period from 8:30 a.m. to noon in New York is the most intense session of the world trading day with London, Europe, and the Americas running full throttle. By noon New York time, it is 5 p.m. in London; London traders deserve a visit to the pub and New York traders can look forward to lunch and a less hectic afternoon, except for a 3 p.m. spike of activity as the Chicago currency futures and options market closes. At 4 p.m. in New York, Wellington, New Zealand, opens up, but the next trading day doesn't pick up until Tokyo opens at 7 p.m. New York time. On weekends, the world trading day effectively ends at 5 p.m. on Friday in New York, when by convention the world value date for spot contracts rolls over to Monday.[6]

Market participants know that if they try to make a currency deal when trading activity is thin, they will face wider spreads, and if they attempt to make a large transaction, they may have difficulty finding a counterparty willing to buy that much, so they waste valuable time. Moreover, in a thin market the mere disclosure of a large offer is likely to drive down the price against the seller. So market participants who are widely scattered about the globe are drawn by narrower spreads to where the most action is at any given time. Electronic networks allow participants located anywhere on the global communications grid to connect with dealers in the most active hub at that moment. Large money-changing banks have central dealing rooms strategically located in different time zones around the globe so that when one dealing room closes, the deal book is kept open by passing it westward to that bank's dealing room in the next foreign exchange hotspot. Thus, the currency market hopscotches around the globe from one enclave to the next. Activity waxes and wanes depending on daily work habits of traders. Like most everyone else, the money changer's biological time clock is set in relation to the sun and the convention of solar time zones.

One might even suspect that money changers had something to do with the invention of solar time zones. In 1869, Charles Dowd, the principal of a school in Saratoga Springs, New York, introduced the idea of dividing the earth into twenty-four time zones of 15 degrees each. That same year the Central Pacific Railroad met the Union Pacific Railroad in Promontory Point, Utah. The transcontinental railroad, which was largely financed with capital from the City of London, gave fast, reliable communication between the east and west coasts of the United States. With wagon trains, stagecoaches, and bandits, travel was slow and much more dependent on the weather, making accurate scheduling impossible. As more railroad lines were built, coordination of schedules was called for, and in 1883 US and Canadian railroad executives agreed on time zones for North America. A year later, a world conference met in Washington DC to decide on a worldwide grid system of twenty-four time zones.

Even more than changes in transport, telegraph service prompted the move towards the worldwide time system. Three years before Dowd birthed the twenty-four time-zone idea, the first transatlantic cable was laid (1866), and in the late 1870s duplex and then quadruplex transmission/receiver systems began sending multiple messages over the same existing cable. For world finance, communications technology sped the transfer of political and economic news that might influence exchange rates, allowing such news to reach New York from London on the same day instead of having to wait a week or two for a ship to arrive. Money could be 'wired' or 'cabled' for rapid delivery instead of having transfer instructions sent by steamer. Currency traders began referring to pound sterling as 'cable.' Even with today's satellite connections, 'cable' continues to be uttered in trading rooms around the world. More precisely 'one cable' refers to a unit of one million British pounds. Financed from London, telegraph poles, lines, and underwater cables spread with the British Empire, greatly diminishing the time lapse between transaction agreements and delivery of funds. This technology placed a premium on accuracy and coordination of time on a global scale. Not surprisingly, the 1884 conference on time zones decided on the Royal Observatory at Greenwich, England, as meridian zero for the world time grid. Contracts around the world began to be written with Greenwich Mean Time as absolute reference, which is equivalent to adding or subtracting hours from the reading on the Royal Exchange's clock in the center of the City of London.

Why do money changers cluster where they do?

Why did small areas of London, New York, Tokyo, Singapore, Frankfurt, Hong Kong, Sydney, and Zurich become foreign exchange hotspots? Six of today's top eight hotspots have seaports that handled massive volumes of international trade for more than a century. Since the twelfth century, London has been the chief commercial link between England and the continent of Europe, but with the increase in British sea power and the Industrial Revolution in the eighteenth century, London's international trade surpassed all other seaports of Europe. The Dutch West India Company built New York's first wharf on the lower tip of Manhattan Island in 1625. This strategic point commands the inland trade via the Hudson River and has storm-protected access to the ports of Connecticut and Rhode Island through the East River and Long Island Sound. Throughout most of the colonial period and thereafter, the port of New York handled more overseas trade than any other seaport of the US. Similarly, Tokyo, with its protected deepwater harbor and inland river access, became Japan's premier port in the nineteenth century and today remains Japan's largest port. Like New York and Tokyo, Singapore, Sydney, and Hong Kong are blessed with deep harbors and strategic commercial locations. Hong Kong has the finest anchorage on the China coast and dominated the South China trade since the first half of the nineteenth century. Sydney boasts the largest natural harbor in the world. Singapore has the best harbor on a series of straits linking the South China Sea with the Indian Ocean. Since the first half of the nineteenth century Singapore has been the most important trans-shipment point for goods entering and leaving Southeast Asia.

The connection between long-distance traders and international banking services is an old one. Since ancient times money changers set up their tables only a short walk from the docks. London's Lombard Street, named for the Northern Italian merchants and money changers who set up their shops and exchange tables there in the twelfth century, is only a few blocks from the docks on the Thames. In the 1450s you could go to Lombard Street and exchange sterling coins for coins of most great cities of Europe. If you did not wish to lug coins on a journey, you could stop at the Medicis' London branch on Lombard Street. With sterling, you could buy a letter of credit – a Renaissance travelers' check – redeemable in a choice of twenty currencies at Medici branches or correspondent firms located in the great trading towns of Belgium, France, Spain, Italy, and Greece. If you needed a loan in sterling to buy merchandise in London for export to Venice (or any of the other nineteen cities where a Medici branch or trusted correspondent was located) you could negotiate a bill of exchange with the Medici branch on Lombard Street. This early form of a foreign exchange derivative would allow you to pay the loan back in ducats ninety days later in Venice.[7]

Next to the old New York customs house, Exchange Place is only three short blocks from the East River docks on the southern tip of Manhattan Island. From Exchange Place north, you pass Wall Street, Pine, Liberty, a half-dozen blocks or so until you reach Fulton Place. This tiny portion of Manhattan, called the Financial District, exactly parallels the East River Docks. It is smaller than London's financial district, but in this small space you find the New York Stock Exchange, the American Stock Exchange, and the Federal Reserve Bank of New York. Until recently when some financial houses moved to roomier quarters in Midtown Manhattan, an exodus hastened by the attack on the twin towers, the Financial District contained the largest investment banks and bond dealers in the US, and the headquarters for five of the ten largest foreign exchange dealers in the world.[8] Similar to London and New York, the international financial districts of Sydney, Singapore, and Hong Kong all lie within walking distance of those cities' first docks.

Concentrated in the Nihombashi, Tokyo's financial district was the earliest area of Tokyo to be claimed from the marsh. It lies directly east of the Imperial Palace grounds and is linked to the deepwater port by the city's busiest canal, which feeds into the Sumida river at its mouth.[9] After the great fire of 1872, the Meiji government 'ordered new buildings to use brick or stone architecture,... [and] London's architectural designs were the guide for reconstructed buildings.'[10] The Nihombashi area, and the Kyobashi district adjacent to it, have since become the home of Japan's largest conglomerates. In 1913, these two areas of the city headquartered 54 of Japan's 159 *zaibatsu*, yet these 54 commanded 90 per cent of the total capital concentrated in conglomerates. The Nihombashi district became home to the Bank of Japan when it was first established in 1882; to Japan's largest foreign exchange bank, Yokohama Specie Bank, in 1899; to Japan's largest mortgage bank, Hypothec Bank of Japan, in 1897; the Agricultural and Industrial Bank of Japan in 1896; and to the Industrial Bank of Japan in 1900. Nihombashi became the seat of the Tokyo Rice Exchange in 1876, the Tokyo Stock Exchange in 1878, and the Tokyo Clearing House in 1891.[11] Nihombashi remains the center of international finance in Tokyo, though, as in the City of London and Manhattan's Financial District, the building boom has spilled over into less cramped space nearby.

Money changing and port activities are naturally connected, but the concentration of international money deals far exceeds those financial centers' relative importance as ports. Rotterdam's port traffic exceeds London's, and New Orleans' wharf activity rivals New York's, but international banking activity in New Orleans and Rotterdam pales in comparison to London and New York. Below the top four foreign exchange centers, there appear two notable ones that are inland transportation hubs, not seaports. With an inland crossroads and a river connection to the Rhine, Frankfurt has been the site of international trade fairs since the thirteenth century. Hamburg exceeds Frankfurt as an international port, yet Frankfurt is a giant compared to Hamburg in international banking activities. Likewise, Zurich is an important inland transportation hub, and in this respect it has served as a conduit for international commodity trade, but Zurich's international banking activity exceeds that of Antwerp, Rotterdam, and Amsterdam, all major ports.

What Zurich does have in common with some of the other great money-trading centers is a history of protecting money changers from political unrest that otherwise might have overturned their tables. Switzerland's armed neutrality and famed laws protecting banking secrecy go back more than a century, but London's protections of money changers go back much further. London's financial district sprang up in the eleventh and twelfth centuries behind the protection of the old Roman walls, which were built in 43 AD. Waterfront protection was enhanced when the Tower of London fortress was first built in 1078. During the fifth century, the one hundred or so guilds of London began purchasing freedom from monarchical intrusion, and in 1192 London acquired an independent charter of self-government, and the people elected their first Lord Mayor. Although Jews did not always fare so well, other groups, including Italians, were protected behind the walls of the city by special exemptions from royal decrees that restricted aliens and their movement elsewhere in the kingdom. Over time the city government grew stronger and developed its own army of sorts, called trainbands. In 1585, Queen Elizabeth I deployed trainbands to counter a potential land invasion by the Spanish, and the trainbands protected the City, its merchants and bankers, from hostile actions by monarchs like Charles I and Charles II. Metropolitan London expanded on all sides, but the message remained that the old city with its 680 acres of docks, warehouses, insurance companies, banking houses, the Royal Exchange, the stock exchange, the commodity exchange, the bond market, the Bank of England, St Paul's Cathedral and the Lord Mayor's Mansion, was not to be tampered with. Today this section of London is still administered by the independent and powerful 'City Corporation,' which guards the rights of its international financial establishment.

During the nineteenth century's age of imperialism the British created protected enclaves similar to the City of London in faraway places. Headquartered in the City of London, the East India Company acquired Singapore island from Johor in 1819 and quickly expanded port facilities in the natural harbor where the city of Singapore is today. The British government gained official control of the island in 1824. Enforced by the British Navy, laws protecting the rights of bankers, merchants, and shipping companies were extended to Singapore. London banks and trading companies set up branches in Singapore, and the port gained the reputation as a safe harbor for business and a refuge from political and economic turbulence on the mainland. Businesses of many nationalities enjoyed the freedoms afforded by Singapore, especially Chinese and Malayan merchants who flocked to the island. Although Singapore became independent from Britain in 1957, the laws and government of the island continued to guarantee freedom of movement for people, commodities, and financial capital, enhancing Singapore's natural advantages as a trans-shipment point and banking center.

British merchants retreated from mainland China to Hong Kong during the Opium Wars (1839–42), and the British acquired the island in the Treaty of Nanking in 1842. Reinforced by a naval base and British law, Hong Kong became a safe harbor for London-based companies and welcomed businesses of other nationalities. Whenever political or economic chaos rocks the mainland, Chinese refugees have fled to Hong Kong. Like Singapore, Hong Kong's laws and government have guaranteed freedom of movement for ships, banks, and merchants, enhancing its natural advantages of location. Perhaps the relative decline in Hong Kong's share of foreign exchange activity in 1998 and in 2001 was based on the fear that the unification with mainland China would tamper with these age-old guarantees.

Far less tangible than protection by fortresses, legal statutes, and governmental structures is an unusual cultural trait found within international banking enclaves. Over the years, these centers have attracted people who are eager to meet foreigners and learn how to pick the trustworthy from the rest. Those who exhibit these traits are rewarded within the community, and some are sent to other financial enclaves as envoys. At times when extreme intolerance or even blind fear of foreigners may reign in the broader society, the political culture of the enclave provides safe harbor for foreigners. There has been a long-run payoff for this behavior, which springs from the nature of banking itself.

The foundation of banking is trust. Geographical distance and cultural difference are enemies of trust. International bankers from the beginning have understood this. They have sent their own sons and most trusted business partners to foreign lands from home centers, where the enterprise already has established ways of judging the creditworthiness of clients and where the firm's own IOUs are accepted by the public. The envoy's job is to build up public trust in the firm abroad and to make prudent decisions about the creditworthiness and trustworthiness of potential clients and borrowers there. Where the envoy is sent is not random. It must be a place where there is plenty of potential business and a place where it is possible as a foreigner to live and become accepted. The reward to the host enclave is large. Once it is known that an enterprise from another land is trustworthy, that enterprise's services – lending, transferring money geographically, and others – can be used wherever that enterprise has branches or agents. This extends the business horizons of the entire enclave.

In medieval times, Florentine merchant houses set up branches in major European cities first to facilitate their own exports and imports of merchandise. Once established in foreign cities, they carried out consignment business for other merchants who could not afford to post someone abroad. Having access to local currencies and currency exchanges in the cities where they had branches, the largest of the Florentine merchant houses were positioned to extend their business from commodity trade into international banking. Between 1300 and 1345, the largest international banking firms in Europe were the Florentine firms of Bardi, Peruzzi, and Acciaiuoli, all of which had branches and networks of agents in the major financial and merchant centers of Europe. The records from the second largest of these enterprises, the Peruzzi, reveal the firm had 'fifteen branches scattered all over Western Europe and the Levant, from London to Cyprus and employed a staff of ninety clerks or factors.'[12] Peruzzi sons were partners of the firm and branch managers in Bruges, Paris, and Naples in 1335; partnerships with branch managers who were not family members were in the other locations.[13]

The famous Medici bank of the fifteenth century never achieved the size or geographical spread of the houses of Bardi and Peruzzi. Their organization of branch partnerships, with the branch manager investing a portion of the capital, was similar, and the Medici perfected some of the banking instruments and organizational structures invented by earlier banks. The Medici sent family members to be branch managers in enclaves abroad and set up partnership arrangements with non-family branch managers, who were sometimes sons or grandsons of former international bankers, especially heirs to what was left of the Bardi fortune.[14]

Branch managers of the Florence-based holding companies of the fourteenth and fifteenth centuries sought to become members of the business communities wherever they were stationed. They lent to princes and heads of state, not always to their financial benefit.[15] Branches would accept bills of exchange not only from Florentine merchants but from enterprises based anywhere in the network, provided the counterparty's credit rating was sound. The papacy found it convenient to use these banking firms to transfer revenues, payments, and subsidies all around Europe, much to the profit of the bank so long as the pope did not spend beyond his means.[16]

Ironically, the same firms that serviced the papacy circumvented the papal ban on usury through a clever use of bills of exchange. To charge interest was a mortal sin, but to change money was not. What the Florentine bankers figured out was how to lend florins and get paid back more florins without running the risk of damnation or loss of the papal account. A borrower wanting a six-month loan, for example, would draw a bill of exchange payable in sterling ninety days later in London by the borrower's agent. The London agent would refuse to honor the bill, but would rewrite it payable in florins ninety days later to the Florence branch by the original borrower. Six months later and after passing through two adverse exchange rates, the revolving bill yielded implicit interest to the Florentine banker on the original loan. 'Dry exchange,' as it was called, facilitated no transfer of goods, but it made an otherwise immoral act moral. For a four-month loan, a 'dry exchange' would be arranged through Barcelona, Valencia, or Bruges, which carried sixty-day one-way bills of exchange; and for a two-month loan, dry exchange could be arranged with Avignon, Palermo, or some other city that was thirty days one way from Florence. Shorter-term loans could be made through dry exchanges with closer banking centers like Venice, Siena, or Pisa.

The papal ban on interest charges meant that pawnbrokers and small-time lenders had to pay exorbitant license fees to local authorities for permission to practice the mortal sin, while bankers like the Bardis or the Medicis, who could afford branches in faraway places, monopolized the market for 'legitimate' lending. Medieval banking practices foreshadowed practices half a millennium later. Whenever modern-day governments or central banks place restrictions on banking activities, large banks with branches in foreign enclaves invent ways to avoid the restrictions, while smaller banks without those connections do not enjoy such an array of options. And great concentrations of banking activity tend to crop up in hothouse atmospheres outside the jurisdictions of interventionist states.

The greatest banking enterprise of the nineteenth century displayed a similar pattern to the Florence-based banks of the fourteenth and fifteenth centuries. The House of Rothschild had its beginnings in Frankfurt, a banking and merchant enclave from the Middle Ages. Mayer Amschel Rothschild (1743–1812), the son of a Frankfurt money changer, became the trusted financial agent for Count William IX of Hesse-Kassel, and acquired a small fortune in the French Revolutionary wars. His oldest son, Mayer Amschel (1773–1855) remained in charge of the Frankfurt parent company while his four other sons were sent to set up partnership branches in Vienna (Salomon, 1774–1855), London (Nathan, 1777–1836), Naples (Karl, 1788–1855), and Paris (James, 1792–1868). The Naples branch was closed shortly after Karl died, but in London, Paris, and Vienna the branches prospered as the original emissaries and their offspring became trusted bankers to private enterprise and heads of state. Everywhere the Rothschilds went, they participated in the cultural and political life of the financial enclaves where they did business, and, like the Bardis and Medicis, the Rothschilds set up in lesser centers agents who were not members of the family.

The Rothschild network came to be appreciated by kings and members of the business communities where they resided. Connections in Vienna led to all five brothers receiving the Austrian title of baron, which was inherited by their offspring. In London, Nathan's son, Lionel, was first elected to represent the City of London in parliament in 1847, a decade before Jews were allowed to vote in Great Britain. In Paris, James became well enough connected in financial circles to ride out political storms and expand the enterprise. James's connections with the French government remained untarnished, even while his brother in London was lending great sums to the enemies of Napoleon. James's eldest son, Alphonse, headed the Paris branch after his father's death and was later appointed to the powerful, trusted position as regent of the Bank of France.

The Peruzzis, the Medicis, and the Rothschilds provide personal sketches of the way trust networks are linked from one international financial enclave to the next. It may take years for a newcomer's creditworthiness and trustworthiness to be accepted by the local bankers' club. Once the newcomer passes scrutiny, the local club benefits from the linkup, and the foreigner may be propelled into powerful positions within the enclave. Even when xenophobia dominates the public consciousness outside, the walls of the enclave protect the foreigners who do business there.

The paradox of clustering in a computer-linked world

With today's international communications grid, banks in the most remote areas can connect with world currency markets. One might expect the excellent connections from any location to have eroded the walls of the traditional money-changing enclaves. After all, a bank in rural North Carolina can now trade directly with a bank in rural Italy through a Reuters' direct dealing network without having to go through a New York or London currency dealer. Paradoxically, money changing remains as geographically concentrated as ever. Throughout the information technology revolution of the 1990s, the top seven currency trading centers continued to capture more than three-quarters of global currency market activity. And the very top of the pyramid actually increased its market share. London's daily foreign exchange turnover grew from 27 per cent of global turnover in 1992 to 31 per cent in 2001 and 2004. Except for Hong Kong, which moved from fourth to seventh place from 1992 to 2001, the relative rankings of the seven hotspots remained stable, with the US in second place, Tokyo in third, followed by Singapore, Frankfurt and Zurich. The only recent newcomer to the top tier was Sydney, which in 2004 pushed Zurich into eighth place.

The continuation of national financial centers as key foreign exchange hubs is not so difficult to understand. New York, Tokyo, Frankfurt, Sydney, and Zurich are market centers for domestic exchange of money instruments, bonds, stocks, financial derivatives, and commodities. So long as trading in domestic financial instruments remains concentrated in national centers, it's logical that those centers will be the main hubs through which international finance flows.

In contrast, London, Hong Kong, and Singapore are more difficult to explain. These cases suggest that once a financial center gains international status and establishes deep connections with foreign financial centers, it can continue to work as an international money hub even when the original causes of international status have diminished. The sun has set on the British Empire, the Royal Navy no longer rules the seas, British goods have lost out to competitors elsewhere, and the pound sterling has lost ground to the dollar, the yen, and the euro. But London still rules the world of international finance, and former colonial outposts of the City continue as important offshore financial centers.

The City of London's nest of supporting institutions took several centuries to develop, yielding the rare combination of robust self-regulation and protections from government interference. There are few places in the world where private decisions can be made with such minimal interference from national political forces. At the same time, the City benefits from the strong and politically stable national government that surrounds it and the British legal system that undergirds it. Within the City, there are exceptionally strong standards, disclosure rules, regulatory and supervisory commissions, and unwritten codes of conduct that encourage transparency, safeguard against fraud, and provide a secure basis for making deals and settling them quickly. The trading culture that has evolved in the City does not seek special privileges for British companies over foreign companies, but thrives on open competition. London-based organizations like the City Corporation, the Bank of England, the Association for Payment Clearing Services, and British Invisibles work proactively with private businesses regardless of nationality to enable successful adaptations to change.

In September 1998, I had lunch with the London chief of Germany's second largest bank. His bank had considered moving its international trading operation from London to Frankfurt but had decided against it. I asked him why, and he said, 'We would have had difficulty in Frankfurt finding and keeping the skilled personnel we rely on to run this sort of operation.' In addition to London's abundance of people with the trading savvy and risk-management skills the German banker was referring to, London leads the world in availability of people with other support skills necessary for international business. Fourteen of the fifteen largest law firms in Europe are located in London. Sixty US law firms have offices in London; among these are eight of the ten largest legal firms in the US The world's largest accounting firms have London offices, and London is the leading provider of financial information services through firms like Reuters, which is headquartered in the City. People with actuarial skills have long been attracted to London by the booming international insurance business. The world's leading insurance underwriters have offices in London. The City abounds in management consultancy firms, which gather a variety of skilled personnel under one roof.

William Clarke, former head of British Invisibles and author of the book *How the City of London Works*, explains that the variety of services offered by London are broader than those offered by other financial centers. He notes that Tokyo is prominent in banking and investment. In addition to banking and investment, New York is strong in insurance, accounting, and legal services. London has all of New York's strengths, but it also has international shipping services, along with Chicago's strength, the commodity exchanges.[17] In a personal interview in July 1999, William Clarke stressed that all of London's services are available in a very compact space, the square mile. Big deals, he explained, involve trust. Despite all the modern-day improvements in communications technology, high-level decisions still require seeing the right people face-to-face. 'In London,' he said, 'anyone you need for advice or a handshake can be found within walking distance or a short cab ride. Deals can be made swiftly. Compactness is a great advantage for the City.'[18]

There seems to be a momentum at work. Once markets find a center, support services cluster there, suitable office space is built there, communications networks lead out from there, and business people from all over come there to do deals. Success feeds on itself. But there are forces that can disturb the momentum. Panama and Beirut were once major offshore banking centers, but political disruptions tarnished their 'safe haven' status, and office staff and equipment were quickly moved out. Bahrain supplanted Beirut as the location of choice in the Middle East. Cayman Islands and Nassau took financial business from Panama. Will Hong Kong suffer a similar fate if the Chinese authorities tamper with the port's traditional freedoms? Hong Kong lost currency market share in 1998, following the transfer of power to the mainland, and its sharemarket share fell again in 2001, as some businesses moved to Singapore and Sydney. Will New York regain its dominance after the rebuilding of lower Manhattan is complete, or will offices be permanently relocated across the river or move further south to Charlotte, North Carolina?

London has not rested on its laurels. Leaders of the City are acutely aware of competition from other centers and they actively work to stay in the lead. In the spring of 2000, City leaders and financial houses lobbied hard through British government officials to defeat a proposal from the European Union for a 20 per cent withholding tax on foreign savings. They argued that the tax would force the Eurobond market to move from London to offshore centers outside of the European Union.[19] On the issue of technological change, City institutions have readily assisted private-sector initiatives to keep on the leading edge of the communications technology revolution. Rowan Douglas, the managing director of WIRE, the company that completed the electronic infrastructure for the World Insurance Portal, makes a broad argument that improved communications technology should not be expected to decentralize global finance. 'Far from equalizing places,' Douglas argues, 'improved communications empower the center to control a world periphery. The twentieth century's communication revolutions led to the rise of three leading world cities – London, New York, and Tokyo – serving the globe's primary need for capital and professional services. The networked world of the twenty-first century will lead to further concentration towards an international apex of information and capital. It will not be Tokyo. New York, massive though it is, remains a domestic center. The international winner will be London.'[20]

6

Professor Smith Gets FXed in Tokyo: could he have profited from a currency forecast?

Jonathan Smith, young and adventurous professor of literature, yearns to study the *Tale of Genji*, the eleventh-century novel of palace intrigue, using twelfth-century scroll manuscripts housed in two museums in Japan. In his grant proposal to the National Endowment of the Humanities, he makes no mention of the sensual character of these tales. He lucks out and avoids the scrutiny of certain Southern evangelicals on Capitol Hill and is awarded a grant that pays his airfare at the outset and $2,000 in monthly installments for the six months he will be living in Tokyo. Smith buys his round-trip ticket and finds an apartment for rent from an ad placed by a Japanese professor going on leave. He arranges for monthly stipends to be directly deposited into his US bank account, which has a Visa card attached allowing him to withdraw up to $1,000 worth of foreign currency a day.

Professor Smith arrives in June and finds the apartment small but comfortable, airy, efficiently arranged and close to the university. The rent seems a bit steep at 160,000 yen, but other professors tell him this is a bargain for the area. His first rent payment translates into $1,000, which he withdraws in a single transaction. The following day he returns to the bank and withdraws the remaining $1,000 worth, which leaves him 160,000 yen to budget for the rest of the month's food, entertainment, and weekend excursions.

June and July are wonderful months. Each weekend, Professor Smith tries another *onsen* in the mountains, where he takes long hikes in the brisk air in the mornings, relaxes in the hot baths in the afternoons, and gets geisha rubdowns at night. The inns cost him about $100 for an overnight stay or 16,000 yen including meals. He finds these spiritually uplifting and affordable to do four times a month, leaving him $600 or 96,000 yen to provision his cupboard and refrigerator, allow him a Kirin or two every night at the local pub and a once-a-week splurge at an upscale sushi bar around the corner, where he can try everything for 5,000 yen, or a little more than $30.

The manuscripts are more tantalizing than in his dreams; he meets some intense literary scholars, and he gets a brainstorm idea for a comparative project for his next sabbatical involving the *Kama Sutra*. This he figures would support a grant to go to India by way of Japan. One night at the pub he muses, 'Now this is the way to begin my first sabbatical.'

In August Professor Smith goes to the bank to make a withdrawal for the rent and asks the teller why she only gave him 150,000 yen. The teller politely points to the exchange rate sign, which reads USD = 150JPY in exactly the spot where it read USD = 160JPY a month before. He pays the rental agent the 150,000 yen from the withdrawal plus a 10,000 yen note he has tucked away as an emergency reserve. He decides he can make up the difference this month by cutting out two trips to the sushi bar. When September arrives, the teller gives him 140,000 yen for his maximum withdrawal, forcing him to return to the bank the next day to collect enough to pay the rental agent the extra 20,000 yen. This setback, he figures, will mean one less weekend in the mountains and only one trip to the sushi bar for the month. As the month wears on, he notices his supply of yen running out earlier than expected. The prices at the Hoshi Onsen and the pub have not changed, so he drinks a beer while he figures it out on a napkin.

6.1 / Professor Smith's napkin

MONTH	STIPEND	¥ PER $	¥ RECEIVED	RENT	SPENDING MONEY LEFT
June	$2,000	160 ¥/$	¥320,000	¥160,000	¥160,000
July	$2,000	160 ¥/$	¥320,000	¥160,000	¥160,000
August	$2,000	150 ¥/$	¥300,000	¥160,000	¥140,000
September	$2,000	140 ¥/$	¥280,000	¥160,000	¥120,000
October	$2,000	?	?	¥160,000	I think
November	$2,000	?	?	¥160,000	I'm getting
December	$2,000	?	?	¥160,000	FXed...

6.2 / Monthly average exchange rates, Japanese yen to US dollar

Source: Based on data © 2001 by Prof. Werner Antweiler, University of British Columbia, Vancouver.
Time period: 1 January 1985–31 December 2000.

It dawns on Professor Smith that on September 1st, he was really down 40,000 yen from his summer budget for food and fun, not just the 20,000 down that he had had to scrape up for the rent. He decides to call the hot springs and cancel his last weekend's reservation. On Saturday night he eats a bowl of noodles and watches sumo wrestling on television in his apartment, hoping October will be better.

The leaves are starting to change when he goes to the bank for his October rent money, and he's relieved to find the rate has dropped only to USD = 138JPY. At least he knows at the beginning of this month what to expect. However, entering the bank in November, his spirits drop when he glances up at the exchange rate. Before going to the rental agent to tell her he'll be a day late again this month, he stops by the pub and orders their largest bowl of hot sake. He figures that at 130 yen per dollar, he'll have 60,000 yen less during his final month than he had when he arrived in the summer. He calculates that with a 100,000 yen budget and an intense desire for one last visit to his favorite *onsen*, he'll have to make do on rice, tofu, and ginseng tea. As the sake steam drifts through his sinuses to penetrate his brain, he grumbles to himself, 'Why didn't the grant give me all the money up front; I could have exchanged it all for yen in July and not have had to go through this humiliation.' He crumples the napkin, pays the bill, and stumbles out the door on his way to the rental agent. 'Boy, I'm glad I'll be home for Christmas,' he burps.

What our young scholar doesn't realize is that with the exact same stipend in dollars, things could have gone quite differently. Smith happened to be in Japan during the summer and fall of 1990. If he had gone to Japan six months earlier, he would have experienced a dramatic improvement in his living standards during his stay, and he would have blessed the National Endowment for doling out stipends on a monthly basis. If he had been lucky enough to go to Japan in 1985, he could have lived like an emperor; the dollar was worth between 230 and 260 yen at that time. On the other hand, if his sabbatical had been postponed until the winter of 1994–95, he would have been fortunate to have survived on noodles and tap water; during that period the dollar dropped from 100 yen down to 80 yen, which would have only paid his $2,000 monthly rent, leaving nothing in his wallet for the remainder of the month.

How predictable are exchange rates?

Could Professor Smith have planned his trip to coincide with a favorable exchange rate? The answer is most certainly no. He must submit his requests for sabbatical and grants at least a year in advance, and with that lead-time the best forecast from the world's greatest currency wizard will most likely prove wrong.

Mr Roberts, the thirty-year veteran of the money changing business who gave us a tour of his foreign exchange department in earlier chapters, described it to me this way: 'Exchange rates are less predictable than the weather. Make a forecast far enough in advance and you're sure to revise it several times. It's like forecasting the weather but with politics and human psychology thrown in.'

The weather forecasting analogy is apt. With exchange rates there also appear to be seasons, but their duration and degrees of variation are so uneven that one is not certain a new season has arrived until well after it has begun. Currency traders, corporate treasurers, international fund managers, and others whose fates and fortunes are exposed to world currency markets are keenly aware of the market's most salient feature – uncertainty. Most participants have experienced periods of fair sailing when currency prices move in the direction they expect, only to be hit by a squall when some statistic is released that calls into question a prevailing trend. A good foreign exchange strategy contains contingency plans for outcomes extremely different from one's best forecast. The most seasoned forecasters are wise enough to admit this up front. Speaking to a group of financial market professionals, Alan Greenspan – one of the best financial market analysts in the business – confided, 'Having endeavored to forecast exchange rates for more than half a century, I have understandably developed significant humility about my ability in this area.'[1]

You might ask, if future prices of currencies are so unpredictable, then why even try to forecast them? The answer is the same as for forecasting major storm events.

Starting in June and lasting until November, inhabitants of coastal areas along the Gulf of Mexico and the Atlantic Ocean watch satellite images for storms that might be brewing off the West Coast of Africa, where the dreaded Cape Verde hurricanes spawn. Counterclockwise cloud motion signals that one's life could radically change within the next two or three weeks, though because the forecast is so uncertain that far ahead one doesn't change plans other than to watch every few days to see if this storm cell will turn into a tropical depression. If the storm becomes a hurricane and the National Hurricane Center shows the eye of the storm tracking through one's home in 5 days, it might be a good idea to check the emergency supply kit from last hurricane season and restock it, but because of the uncertainty in the 5-day forecast, it is generally unwise to begin nailing boards over the windows or evacuating for higher ground. The National Hurricane Center (NHC) is upfront about the degree of uncertainty in its forecasts. The NHC shows its best forecast of the path of the hurricane's center for the next five days, but around that forecasted track is drawn an uncertainty net, based on past forecasting errors, showing the likelihood of the eye actually hitting within that area.

People or companies exposed to exchange rate movements make use of currency forecasts, but instead of having one central forecasting team, there is a plethora of currency forecasters to choose from and a much wider array of models than the number used by the NHC for forecasting hurricanes. Similar to the weather, currency forecasts must be continually updated to be useful, and exchange rate forecasts are more accurate the shorter their time horizon. You'll have a better chance of guessing the dollar price of Japanese yen one hour from now than one week from now, just as you'll have a better chance of guessing whether it will be raining an hour from now than a week from now.

There is a crucial place where the weather analogy breaks down. No matter how many people watch the weather channel and base their decisions on forecasts, their actions will not change the weather. This is not true of the currency markets. Beliefs about the future direction of currency prices greatly affect the timing of decisions to buy or sell, and when enough major actors share the same beliefs and act on them, prophesies become self-fulfilling, with occasionally cataclysmic results.

If beliefs about the direction of future exchange rates influence decisions to buy or sell today, then how do the players form their views about the direction of the market? Let's go to a trading room to catch a glimpse of the way the players think.

7

Inside the trading room: philosophies behind trading strategies

Inside the trading room, the air is electric. It smells like a classroom in the midst of a tough exam. A tropical fish tank, embedded in the wall, casts a soothing, dappled light on the dark side of the room. On the opposite wall a dazzling ticker tape with a half-dozen tracks displays foreign exchange quotes in running red lights, and high on a third wall are clocks posting times in London, New York, Tokyo, Hong Kong, Singapore, and Frankfurt. One trader shifts from foot to foot, another paces with eyes fixed on the ticker tape, a third frantically punches an order on the terminal, a fourth tips back in the chair and breathes deeply. The only calm is inside the tank; a Picasso fish glides behind a rock.

A woman looks up from her terminal, makes eye contact, and with a smile walks over to greet me. She's slender and graceful as she approaches, but the most striking feature is her eyes. They have the alertness of a serious surfer momentarily distracted from studying a turbulent sea.

'You're here at a great time,' Genevieve says. 'In fifteen minutes the Fed will announce its decision on interest rates.'

'Check this out.' Her eyes shift to a computer screen; she remains standing, her fingers – like those of a concert pianist who has played this many times – effortlessly transfer her intent. A graph pops up, showing a jerky movement up then down. 'Look how nervous the federal funds market is.' She' plays another chord that brings up thirty-year Treasury bonds. 'These are so far out they're not moving much today.' A third chord shows yields on two-year treasury notes. 'These are short-term enough to move around some. Let's magnify this,' and the scale of the screen changes to exaggerate the movements up and down.

I ask her, 'What's the market sentiment? Is everyone believing the rates won't change?'

Her eyes watch the movement and her hands hover lightly over the keys as if she's checking a pulse or contacting the spirits. 'No, looking at the federal funds futures, I'd say it's a closer call, maybe 60:40 that the Fed won't do anything this time, which means if they *do* notch it up, you'll see this graph shoot way up as traders who've bet on no change will try to exit their positions. If the Fed holds rates steady, you'll see the graph go the other way but not by so much.'

'We'll go back to two-year notes in a second, but first let's check out the spot market for yen.' The screen for yen pops up. 'A few weeks ago the dollar was trading at 127 yen, now it's down to 114, and look at it moving around. If the Fed raises rates, we'll see the dollar move up, and if it keeps rates unchanged, I expect this graph will drop down fast and then recover a little.'

She flips back to the two-year treasury notes and looks around the room. With a sparkle, she whispers, 'This place turns into a kindergarten before an announcement like this. I'm not betting on this one, so I can relax.'

Across the room, a tall, wiry chap with a British accent bangs in a last-minute order. He jerkily picks up a closed umbrella, aims it at the ticker tape and begins firing his ersatz machine gun. Sixty seconds to go, no more clicking of keys, all eyes channeled into their own screens, their own markets, hoping they're right, fearing they're wrong, but ready to act in any event. Someone cracks a bad joke, giggles uncontrollably, and a chorus of boos and laughter follows.

Everyone's eyes are on the Reuters screen overhead. Suddenly the message they're waiting for appears: '2:15 p.m. EDT The Federal Reserve Open Market Committee decides to keep the target federal funds rate unchanged.'

A woman screams, 'Yipes,' and punches frantically an exit trade. Others cheer. One trader jumps to his feet, springs straight up in the air, yells 'Yessss' in mid-air, and dunks an imaginary basketball. He sits down, looks euphorically in Genevieve's direction and comments, 'I see dollar signs.'

Genevieve reminds him, 'You know our motto, Jim, don't cheer so long you forget to sell.' Jim moves up to his screen and with a grin on his face waits for the right moment.

We watch the USD/JPY graph, and Genevieve exclaims, 'Whoah, look at that, the dollar dropped to 111.6 yen... but now it's coming back up.'

Genevieve has worked as a trader for this financial institution for six years, and before that she traded foreign exchange for a large commercial bank in the same city. She explains that since she arrived, her financial institution has become more global in its investments, especially in the area of foreign bonds. This means more foreign exchange orders coming down from the investment department, which looks at the entire balance sheet and makes strategic investment and borrowing decisions. In addition to these orders 'from above', as she puts it, the investment department has allowed a portion of the company's liquid reserves – what might otherwise be earning low rates of interest in treasury bills or institutional money market accounts – to be put to work 'by us' in the trading room. Each trader is allowed a limited amount to work with during a session, and traders are only allowed to speculate on short-term price movements of high-grade assets, like top-rated government securities and very liquid currencies, and derivatives of those underlying assets. She comments, 'In our overall portfolio we hold considerable liquid reserves. We have a stellar credit rating with the banks and securities firms we do business with, so the spreads they give us to execute our orders are very thin. We have found that our little trading operation is a way to substantially boost returns on capital.'

'How do you direct all these traders?' I ask. 'It looked like they were betting every which way.'

'Instead of trying to decide the day's strategy in committee, which would give us erratic gains and losses as a unit with everyone betting the same way,' she draws a zigzag line with wide swings on the paper, 'we've decided to decentralize and allow each trader to design his or her own strategy, while placing strict daily loss limits on each trader. This gives lots of little zigzags, each with a floor,' which she draws, 'but gains and losses are staggered, so our total performance is smoother.' She draws a smoother, less amplified wave motion above the asymmetrical zigzags.

'This sounds like a portfolio diversification technique.'

'Yes, but it's trading-style diversification, and it allows individual traders the flexibility to respond to the unexpected in markets they know, quite unlike decisions by committee. Because it places responsibility on the individual trader, this setup raises the anxiety level when a government announcement or relevant statistic is released. I like it because it allows some wide-ranging views to coexist in the same room. You learn more that way.'

'How do you find balance in your daily life when your work involves riding the waves of uncertainty?'

A flash comes to Genevieve's eyes. 'Trading Tokyo is the way to go for a working mother.'

'What are your days and, should I ask, nights like?'

'I get to spend all morning with my two-year-old daughter, playing, reading, painting, watching our small garden grow. After lunch, I take her to the babysitter, and I drop in at the trading room for an hour or so to see how London closed, and to see what's happening in New York. I read market newsletters, talk with traders who specialize in different markets, and generally prepare myself mentally for the evening's trades. I pick up my daughter, fix an early supper for her and dinner for my husband, and at seven I turn on my computer and begin trading, while my husband spends time with Amy. The first two hours of trading I need complete concentration. During the first hour is when Japanese data is sometimes released and markets go wild. Often about nine thirty I can take a short break, read Mother Goose and put Amy to bed, or, if she's already asleep, go downstairs and have a glass of wine with my husband, and return for a lighter session between ten and eleven.'

'Do the nursery rhymes influence your late-night trading style?'

'Well, yes,' she quips, 'Humpty Dumpty makes me look for a good short' (a bet that a price will fall).

I'm amused as she continues. 'Tokyo winds down for lunch about eleven our time, so I generally close-out by then. There is a pick-up in Tokyo between two and four in the morning here when they're finishing their day. I have my broker beep me if there's a major market move. Usually I get to sleep right through it, and in the winter, all this happens an hour earlier.'

She has an hour before leaving to pick up her daughter at the babysitter, so I ask an open-ended question: 'So, Genevieve, what makes exchange rates change?'

Vision one: 'it's all supply and demand'

'When it comes to daily, hourly, minute-to-minute, or second-to-second fluctuations of currency prices, everyone in this trading room and upstairs and in rooms like this from London to Singapore agrees on one thing: supply and demand moves the market. When there are more orders to buy a currency than to sell it, the sellers will have the advantage, and they'll be able to raise their prices. When there are more sell orders than buy orders, the buyers gain the upper hand and can bargain between sellers for lower prices.'

Genevieve continues. 'A few minutes ago, immediately after the announcement about US interest rates, the dollar plunged to 111.6 yen. Those who had been betting on a rate hike were also betting the dollar would rise relative to the yen. When the announcement shattered their expectations, some who had entered into contracts requiring them to deliver yen, rushed to sell off their dollar holdings to get the yen they needed to cover their short positions. This rush of dollar sellers or, another way of saying it, yen buyers, drove down the dollar relative to the yen.'

'Yes, and then the dollar popped back up to 114 yen,' I recall.

'Right. The low-priced dollar sales that everyone saw on their screens triggered some bargain hunting, and these dollar purchases quickly pulled the dollar back up.'

I toss out some bait. 'So all you need to know is the law of supply and demand, and you'll make a good trader.'

'A new trader will discover this obvious truth within the first hour of trading, even if he hasn't taken Econ 101. The imbalance between supply and demand tells you the direction that prices will move, but it can't tell you by how much they'll move.'

Genevieve turns up the volume on a small speaker box. Static is broken by a voice blurting out some numbers. 'The voice traders are an endangered species, but you can hear an imbalance in the market by listening to their trading room where some jumbo orders still come through. I've heard situations when lots more orders are out there to buy a currency, but there's no sense of urgency, and the price barely changes. I've also heard situations when a single order to buy triggers a price surge.'

She explains that the sense of urgency or complacency at a single moment depends on what the buyers and sellers 'believe' is going to happen to the price in the future. If many market actors think prices will rise in the next few days and an excess supply happens to appear, the price won't fall much, 'because sellers are willing to wait it out, hold out for more later, and the small drop in the price will pull in lots of buyers who see it as a bargain situation that won't last.'

'Well, what shapes the actors' views about future prices?'

Genevieve sighs. 'On this there's great disagreement. I, myself, have had to change my views on how this works.'

Vision two: 'it's all fundamentals'

'When I first began working foreign exchange at the bank, I was just out of graduate school, and my training in economics drove my trading style. I'd look for real economic causes or what we call "fundamental" forces behind the movements of supply and demand. It was easy to recognize all sorts of temporary causes that will make a currency's price rise above or fall below its "long-run equilibrium value" or natural resting place. The way I used this in trading was that if a short-run price got out of line with what I believed to be the long-run equilibrium value of the currency, I'd bet that the currency would move back toward equilibrium.'

'Well, then what determines the long-run equilibrium?'

'That depends on which fundamental theory one adopts, and there are many theories.'

'Which one did you use when you first started trading?'

'One of the theories I learned in grad school was purchasing power parity. It says currency prices adjust to make goods and services cost about the same everywhere. So what you look for are relative inflationary pressures between one economy and the next. If you see much higher inflation rates in one country, its money has lost purchasing power over local goods, so you'd expect that currency to depreciate to bring back parity with prices of goods abroad.'

'So what's the mechanism that would make the currency depreciate?'

'Trade flows. If the currency's exchange rate didn't depreciate at first, people inside that country would increasingly import less expensive goods, and foreigners would gradually stop buying that country's products. The trade deficits would produce strong sales of local currency for foreign currency to buy the imports with, and the local currency would depreciate until its local purchasing power was the same as its purchasing power abroad. At that point, trade flows would come back in balance and the exchange rate would be in equilibrium.'

'So, how did you use that theory in making trades?'

'I'd look for leading indicators of inflation.' She explains that some economists look at growth of money supplies.[1] If one country's money supply is growing at twice the rate of others', the theory predicts this will lead to greater inflation. They'd predict that currency's price would trend downward, so its power over buying foreign goods wouldn't be more than its power to buy local goods for very long. 'I'm not a monetarist, so I preferred looking at business cycles, labor market conditions, capacity utilization rates, and other signs of overheating. Because these cycles rarely coincide with each other internationally, one country's economy might be overheating while another is in a recession. I'd predict that the currency from the economy with heavy inflationary pressure would decline in value to bring about purchasing power parity. I'd wait until just before announcements on price indexes, unemployment rates, and so forth, and place bets accordingly.'

'How did trading on purchasing power parity work?'

'I sometimes made great trades, but only if I incorrectly forecasted the direction of a statistical release. When I guessed the direction of the statistic correctly, I usually lost money. With the currencies I was trading, the actual exchange rates often moved in the opposite direction that purchasing power parity predicted.'

'What accounts for that?'

'If a statistic were released that signaled increasing inflation, the central bank of that country might raise short-term interest rates, and so instead of the currency going down in value, it would rise. International actors were more concerned about finding interest rate deals than worrying about what was happening to prices of real goods and services – the balancing act of purchasing power parity.'

Genevieve's brow wrinkles. 'I had to question this theory.'

'Did you completely toss it out?'

'No. I think it's useful, but in very limited circumstances.' She gives the example of countries that have poorly developed capital markets, or controls that limit capital flows. The main reason for buying or selling such a currency is for trade purposes, not financial reasons. 'If that country's inflation rate were to soar, I'd expect its currency would depreciate, just as purchasing power parity would predict, though government policies might delay the decline.'

'So, what about purchasing power parity and the Tokyo market?'

'The financial capital that moves in and out of Tokyo swamps the money that moves due to trade in real goods and services. You see, the Japanese have a very high savings rate, they've maintained international competitiveness in production of goods for many decades, and they have financial surpluses that accumulate in pension funds, insurance companies, trust companies, and the like. The managers of these funds must look globally for placing financial investments. Relative changes in interest rates are likely to have a larger impact on the dollar–yen exchange rate than how large the trade surplus is.' Genevieve smiles. 'Have you seen the London *Economist*'s spoof on purchasing power parity?'

'No. What is it?'

'I always get a kick out of this article.' As she looks through her satchel for the magazine, she comments how poorly purchasing power parity theory stands up to empirical tests. In the economics literature, one of the controversies is how to get a standard bundle of goods and services to compare purchasing power when people in different countries consume such different stuff. 'Every April *The Economist* runs a spoof on the controversy.'

7.1 / The hamburger standard

Country	Big Mac in local currency	Big Mac in US$ at today's exchange rate	Big Mac purchasing power parity exchange rate	Actual exchange rate local currency per US$	Under/over valuation (-/+) against $ (%)
United States	2.54 US$	2.54	1.0	1.0	0
Argentina	2.50 pesos	2.50	0.98	1.0	-2
Australia	3.00 $ Aus.	1.52	1.18	1.98	-40
Brazil	3.60 real	1.64	1.42	2.19	-35
China	9.90 yuan	1.20	3.90	8.28	-53
Denmark	24.75 DKr	2.93	9.74	8.46	+15
Euro area	2.57 €	2.27	0.99	0.88	-11
Switzerland	6.30 SFr	3.65	2.48	1.73	+44

'What does *The Economist* use for its standard bundle of goods?'

'One item.' Genevieve turns to the article and slaps it down in front of me. 'The Big Mac.'

I laugh. 'Not a very large bundle of goods, but Big Macs are the same no matter where on the globe you happen to be!'

She points to the table that shows the cost of a Big Mac in different countries.[2] We look at the most undervalued currency. According to the Big Mac index, the Chinese yuan is 53 per cent undervalued relative to the dollar. A Big Mac in Beijing back in April cost 9.9 yuan, and there were 8.28 yuan to the dollar, so in dollar terms that hamburger would cost $1.20. At the same time, in the US the average cost of a Big Mac in four major cities was $2.54. So the dollar is much too high relative to the yuan – and to all the other currencies except the Swiss and Danish. To bring about equal purchasing power, the yuan would have to rise 53 per cent in value, and a Big Mac would cost the same in both places.

I say, 'I know this is hokey, based on one item, but it sort of fits the situation with China. Their undervalued currency makes Chinese labor appear even cheaper, so Wal-Mart and Target fill up on clothing, footwear, and sporting goods "Made in China." But would you bet on currencies using the hamburger standard?'

She laughs. 'Not unless a bunch of London traders started using it! Actually, several years ago, an economist at Georgetown found that the Big Mac index correctly predicted the direction of exchange rates for eight of the twelve currencies of the large industrialized countries. And out of seven currencies that moved more than 10 per cent in value that year, the Big Mac index predicted the correct direction in six cases. That's a better track record than some of the highest paid forecasters!'[3]

'But you didn't get good results using this theory in your betting strategy?'

'Terrible. But, the commodity basket problem aside, even advocates of purchasing power parity would argue that adjustments might take a long time, and the trading game is short run.'

'So, what guided your trading strategy after you dumped purchasing power parity?'

'For a while I kept relying on real, "fundamental" causes, but I expanded the variables I watched for. In addition to watching inflation and trade balance indicators, I began watching forces that would cause interest rates to change. And I became more attentive to other fundamental factors in addition to interest rates – corporate earnings, for example, that would influence capital flows.'

'How did this work for you?'

'I got much better trading results, but I was still under-performing relative to some of the other traders. What kept happening – to the extent it was not merely coincidence – was that just when I felt comfortable that I'd found the right causal variables, some wild card event would come into play and completely stir up the deck.'

'How did you process this?'

'Well, this may sound New Age, but I had a sort of... conversion experience.'

'What triggered it?'

'One day, it hit me. I recalled a conversation I had with the senior trader on my first day of work at the bank.'

'What did he say?'

'Mr Anton said, "Genevieve, with your educational background, you're going to quickly understand traders when they speak of money supplies, inflation rates, current accounts, interest rates, business cycles and the like. Then you're going to see someone over at his desk in the corner with a ruler and a pencil, all bent over, intently drawing lines. You won't have too difficult a time sensing his meaning when he speaks of support and resistance levels, trading ranges, up-thrust and down-thrust days, but if you keep talking with him long enough, pretty soon you'll think he landed from Mars. He'll be sketching away on his chart, and go 'Oh, gosh here's a descending triangle', or 'there's a "head-and-shoulders" formation,' or 'look at that flag,' or 'check out that pennant.' Immediately after he's discovered this image on his chart, he'll rush over to make a trade."'

Vision three: 'it's all technical'

I ask Genevieve, 'So did you get to know the Martian?'

'Yes. He was this little guy with coke-bottle glasses, and I must admit I thought his approach was rather silly. All he looked at for making trading decisions was past prices; he didn't even consider what might be moving supply or demand. I confronted him on this during a coffee break.' With dilated pupils, she mimics the Martian. 'He looked straight at me like an owl and said, "Genevieve, you'll never find all the causes that move supply and demand, so what you expect to happen will rarely occur. Past prices contain the resolution of all of the forces moving supply and demand – those that make their way into economists' models and those that don't. It's impossible to identify each force separately, but past prices are knowable and readily available. So at least I'm basing my decisions on something real. If I detect a trend forming, I don't stop to question *why* it's forming. I've watched these markets for a long time, and there are some repeated patterns. I just go with what I see taking shape. In my strategy, I build in ways to prevent myself from jumping in too early before a trend is confirmed and I build in some good stops in case my chart interpretation is wrong. This may not sound scientific to you, but it *is* practical."'

'So, what made you take him seriously?'

She laughs. 'I assure you it wasn't what he said. It was what he did. I found out from some co-workers that this guy consistently outperformed the other traders in the group. Now he's making big bucks at Goldman Sachs. Before he left, I got a reading list from him on technical analysis.'

'So,' I query, 'now you have a ruler and a pencil?'

'Better than that – I've got Bloomberg's.' Genevieve punches in an order for a 24-hour trading chart of USD/JPY spot rates beginning two weeks before. It shows the great slide of the dollar from 127 yen to 112 yen, then wave-like patterns staying fairly well-behaved between 114 and 116 yen per dollar, with occasional steep ups or downs. 'Just eyeballing this, it looks like a trading range is forming between 114 and 116 yen. In using charts, more recent price developments are more significant for trading than more distant ones. For example, nobody is expecting to buy yen at 127 per dollar now – the market has moved into a different phase – but it appears highly probable that you could buy yen for dollars at 116 and sell yen for dollars at 114. If you did enough trades like that, you'd make money.'

'What would the chart analysis instruct you to do if prices broke out of the trading range – say went to 117 yen per dollar? Would you sell off dollars at that high price?'

'Probably not. It would depend on the chart model you've found most useful in trading this market. And it would depend on your own decisions about timing, probabilities, risk, and your own gut feelings, but this kind of breakout could imply a move to another trading range, which would mean you'd sell off yen and buy dollars before the dollar moves up further.'

'Can you show me an example of a chart model?'

Genevieve punches 'Mac-D' on the menu at the top of the screen. 'Here's a stochastic model I've found useful for dollar–yen trades of five to sixty minutes' duration in and out. For such fast trading, I'd have to accept much thinner ranges than buying dollars at 114 and selling at 116, or else I wouldn't be making many trades. Let's chart Mac-D with an initiation of twenty periods back, just as an example.'

The vital signs of a patient appear on the screen and dotted lines form well within the limits of peaks and troughs. 'Those dotted lines are recommended buy and sell points from Mac-D's perspective. You don't try to hit the peak or trough of the trading range; instead, you do lots of trades in between, working in the same direction the market is going.' Genevieve turns to a fresh sheet of paper and picks up a pencil. 'It works like this,' and she draws a wave-like motion. 'Chart-traders are basically trend followers. Here on the upswing there is buying. When the price approaches the top of the trading range, buying slows down as traders who don't expect it to go higher wait to see if there will be a breakout or if the trading range will remain intact. If the price starts to fall as expected, the traders who bought in higher up during the previous upswing will begin selling to make sure they secure a profit on the trade. As they sell, the price continues to slide down and others who bought in lower sell, and so forth until you reach the bottom of the trading range. Then there's a suspension of activity as traders try to see if an upswing will occur as expected or if there'll be a breakout downwards. It's all action/reaction, where everyone is trying to buy low and sell high.'

'That makes sense, but what's behind Mac-D's dotted lines?'

Genevieve's index finger instinctively punches a key. On the Bloomberg screen appear mathematical formulae showing the derivation of Mac-D's dotted lines. Without working out a full understanding of the action/reaction assumptions, I note, 'It looks like past closing prices are being compared with daily trading ranges to arrive at the dotted lines.'

'Yes,' Genevieve says, 'in many of these charting models, closing prices play an important role.'

'Why is closing more important than mid-day?'

'One reason is that longer time horizon investment managers who do not engage in short-term trading are more likely to read or hear about yesterday's closing rates than any other statistic about the market. These are the statistics most quoted in all the newspapers. For example, while I'm fixing Amy's oatmeal in the morning I hear the dollar/yen closing rates in Tokyo on NPR's "Morning Edition." Of course, I already know that, but financial managers listen to the closing prices on their way to work. If they hear a favorable rate or a closing rate that worries them, this can be a signal for them to enter the game, and their combined actions influence the market.'

Genevieve shifts attention back to the screen. 'Here's a different chart model I'm just learning about.' She punches an item on the Bloomberg menu line. 'How far back should we go?'

'I'd like to see all the way back for the lead up to the crash of the dollar against the yen.'

'OK. Here goes.' The daily average dollar–yen spot rates for worldwide trading appear. The screen shows the buildup to 127 yen and then the plunge. Below that jerky line two smoother lines are fitted, and after these smoother lines are drawn, the computer fills the distance between them in blue. 'Those are the clouds,' she remarks. 'This charting model is popular in Japan.'

'How would you use this?'

Genevieve says, 'I'm just starting to learn a little about this charting scheme, so let me see if I can get Yoshi; he's our cloud expert.'

She calls over to see if Yoshi has closed out his trades, 'Professor Williams wants to know about the clouds, Yoshi. Can you explain them to him?'

Yoshi humbly prefaces the lesson. 'I am just a novice on this.'

'How would you use this scheme in trading?'

'In the most simple way...' Yoshi explains there are much more sophisticated interpretations of this used in Japan. 'If the average spot rate rises over the cloud, like in the first five months of the chart? It's a bullish sign for dollar; you make trades that the dollar rises against the yen. Look... here,' he points to a narrower place on the chart, 'See at 124–126 yen, the cloud gets thin? That's a warning sign! Keep on the lookout for change of weather. But wait until the spot rate drops through the cloud; then sell off. See when the dollar dropped under the thin cloud at 120? The dollar slid! All the way down to 112.'

'What's behind the cloud formation?' I ask.

Yoshi punches the command for the derivation of the two lines defining the clouds. One line charts a moving average of the spot averages of the past nine days and the other for the past twenty-six days. I figure out loud, 'This would mean that if the dollar is rising as a general trend, the spot rate would be above the nine-day moving average, and the nine-day line above the much smoother twenty-six-day moving average. It's just a way of seeing if a real trend has been taking place.'

'Right,' says Yoshi, 'but it is much more than that.' He explains that the man who developed this trading method is a Buddhist philosopher who began earning money on the side as a trader. The more the philosopher studied the charts, the more he saw patterns that repeated patterns found in nature.

'So, the numbers nine and twenty-six are magic numbers?' I ask.

'Yes, they're in the snail shell and sacred objects in Buddhist temples.' He says that the philosopher gained a reputation in Tokyo as a very successful trader. When his book was published, it sold thousands of copies in Japan. 'Technical traders,' he explains, 'follow trends, but this tells you more. It tells you: "in two weeks be careful! Rough weather comes."' Yoshi says that the author was concerned that people would turn his method, which he views as a deeper philosophy, a unity of living things, into a mechanical rules guide, and he warns against this in his book. Yoshi laughs, 'it is not in English yet, so the Japanese have a monopoly!'

I ask the name of the book and Yoshi writes on my legal pad, *Ichimoku kinkou byou*, and below in English 'Overview equilibrium table.'

I ask, 'Of traders you know who use this method best, how do they use it?'

'Many use it in a loose way. All traders in Japan know this. But the best traders? They are always reading the book closely, over and over.' He explains that the most successful traders read the book and watch the cloud formations. He describes it as if they're repeating a religious chant. If they are given signs, they follow through and act on the signs, even when rational doubts creep in. He says that not many traders in Japan are disciplined like this and confesses, 'I am not disciplined either.' He says that when the chart tells him a break is coming, 'like two weeks ago when the dollar dropped through the cloud? I saw the sell sign, but I waited.' He explains that before he acted on the signal, he looked at fundamental factors that might reinforce a more permanent move downward. 'If I see other good reasons? I sell.'

'How has this method worked for you, Yoshi?'

'I'm just a beginner. I do not use *Ichimoku kinkou byou* in other markets, but in the Tokyo market' – he gives examples of securities and currency trades involving the yen – 'in the Tokyo market, it works.'

I thank Yoshi, who appears anxious to return to trading.

I want to understand more about Genevieve's views on this. I can't recall meeting someone so rigorous and well trained, but also so open in her thinking.

'Is there somewhere less hectic we can go to?' I ask her. 'I don't want you to sneak off without hearing your answers to some big picture questions.'

She looks at her watch and says, 'Yes, we have a soundproof break room. But I must leave to pick up Amy from the babysitter's in forty minutes.'

Behind the fish tank:
what causes rates to change?

Genevieve opens the door through the aquarium wall, and we enter the break room, where traders can escape the erratic pace of the markets, meditate, watch the fish, and view the commotion in the next room through the calming water. We pick from a basket of teabags, fill our cups with hot water, and sit at a table next to the fish tank.

I jerk the teabag a couple of times and look up at her. 'Genevieve, we both have training in economics, and we've pretty much kept up with the professional debates on foreign exchange, but you have an advantage. You've directly felt the pulse and faced extreme market conditions. I want to see the big picture through your eyes.'

Genevieve blurts out, 'Well if you're looking for a religion with a credo to follow, you've come to the wrong person. The more I trade, the more agnostic I become.'

'So what's your take on the view that when a major news event is received, the market reacts by overshooting the new long-run equilibrium, after which it slowly adjusts back toward the new equilibrium?'

'I was excited at first about the overshooting model,[1] because I noted that when a financial news event hits our screens, like we witnessed a few minutes ago, there's an extreme movement of price. But if there is a reversion to a new trading range – the closest thing to an equilibrium I've seen – it doesn't take months, as the overshooting model suggests, but happens fairly quickly. The jump in prices we just witnessed was sudden, lots of movement within the first few minutes after the announcement

– just as the overshooting model suggests. The groping for a new trading range is still going on in there.' She points through the water to the traders still active at their terminals. 'But wild currency swings and high volume of trades will dampen down to more normal levels in another 45 minutes, not the months it would take for the real economy to adjust to the money policy as in the overshooting model.'

'So it takes about an hour after a news flash to get centered again?'

'That's a rule of thumb when the timing of an announcement is known in advance. When a news event pops up out of the blue, unannounced, the wildness lasts longer – up to a couple of hours – unless, of course, it triggers a major storm.'

'So, you mentioned you have a problem with the idea of "equilibrium"…'

'Well, in the overshooting model and in others, equilibrium is grounded in real economy fundamentals. The harder economists have worked to find "equilibrium" currency valuations based on real fundamental variables – prices and production of real goods and services, trade balances and so forth – the more elusive the search has become. I've become convinced that in the world of foreign exchange, equilibrium muddies the water.'

'Then do you see the market moving like a "random walk"?'

She mimics W.C. Fields's monotone, 'Close… but no cigars.' Then she explains that a pure random walk with no drift says that the next period's spot rate is just as likely to go up as it is to go down, and the size of the movements one way or another won't vary much.

'Can you give me an image?'

Genevieve grins. 'Imagine W.C. Fields in a perfectly flat open field. He's had way too many whiskeys to walk straight, and he's almost but not quite knee-walkin' drunk. Each step is about the same size, but who knows where the next step will take him: forward, backward, left, or right? If you were to place bets on his movement, you'd do better not to place a big bet on where he'll be fifteen steps later. Since you know where he is after each step, you'll do much better making a lot of little bets, one after each step. If it's a true random walk, the best bet is that he stays in the same place, in other words you'd do better betting that tomorrow's spot rate is the same as today's.'[2]

We discuss an empirical study that raised eyebrows in the economics profession. The study tested out of sample a number of fundamental models of exchange rate determination. 'The out of sample tests using real economic variables performed miserably,' Genevieve recalls. 'None of those models and none of the forecasts from market surveys beat a pure random walk in explaining currency movements.'[3]

'So, what's your take on the efficient markets hypothesis, that the random walk happens as market players efficiently digest unpredictable news?'

'The efficient markets view is right about market players reacting to unexpected news – this is a stylized fact of the markets – but I have trouble with the notion that the digestion of the news produces a "correct" price... You saw how fast the traders reacted to the announcement, but the volatility is still happening in there. The information they're reacting to is full of uncertainty and open to multiple interpretations.' She gives examples of ambiguities in the wording of Federal Reserve announcements and the measurement errors and uncertainty contained in government statistics and corporate reports that make them subject to spin. 'And as we saw in the trading room, there are many trading styles and views of cause and effect.' Her nose wrinkles with disdain. 'To believe that all of the players come together in the market and arrive at some efficient, correct price, is a fairy tale that may give a calming effect to those who believe in it, but the efficient markets hypothesis way understates the uncertainties we face.'

I ask, 'Then, why do you think the movement of exchange rates resembles a random walk?'

Genevieve stares at her teabag for a few seconds and then glances up. 'It's not like pricing something real, like a car, where there are tires, steel, parts, labor, physical stuff with costs that give some reality base to valuation. Maybe currency prices used to be connected in a clear way with real commodities, but, as we discussed in the trading room, the bigger linkage now is with financial markets, where prices don't have easy reality checks, so they're much more subject to shifting whims of the players.'

'Keynes's animal spirits of investors?'

Genevieve nods affirmatively. 'Yes. Keynes was on to something.' Using the example of the US and Japan, she says that in today's world, currency markets link highly diverse financial markets, each with its own peculiar legal and regulatory frameworks, accounting standards, and trading practices. She explains how this adds to the uncertainty. 'Foreign exchange is like the stock market with gasoline thrown on it.' She goes on to say that players in the currency markets have no way of knowing what will happen three weeks or even three hours from now. The only thing knowable is what currencies are trading for now and the rates they were trading at in the past. 'Because of the extreme uncertainty about the future, all of us, fundamentalists and chartists alike, use the most recent trading prices as our reality base, and then we either chart projections or look for fundamental causes that might move the rate up or down off that temporary benchmark. That's why the prices move off recent prices. It's not that the current price is "correct" or "efficient"; it's just about the only thing real we have to go on.'

'So, how do institutions control for the risk that what they bet will happen doesn't come to pass?'

Genevieve says, 'Active players know the dangers of making long bets on where W.C. Fields will end up. They know that currencies move much like a random walk, up or down off recent prices offered in the market, so they'll only allow short-term bets on currency movements. For this reason, many banks have policies that strictly forbid long-term bets. If, for some reason, a long-term currency exposure were discovered on the books, executives would counter the exposure with a hedge of some sort.'

I remind her, 'You said close to a random walk, but no cigars.'

'The movement may resemble a random walk in that today's rates seem to make moves off of yesterday's, but I've become convinced by empirical studies that exchange rate changes don't fit a pure random walk.'

'How not?'

'In a couple of ways. First, the stride of the walk can vary tremendously. Right after important data releases, there tend to be big jumps. Then there are certain periods when our drunk gets stung by hornets, and we see wildly oscillating, chaotic movements. That happens during crises, when two-way trading breaks down and normal sources of liquidity dry up. Then there are periods when the stride is more even. Second, if it's a pure random walk, steps taken before wouldn't influence the direction of steps taken later, but studies show past steps are auto-correlated with more recent steps. In other words, some trending takes place. Our drunk happens to stumble, his weight is tilted, so the next steps drift in the direction he was leaning when he stumbled.'[4]

'Well,' I ask, 'if it's not a pure random walk or a rapid return to equilibrium, what about the view that speculative behavior leads to "bubbles" that can last for a long time, only to be followed by a big pop?'

'I admit the "speculative bubble" models[5] are appealing. They take into account that actors in this market are divided on their views about what makes currency prices change. So there can be episodes when the chartists dominate and the markets completely defy fundamental economic forecasters. The chartists see the price of a currency rising, and they bet it'll continue rising, and their bets reinforce the speculative mania. The bubble can keep inflating for a long time.'

'What example do you recall of a bubble path?'

'Of course, the tech stock bubble, but a classic currency example,' she says, 'was the mid-1980s, when the US dollar remained strong despite repeated evidence that the US current account was going to hell in overdrive, real interest rate differentials were narrowing, and other fundamentals were no longer there to support the dollar's continued strength. The best-predicting fundamental model during the period, the one based on relative interest rates, forecasted a downturn of the dollar an entire year before it happened. Those who believed in this forecast got creamed; they missed 20 per cent of the dollar's total rise from trough to peak. And a similar scenario happened with the dollar from 1999 through 2001.'

'So, from a macroeconomic fundamentals point of view the dollar defied the law of gravity.'

'Yes, and the bubble path analysis gives a reasonable account of strong momentum episodes like this. But it gives no clue as to how long the bubble should last before it pops, so it offers very little to traders. And it doesn't account for other episodes when bubbles seem to get started but they don't fully develop. It's a partial theory that still holds to a notion of equilibrium, one that moves in a path. Like the overshooting model, the speculative bubble models provided building blocks for later generation dynamic disequilibrium modeling.'

'Are you speaking of applications of "complexity," or what's more popularly called "chaos" theory?'

'Yes. Some strong insights into the actual working of the currency markets came from working with these models.'

I ask, 'Have you seen the work by the group of Belgian economists, or are they Dutch working in Belgium? Back in the 1990s they did some computer simulations of the foreign exchange market.'[6]

Genevieve squints her eyes trying to get clear recall, so I summarize their work to jog her memory. In the simulations they have two types of participants, "fundamentalists," who bet that future rates will move in the direction of purchasing power parity, and "chartists" who look at past behavior of exchange rates, stylized versions of the two views we observed in the trading room. The approach differs from the overshooting model and the bubble path model in that the structures through which adjustments take place are non-linear. This means that instead of getting solutions in the form of equilibria or steady-state growth paths like the earlier models, the non-linear structures combine with interactions between traders' expectations yielding complex behavior. There's no "solution" in the traditional sense, but once initial conditions are set, simulated currency prices can be watched on a computer screen and you can look for patterns in the movement.

Genevieve recalls these. 'Yes, a while back I read a book titled something like *Chaotic Models of the Foreign Exchange Market*. When the authors watch their simulations play out on the computer screen, they see apparent cycles, but each one is unique and sensitive to slight changes in initial conditions. This is what's called the "butterfly effect" – the flapping of a butterfly's wings in the beginning can have a magnified effect much later on because of the dynamic interactions embedded in the system.'[7]

'Do you remember what happens when they administer a shock in mid-stream?'

'Yes, that's one of their best results.' She recalls how a sudden change in the money supply of one country sets off strange behavior in the market, unlike anything a fundamental model would predict. 'You've got chartists in there, not reacting to the money supply at all, and their speculative interactions with fundamentalist traders leads to unpredictable behavior.'

She pushes back in her chair. 'Another result of the "chaos" models strikes a chord with me. After initial conditions are set, the patterns observed on the computer screen appear as if the market is reacting to unexpected news – large moves in an opposite direction for example – even when no news shocks are administered. In my own trading, it's sometimes very difficult to tell if a market move is really a reaction to a news event or a reaction to a previous action, though the financial press is always looking for a story and reports it as a reaction to a news event. Lots of "false stories" are introduced this way that have a short life span.'

'You've noted the insights of the chaos models. How does reality differ from the ones you've seen?'

Genevieve counts the ways on her fingers. 'First of all, and the authors would be the first to recognize this, the underlying economic structure is not simple and not known ahead of time, in fact it evolves, so there's lots of room for competing fundamental perspectives to shape expectations. Second, shocks to the world system are not singular. Before the effects of one shock can be fully transmitted through the markets, there have been a half dozen other shocks coming into play, so with the dynamic interactions of the system it's hard to tell which shock did what. Third, as we've seen in there,' (she points through the fish tank) 'there are just as many competing perspectives within the "chartist" camp as there are in the fundamental camp. If you talk with the people who're making decisions to buy or sell currency, you'll find very few who fall 100 per cent in a single camp. And some players in the market have more chips to bet with than others.'

'Haven't the microstructure analysts taken a more realistic approach along the lines you're suggesting?'

'Yes, in my opinion,' Genevieve taps her finger on the table, 'that is the most promising direction for understanding exchange rate dynamics.' She says that when the logical deductive macroeconomic models failed time after time to explain exchange rate movements, some financial market analysts began taking a different tack. Instead of making grand assumptions about the economy and investor rationality, deducing logical results from these assumptions and testing the results against evidence, the microstructure theorists started by looking closely at the evidence. For example, they would measure actual market behavior following macroeconomic news announcements, examine response patterns in the data to find the channels through which the information in the news is transmitted through market structure to produce changes in prices.

'How is this approach different from technical charting?'

'The technical chart analysts are looking for past patterns in order to project these into the future – history repeats itself – the microstructure theorists look for structural causes of the patterns. They're building theory from the ground up with careful attention to the institutions, conventions, technologies, and groupings of major actors that constitute a particular financial market.'

'Wouldn't they need very detailed data compared to the fundamentals forecasting approach?'

'Yes, and the high frequency data they needed on the foreign exchange market was harder to come by back in the 1980s and early 1990s when this branch of research got going.' She explains that microstructure analysis of the stock market was more advanced empirically because stocks traded on central exchanges, and the volume of trading and minute-by-minute price data for the whole market was available from the exchange back in the 1980s. Although the treasury bond market does not work through a central exchange, researchers of the bond market had a leading advantage because most of the trading at the center of the market goes through six or seven inter-dealer brokers, most of whom by the early 1990s were reporting high-frequency trading volume and prices to a company called GovPX, which released the data through information distributors like Bloomberg's.[8] The currency market was not so centralized, so it was much harder to get continuous market-wide data.

'But didn't the electronic currency trading platforms change that?'

'Exactly. And as more dealers began trading through a particular dealing system, researchers with access to the platform provider could mine the data needed to test for the currency markets some of the detailed tests that had been run on the stock market and the treasury bond market.' She says that in the mid-1990s a significant portion of the inter-dealer currency market was going through Reuters' direct-dealing platform, and some pathbreaking work for foreign exchange was done with that data.[9] And now with such a large share of the inter-dealer spot market going through electronic brokers, researchers with access to those centralized databases can watch the 24-hour market second by second over long periods. It's like having a high-resolution video recording of what actually happens at the center of the world's largest market.[10]

'What kinds of things are they looking for?'

'Like the earlier work on stocks and Treasury securities, they're testing market reactions to pre-scheduled government data releases, but with this high frequency footage all sorts of other things can be learned about the structures and dynamics of currency markets.'

'For example?'

'It would be possible to analyze closely major episodes like the financial turmoil following the September 11th attacks, how currency market storms get brewing, and the dynamic linkages between currency markets and other financial markets. You could even test for regional/cultural differences in interpretation of market headline events, because in a 24-hour market day there are short periods when just Asia is trading, just Europe is open, or just America is in the driver's seat.'

'So, I guess with all this micro-structural research currency forecasters will be able to predict the future.'

'Well, I wouldn't go *that* far. Knowledge of the structures can help me sort out how to respond better to a dynamically changing context, it can help central banks know when it might be more effective to intervene,[11] and it may help big players know how to use private information better to their advantage, but a better understanding of the structures will not reduce their inherent instability or the uncertainty surrounding the future. I'm almost where Alan Greenspan is on currency forecasting.'

'Where is that?'

'Greenspan says that despite all the efforts put into it, no currency forecasting model has a success rate better than a coin toss. Out of the thousands who try, some are quite successful, but so are winners of coin-tossing contests.'[12]

'Genevieve, all this uncertainty is getting to me. To do your job, you must have a visualization that helps you manage the uncertainty. How do *you* see it? I wish we had another hour,' I look down at my watch, 'but you have twenty minutes before you must go.'

'In that case,' she laughs, 'I'll have to find a sloppy metaphor.' She stares up at the lights for a second and begins. 'Keynes spoke of the animal spirits of investors as ruling the markets, and there's the hackneyed image of a herd of cattle, stampeding mindlessly in one direction. These people, Lord Keynes included, were mostly city folks who've never observed a herd of cattle, but during my childhood I spent a month every summer on my grandaddy's cattle ranch in East Texas, so I got a chance to watch.'

'How does a herd move?'

'A real herd of cattle doesn't move in a single way; it has many modes of behavior. In a huddle phase, a herd will stay around the same spot, though it's always moving. A bull mounts a cow and the others have to get out of the way, a calf runs out on the edge and the mother chases it. A steer kicks another one. When a herd is excited, the cattle don't move in one direction at once, otherwise it would be easy to round 'em up. A lead steer on one edge may begin a move toward an opening he sees and others follow, while at the same time another section may be bulging out in a completely different direction. There are lots of followers, but there are usually competing leaders. Only on rare occasions will the whole herd stampede in the same direction as you see in the John Wayne movies, but even then there's a straggler or two that run off into the woods.'

She pauses for a few seconds and continues. 'We're not mindless, though fear and greed sometimes make us appear that way. We're rational. Everybody wants to buy low and sell high and do it without incurring too much risk, but we're not equal. There's no such thing as "a typical cow" in this herd. Each participant or group of participants has a different purpose for exchanging currency, and the purpose influences the strategy. As one fascinating study shows, the purpose for engaging in the market may even influence an expert's forecasts of future exchange rates.'

'Which study are you referring to?'

'A Japanese economist back in the 1980s tracked for two years the dollar–yen forecasts of the leading foreign exchange experts.[13] Twice a month these experts indicated over the telephone what they expected the exchange rate to be in one, three, and six months out. The forecasts were all over the map, and "wishful expectations" were found to be at work in their forecasts.'

'Wishful expectations?'

'Yeah. Exporters in Japan, who benefit from a rising dollar, consistently made higher forecasts for the dollar–yen rate than forecasters from other types of businesses. Importers, who'd benefit from the dollar getting cheaper, consistently made lower forecasts of the dollar–yen rate than the other foreign exchange experts.'

She goes on. 'Members of the herd differ in other ways as well. Some must buy currency for reasons unrelated to price movements; others are in it to make money off price movements. Some are end users; others are middlemen. Some have huge stakes and great influence; others have small stakes and little influence. Some think long run, others short. Some take big risks, others none. Some play the game daily, others rarely. Some lead, others follow. Some are in a position to see a movement happening early on, others must wait until the move is well under way.'

'How do you use this herd theory in trading?'

She looks straight at me with honest eyes. 'I try to keep track of the herd.'

'How?' I ask.

She peers into the fish tank. 'I envision clusters of participants. At the very center are the middlemen, the biggest foreign exchange dealers, huge banks with operations in all the financial centers. They're key because they hold inventories in all the major currencies, and they stand ready to buy or sell whatever currency the rest of us might be interested in. They're the liquidity center that everybody else relies on. Their customers I group according to motives for engaging in currency transactions, smaller banks, fund managers of various sorts, corporate treasurers, and central banks.'

To stay focused on Genevieve's vision, I draw what she's describing and add details as she goes. Here's the drawing I ended up with.

8.1 / Genevieve's view of currency market structures

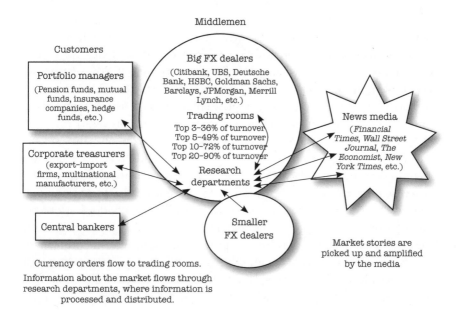

Currency orders flow to trading rooms.
Information about the market flows through research departments, where information is processed and distributed.

'To simplify, I look from the center out, paying particular attention to the biggest middlemen, who make a market in currencies by offering continuous two-way prices.' She points out that the three largest dealers together handle more than a third of the entire market turnover, the largest five do about almost half the total volume, and the top ten manage more than two-thirds of the market. Everybody else, including the smaller dealers, ultimately rely on this concentrated center for liquidity, the place where they can make exchanges when everywhere else dries up. 'When these big ones at the center stop offering two-way prices or if they increase their spreads abruptly, the rest of the market – the smaller dealers, the customers, the futures exchanges – everywhere else goes into a panic. Everyone watches what's happening at the liquidity center.'

'And the biggest dealers have the best spot for watching everyone else,' I comment.

'Exactly. They have periscopes on the market.' She gives the examples of UBS (Union Bank of Switzerland) and Deutsche Bank, who handle more than a tenth of the market each. And then she speaks of banks like JPMorgan Chase, which are custodians for Treasuries and other securities in addition to having huge currency turnover. 'They can see changes in overall market flows ahead of smaller dealers. And because their clients include all types of end users positioned around the globe, the top tier dealers have early receptors of information on sentiment changes.'

'Do you see the top five currency dealers as controlling the market?' I ask.

'No, they can't control the market, but they respond quickly to what they see happening in their customer base, and smaller middlemen tend to follow their leads. I remember on my first day at the bank, Mr Anton warned me, "no matter what you believe will happen, if you see the big guys moving in another direction, *never* bet against them."'[14]

'But, Genevieve, these are complex enterprises. Is there some nerve center where all this information gets channeled and processed?'

'Yes.' Genevieve's eyes light up. 'The research departments.' She explains that all the big dealers have in-house research teams that keep tabs on government statistical releases and other information that influences the currency markets. These analysts have real-time access to the internal database of orders flowing through their bank's worldwide network of trading rooms, and they walk the trading room floor and talk with traders. The best researchers not only brief upper-level management and proprietary traders on currency market issues, but they have telephone contact and sometimes meet with the firm's best clients, so they hear the daily concerns of the world's big fund managers and corporate executives.

I interject, 'It sounds like the research teams are the intelligence gatherers, the eyes and ears of the middlemen.'

She replies, 'Yes, but they're also the mouthpiece or transmitter of the intelligence gathered.'

'How does that work?'

'First dibs on the intelligence goes to the chief economist of the firm and higher-up executives, who use it for in-house strategic decision-making, and I'm sure some banks have figured out how to use this information to improve the returns of their proprietary traders. Then the most important clients of the firm have telephone access to the firm's best analysts, who, in turn, pump the clients for information while they're giving them advice. The next in line are those who have access to the team's research products.'

'Research products?'

'Yeah. It used to be that we would get hard copy of market developments from research analysts at the big dealers and we'd place the newsletters in little stacks on the windowsill of the trading room. Now we use FXall, a multibank portal that allows us access to all the research products of the dealers we do business with.'[15]

I draw the arrows feeding into and out of the research departments. 'OK. I think I'm starting to get the picture.' I make a stab at it. 'The larger the customer base is, the more comprehensive is the sample available for the research department to analyze, and the greater the impact of their research will be on the direction of the market.'[16]

'Almost,' Genevieve reflects. 'But portfolio managers and traders don't have to read the material sent out, and we don't have to believe what we read. These reports differ greatly in quality and mode of analysis. Sometimes large FX dealers don't have the best analysts.' She gives the example of one of the biggest dealers in the world that had a researcher in New York reporting on political and economic developments in Germany. 'The analysis was shallow and hardly worth reading. Portfolio managers and traders have limited time, so we're selective.'

'How do you select?'

'I know who's doing the best job on the Tokyo market right now, so I make sure to read those reports, but I get leads on other markets and analysts from the financial press.'

'Where do you look and what do you look for?'

'I look through the 'Money and Finance' section of the *Wall Street Journal*, the *Financial Times* (of London), and *The Economist*. When you read these reports, notice the names of the individuals quoted. They're frequently the heads of research departments or currency strategists for very large dealers. If an analyst quoted appears to be on to something that others in the market might be swayed by, I'll check out the research products for the deeper story, and I'll follow that story line in the broader financial press.'

'I've heard you use the term "story" in place of "analysis" more than once. Why?'

Genevieve reflects for a few seconds. '"Story" better fits the human situation in there.' She looks through the tank. 'You saw how fast decisions had to be made.' She explains that there's rarely enough time to ponder ambiguities in data releases, to sort carefully the meaningful information from the noise, or to work through a complex chain of cause and effect to arrive at the real implications of an unexpected shock. 'In this fast-moving world, a simple story that has already captured the imagination of a large portion of the herd will guide their actions more than some sophisticated model that's hard to digest or alien to the belief system.'

'So, that's why you're paying careful attention to the cloud theory?' I question.

'Yes. That's a fascinating example. *Ichimokusanjin* touches something primal in Japan, a belief in patterns in nature that takes on a mystical, religious power. This is the sort of story that gives people a sense of order in a disorderly world. The book is a bestseller in the Tokyo trading community, and popular articles in Japan refer to it all the time. No wonder Yoshi is finding it useful in yen trades. It has become integral to the action–reaction process in Tokyo.'

'The cloud theory is a technical story; what about fundamental stories?'

'They work the same way. The best ones give a sense of order to a disorderly world, and they fit within a broader belief system. Also they have a natural history that intrigues me.'

'You mean survival of the fittest?'

'Just that. Broadly speaking, stories must fit within the acceptable mode of discourse. For fundamental stories it's the language of economics, supply and demand as applied to money and finance. For technical stories, it's the language of patterns. Within this acceptable mode of discourse there's a huge range of interpretive scenarios. What's interesting is that at any moment, out of this huge range of possibilities only two or three stories will dominate in the minds of market participants. So that all the news is being watched and reacted to through this dominant story medium.'

'So, how does this natural history of market stories influence your trading style?'

'In trading, I find it essential to stay current on the story medium. If I've been away on vacation for a week, it takes some catch-up reading and three or four trading sessions to get back on track.' She says that awareness of the current story medium helps her know what kind of news to watch for, and it helps her gauge the degree to which prices will swing when a rogue event happens or a statistical release is above or below the forecasts.

'How does the story medium change?' I ask.

'There may be long periods of subtle change when a dominant story holds. But, if you notice, fresh material flows in that doesn't relate to already established stories. This usually comes in the form of side comments by market analysts in the news. The fresh material serves as a mutation pool, out of which there's natural selection of new story lines.'

I ask. 'What, then, is the principal device that discards already established stories and selects new ones out of the mutation pool?'

'Actual price movements.' Genevieve waits for this point to sink in. 'How long can traders continue to believe a story and use it in trading when we suffer a string of losses or missed opportunities from using it?' She goes on to say that when price moves begin to contradict an established story, reporters unearth analysts who don't believe in the dominant story. All of a sudden a contrarian's statement makes headlines. The reporting of non-believer views, coupled with price movements consistent with those views, reinforces doubt in the once strongly held story. So the old story migrates to the back of money managers' and traders' minds.

Genevieve continues on a roll. 'And the market newsletters and the financial press are constantly looking for new stories. I've noticed when there's a very large price move in an unexpected direction and some currency analyst with a plausible hypothesis happens to get interviewed that day, his or her account can be pushed toward the front of the story medium. This shifts the attention of traders and customers. They begin to look for different kinds of evidence than was being looked at before, and in the days that prices continue to move in ways unexpected by the old story, reporters will scrape around and find someone who has a story consistent with the new direction of price. After a week or so, enough market players have become sensitized to the new story that a comment by some public official or a statistical release that would've gone unnoticed a week before can trigger a major market move in the direction predicted by the new story. After repeated price confirmation and wide circulation in the financial press, the new story will have some staying power.'

'Genevieve, I can see how price movements would validate or discard stories. I can also see how the story medium filters the news and influences the immediate actions of portfolio managers and traders. But this makes me curious. Have you noticed any long-run shifts in story patterns? You've been engaged in the currency markets for more than a decade. How have the patterns of market stories evolved in relation to the changing financial structures?'

She ponders for a moment. 'When I started trading back in the late 1980s, stories were already beginning to change from the meat and potatoes fare – trade balances and short-term interest rates – to include more exotic desserts – such as stories about securities, stock and bond markets around the world. With the communications technology revolution of the 1990s, stock and bond markets got wired. Cross-border trading zoomed. Of course, settlement for a cross-border trade usually requires a foreign exchange deal.'

I interject, 'So now currency traders have to watch what's happening to the Nikkei, the Hang Sen, the DAX, the FTSE, the Dow, and the NASDAQ, and connect those with likely moves in the currency markets?'

'Yes. But to stay on top of the story medium, you have to be alert to the analysts and research departments most in touch with the moves and sentiments of big portfolio managers.' Genevieve looks at her watch and rises.

As we walk by the fish tank to the exit, I comment. 'Genevieve, I wish we had time, because I'd like to tap your mind on chaotic episodes you've experienced like the Mexican peso crisis, the Asian currency crisis, the crash of the dotcom boom, and so forth. Who would best understand the anatomy of great financial storms?'

She smiles. 'For Tokyo, I could give you some names. But overall, I'd say go to the research department of a big currency dealer in London or New York. Talk with a foreign exchange specialist who advises fund managers.'

How currencies are delivered:
snapshot of an evolving system

When the traveler changes dollar bills for foreign currency, the deal is struck and the two currencies are exchanged right there at the money changer's window. Deal – and, seconds later, simultaneous delivery of both currencies. Making a deal to exchange bank account money, the dominant form of money used in world currency markets, is easy, but delivery is tricky. For a deal to be made using account money, all that's needed is for the two parties to have a secure line of communication and for each to trust that the other will make good on the delivery later on. The two parties may be thousands of miles apart, and at one instant in real time they strike a deal to exchange precise amounts of two different currencies. However, the delivery of bank account money takes time. Anyone who has deposited a check knows that the bank may hold the funds for a day or two until the check-writer's bank settles up and the check clears, at which time the deposit can be used. Currency deliveries in bank account money require inter-bank settlement in two different banking systems. Laws, regulatory requirements, technologies, and settlement practices may differ significantly. One system may be fast, the other slow; one reliable, the other less so. The two systems may operate in different time zones. Add these practical differences up, and there appears a mountain of obstacles to a pair of currencies arriving at the same time. It's as if the money changer takes your dollars and, as he shuts the window, says 'Come back later on today and I'll have your foreign currency for you.'

Foreign exchange settlement risk, as it is sometimes called in the banking world, lasts between the time you pay the dollars to the money changer and the time when the money changer returns from lunch and delivers the foreign currency he owes. The amount at risk is the entire principal, the total in dollars you handed to the money changer, and the risk is that something happens to the money changer – anything – so that he cannot pay you the currency he owes. For a traveler to get stiffed in a currency trade there would be few side effects, but for a bank with billions of dollars' worth of settlement exposure from currency deals, a delivery failure could make the bank unable to meet other obligations, and the misfire could lead to a string of payments snafus that could easily spread from one banking system to the next.

Before 1974, bank regulators and private-sector interests paid little attention to foreign exchange settlement risk, but a near crisis event that year revealed the monster lurking beneath the surface of world currency markets. Bankhaus Herstatt was but a small German bank that was trying to grow by becoming an active trader in foreign currency markets. Herstatt had been borrowing money from other banks at relatively high rates of interest and betting the proceeds on currency fluctuations. In early summer 1974, Herstatt suffered a string of losses in foreign exchange trading that threatened the bank's capital base. On 26 June it became obvious that Herstatt could no longer meet its clearing obligations, and German banking authorities shut it down after the 3:30 p.m. final settlement of the German banking system. At 3:30 p.m. German time, it was 10:30 a.m. in New York. The German marks Herstatt had bought in currency deals for that day's delivery had already been paid to Herstatt and settled with finality at the Bundesbank, Germany's central bank. The dollars Herstatt owed in return had not been sent yet or were in the process of being netted at the New York Clearing House, which was not scheduled to settle with finality at the Federal Reserve until 4:30 p.m. New York time. According to German banking law at the time, an insolvent institution's assets would be completely frozen and could not be used to settle outstanding obligations until the bankruptcy courts had decided the case. So banks that had delivered marks to Herstatt that day did not receive the dollars they were due. At 10:30 a.m. New York time, Chase Manhattan Bank, Herstatt's correspondent bank in New York, stopped sending payments messages on behalf of Herstatt's $150 million dollar account, and at 4:30 p.m. Chase did not cover for the payments messages that had been sent to the New York Clearing House prior to 10:30 that morning. First National City Bank (now Citibank), JPMorgan, and other big New York banks took losses of several million dollars each, hurting their earnings but not threatening their solvency. But a bank in Washington State, Seattle First National Bank, had to write down more than $20 million, a threatening amount for such a bank at that time.

Repercussions of the Herstatt crisis were far greater than the monetary damages and system disruptions of June 1974. It was as if the banking community worldwide was suddenly made aware it had been practicing unsafe sex. Before Herstatt, banks thought they might gain or lose from a currency transaction if the currency they bought dropped in value, but the gain or loss would be a small percentage of the total transaction. They were unaware at the time that they could be ripped off for the entire amount. Seattle First was aware that currency market fluctuations could cause a loss of several hundred thousand dollars from trades with Herstatt, but it never dreamed it would be out the entire notional amount of the exchange, $20 million. Herstatt was a relatively minor player in the world currency markets, but it raised the deeper question: What would happen if a *major* player were to fail? The suspended, unsettled payments could be large enough to make other major players insolvent, thereby placing at risk entire domestic banking systems, and, if not contained: the world payments system. The Herstatt crisis galvanized monetary regulatory authorities around the world, setting in motion a process that shaped the evolution of currency delivery systems for more than three decades.

In the summer of 1997, I had the opportunity to interview payments systems experts and to tour CHIPS, the international payments processor for the New York Clearing House and the world's largest currency delivery facility at that time. Twenty-three years after the Herstatt crisis the experts I interviewed used the term 'Herstatt risk' interchangeably with 'foreign exchange settlement risk,' almost as if the event had happened a few months before. Most of the system improvements pointed out to me, whether they were more robust legal arrangements, technological advances, or operational safety features, were rationalized in terms of the overarching goal of reducing settlement risk. After two decades of public- and private-sector attention, Herstatt risk in 1997 was still a deep worry of regulators and weighed on the minds of private payments system architects.

It was not until October 2002 that a privately owned payments facility went on-line that was designed to eliminate Herstatt risk by settling with finality both sides of a currency deal at once. Beginning with settlement in seven currencies, Continuous Linked Settlement Bank (CLS) kept adding currencies and expanding its customer base. By 2004, CLS was delivering gross value of $1.9 trillion in currencies a day on average, about half the world's currency market turnover, surpassing CHIPS' $1.4 trillion per day average in dollar deliveries that same year.[1] By 2005 CLS could simultaneously deliver foreign exchange for its members in fifteen currencies across sixteen time zones and boasted plans of adding more. In brochures published in 2005, CLS explains that 'the main driver behind the development of CLS Bank ... is a response to regulatory concern about settlement risk,' and the brochures advertise simultaneous delivery as the key reason why more banks, brokers, fund managers, and corporate treasurers should settle their currency trades through CLS.[2]

The snapshot of the currency delivery system I observed in 1997 sheds light on the remarkable evolution of currency delivery since then. The payments systems principles revealed to me are fundamental for understanding the variety of delivery channels, along with their associated risks, that coexist in today's world. Once one grasps the logic of currency delivery, it is easier to learn the evolutionary dynamics and vulnerabilities of systems used to complete other financial market transactions involving stocks, bonds, commodities, and derivative contracts of all sorts. The person who first called my attention to the severity of Herstatt risk and gave me basic training on how currency delivery systems work was my central banker friend from graduate school days mentioned in the preface to this book. Franco Passacantando, a career economist for the Bank of Italy, helped design Italy's large-value electronic payments system that was introduced in 1989. In preparation he studied the payments systems of other countries, including the historical development of the United States' payments system, research he completed as a visiting scholar at the University of California at Berkeley. In 1996 Passacantando took a leave from his position in Rome to serve for seven years as Executive Director of the World Bank in Washington DC. The following footage on the basic principles of currency delivery is extracted from notes I took during private sessions with Passacantando during the summer of 1997 in Washington.

A meeting with a payments systems expert

I pick up my security pass at the front desk, walk through the bomb detector, and enter the massive atrium of the World Bank. Cold steel, blue filtered light, artificial waterfalls, and perfectly manicured tropical plants give the futuristic feeling of a space station. The Italian Executive Director has a suite of offices on the top floor. While I wait in the conference room across from Passacantando's office, professional assistants converse in Italian.

Passacantando extracts himself from a briefing on Albania and enters the conference room ready to shift gears.

'Well, maestro,' I begin, 'you've told me about the Herstatt fiasco before, but what were the reactions?'

'The New York Clearing House was in an uproar' over the German authorities' order to freeze Herstatt's dollar accounts in the middle of their netting cycle. Passacantando recounts how this group successfully lobbied for legislation that eventually made it illegal in New York State to freeze assets of an institution before a netting cycle was finalized. The clearing house also began working on its own internal procedures to make multilateral netting safer. The Herstatt crisis, he emphasizes, was the spark that drove central bankers around the world to coordinate with each other and with private banks to promote safer settlement practices.

'At some point, I need a clearer picture of how netting works, but I'm curious, in today's world is it practically possible to avoid Herstatt risk all together?'

'Yes, I'll show you a couple of ways.' Passacantando gives the example of currency traders who use the same international bank which operates branches in the two currency zones. Deliveries move from the seller's account to the buyer's within the two branches of the same bank, so there's no settling up between banks and no chance of a national payments system problem that could delay delivery. The internal operating system of the global bank can schedule it so the two currencies are delivered at the same instant in real time. In that case, the funds have to be there before the exchange of the two currencies is executed, so there's no chance that one side will be delivered but the other not. (Those who prefer pictures should refer to figure 9.1 in the appendix to this chapter.)

'That sounds easy, but how often does this type of delivery occur?'

'It happens a lot more often now than it did ten years ago.' Passacantando explains that a decade before central banks around the world had stricter rules on allowing foreign banks to participate in their systems. Now the largest international banks directly participate in several national payments systems, not just their home base. And the largest banks are merging and acquiring other banks, so the chance is much higher now of customers to a currency deal using accounts at branches of the same global bank.

'How are payment instructions sent when there's more than one bank involved?' I ask. Passacantando says that when an external communications network is needed for a large value payment, the most likely message carrier will be SWIFT, which is considered so efficient and safe that some banks use SWIFT channels instead of private lines to send payment instructions between their own branches in different countries.[3]

'So SWIFT will be used to relay the payment instructions, but how will delivery work if customers use different banks in both currencies?'

'There's the potential rub. The movement of account money between banks requires the sending bank to pay – or settle for that amount with – the receiving bank.'

'How does the currency seller's bank pay the currency buyer's bank?'

'Any number of ways depending on banking laws, customs peculiar to domestic banking systems and contractual arrangements between banks.'

'What's the safest way?'

Passacantando says, 'The safest way for banks to settle up with each other is with central bank money.' He gives the example of a US dollar–Swiss franc trade where banks settle up with each other through accounts they hold at the Federal Reserve and the Bank of Switzerland. The safety of this method comes from two sources. First, no matter how turbulent conditions are, the Federal Reserve and the Bank of Switzerland will not fail, so the receiving bank knows the money from the paying bank is good. Second, the paying bank must have enough money in its account at the central bank for the payment to go through. If the funds aren't there, the payment must wait, so when the payment does go through, it's final, and the receiving bank can use the funds immediately without worry. Passacantando uses the term 'Real Time Gross Settlement' (RTGS) to describe this one-payment-at-a-time method using central bank money. He explains that if a currency exchange uses an RTGS settlement in both countries and there is a period of the day when the two systems are open at the same time – as is the case with Fedwire and Swiss Inter-bank Settlement – it is possible to have both currencies delivered at the same instant in real time. 'The delivery is final. After banks settle using accounts at central banks, nothing can be reversed. The currency traders can then use the delivered funds without worry.'

'So if it's so safe, why might banks use other ways to settle with each other?'

'Real Time Gross Settlement systems are costly for the users.' Passacantando explains that banks using systems that settle with each other for the gross amount of each payment, one at a time, must hold enough reserves at the central bank to cover for what are sometimes large transactions.[4] These accounts at the central bank typically earn zero interest and transaction fees are often charged. Banks prefer to earn money on their working balances and to minimize transaction fees, 'so they've gotten together and developed less expensive ways to settle with each other.'

'What are the most widely used alternatives?' I ask.

'Netting systems.' Passacantando explains that funds move back and forth between banks all the time. Instead of having to hold huge amounts of reserves in order to settle on a transaction-by-transaction basis, banks can agree to settle later for net amounts of an entire batch of back and forth payments. He calls these 'deferred net settlement systems' (DNS) and gives the simple example of two banks that settle bilaterally (see figures 9.3 and 9.4) The net amounts owed at the end of a batch are a fraction of the total payments accomplished, so the banks only have to hold enough in their central bank account to cover for the net amount owed.

'I see the savings in central bank reserves with the bilateral netting example. How would settlement work with lots of banks?'

Passacantando explains that with many banks in a netting scheme, further savings on reserves can be achieved if the members agree to settle for the 'net-net' amounts instead of 'bilateral net' amounts. (see figure 9.4). At the end of the multilateral netting cycle, the system calculates which banks owe money, and that amount is paid into a system settlement account, usually at a central bank. Once those who owe have paid in, the settlement account pays those who are owed. At that time all the payments for the cycle have been finally settled using central bank money for only a few transactions at the end.

'I see, so with multilateral netting the participants save by not having to tie up large amounts earning nothing in central bank money, and they also save on transaction fees charged by the central bank, so what's the problem with netting systems?'

'Payments are not final until the end of the cycle.' If something happens to at least one of the participants in midstream before final settlement, the participants who are not paid may not be able to pay other participants, and the payments batch could be unwound. Herstatt revealed this possibility.

'What other events have prodded the banking community to make currency deliveries safer?'

Passacantando thinks for a few seconds. 'Where should I begin?'

'How about the 1990s.' I suggest.

'In the 1990s, we had some scary moments,' he reflects. He recounts that in 1990 when the Drexel, Burnham, Lambert group collapsed, a gridlock of international payments developed through that firm's London trading subsidiary, which dealt in the foreign exchange and gold markets. 'Fortunately, the Bank of England stepped in and set up a real time settlement facility that resolved the gridlock before the liquidity problem could spread to other actors in the markets.'

The next scare he mentions came on 5 July 1991 when authorities in Luxembourg closed a bank called BCCI, SA. Two firms were never delivered currency they had paid for. According to Luxembourg law, an insolvent bank must be closed during operating hours so the courts can appoint a liquidator. The BCCI case revealed that because of legal practices and time-zone problems, it is practically difficult to time liquidation so that all markets are closed simultaneously.

Then in August 1991 an attempted *coup d'état* in the Soviet Union disrupted the foreign exchange market because of the suspicion that Soviet financial institutions, some active players in the currency markets, would be unable to deliver on currency contracts that were maturing. The counterparties' delays in delivering currencies they had promised to deliver reduced their exposure to settlement risk, but this exposed the Soviets to liquidity risk, which could have made them unable to deliver on all sorts of obligations. 'Fortunately, several central banks stepped in and arranged for special settlement deals with major counterparties to the Soviets, so the liquidity problem did not spread to other sectors.'

Furthermore, he continues, there was the Barings failure in February 1995, which caused a serious clearing problem in the ECU system. A bank discovered on Sunday when Barings was closed that it was too late to stop an ECU payment it had sent to Barings the previous Friday. Fortunately, the sending bank, which owed the multilateral netting system at the end of the following Monday's cycle, agreed to borrow from another bank to cover the net amount it owed. 'Otherwise the ECU system would have suffered an unwind on Monday, and forty-five banks would have been unable to settle some 50 billion ECU in payments.'[5] Passacantando explains that all of these near catastrophes, beginning with Herstatt, led to investigations into the nature of the problem and efforts to reduce it.[6]

I ask, 'So I guess after all this time and effort, foreign exchange settlement risk is no longer a problem.'

Passacantando's mood darkens as he turns to the bookshelf behind him. He pulls out a slick paperback. 'I don't wish to alarm you, but you should read this.' He slides the volume over to me. The title reads *Settlement Risk in Foreign Exchange Transactions*, published by the Bank for International Settlements in Basle in 1996.[7]

I reply, 'I'll read it cover to cover, but can you summarize the main findings?'

Passacantando says that even after all of the close calls of the early 1990s, banks were still engaged in unsafe settlement practices. This study alerted the banking community to the remaining risks, and it suggested a series of remedies, some of which have since been heeded.[8] The study developed a method for measuring settlement risk and it surveyed eighty banks on their actual practices to determine their exposures. It was found that many banks were engaged in bilateral netting, which exposes them to much larger settlement risks than if they sent their currency deliveries through an appropriately managed multilateral netting arrangement.[9] The study found that the total settlement risk for a bank under the practices at that time could easily amount to the sum of two to three days' worth of foreign exchange trades. And exposures to individual counterparties were found to be large. Many banks reported conducting in excess of a billion dollars' worth of currency trades with individual counterparties on a daily basis. So currency deals exposed even very well capitalized banks to serious risks that could, in turn, endanger whole banking systems. Additionally, the study found that many banks believed central banks would step in to prevent settlement risk from actually occurring and so most banks were not properly accounting for the exposures. Banks were encouraged to move deliveries through multilateral instead of bilateral netting arrangements, and safer standards were proposed for multilateral netting schemes, some of which, Passacantando notes, have been introduced.

'What are some ways to make multilateral netting safer?'

Passacantando explains that all sorts of risks to final settlement occurring on a timely basis have to be addressed. Legal risks to netting have been reduced in many jurisdictions following New York State's lead, but he notes that legal risks remain. Operational risks to all types of payments systems, netting arrangements, real time gross settlement systems, and hybrid systems, have been lowered by developing secure lines of communication and backup systems that can be brought on line if the primary processing center is disrupted by a power outage or sabotage. And financial risk control measures have been applied to multilateral netting schemes that make final settlement less likely to be disrupted.

I ask Passacantando to outline some of the financial risk controls. He says that one way is to make netting cycles shorter so finality is achieved more quickly and large credit imbalances are not allowed to build up; some of the European netting arrangements settle in shorter batches several times a day. Another way is to set credit limits on participants, so if a bank tries to send a sizeable payment that pushes it over the credit limit, the payment is either returned for later submission or put in a queue to allow the sending bank to build up enough credits to cover the large payment it needs to send through. He mentions a third way, settlement loss agreements, whereby participants agree on how to distribute the losses if one or more members fails during the cycle, and they post collateral at the beginning of a cycle to cover for that event.

'But don't these financial risk control measures carry costs with them?' I ask.

'Most do.' He explains that to lower the risk of a system there is a tradeoff that either raises its costs, like posting collateral, or slows down its operation, like setting credit limits. But technological improvements in design features have allowed much better liquidity management, and these have sped up the flows within systems and brought about lower transaction costs.[10]

'What have central banks done to support safer international payments flows?' I ask.

In 1990 only the US central bank had a real time gross settlement system, but 'now in 1997 all of the Central Banks of the Group of Ten industrialized countries have moved to the safer real time gross settlement (RTGS) systems like Fedwire in the United States, so that instantaneous final payments can be made between banks.' He adds that central banks have extended their operating hours to overlap with each other despite differences in time zones. This permits simultaneous final settlements of foreign exchange transactions if banks use central banks to settle.[11]

'So, I'll ask again, are you saying the world financial system is free of settlement risk?'

Passacantando frowns. 'No. Foreign exchange settlement risk is still there because it is cheaper for private bankers to make preliminary settlements with each other before they go to the central bank to make final settlement. So long as there is a gap in the timing of final deliveries in a currency exchange there is the possibility of settlement risk.'

'So the large value international payments flows are delivered through private netting schemes. What's the largest currency delivery system?'

He replies quickly: 'CHIPS.'

'It sounds like a snack. What does CHIPS stand for and where is it located?'

'The letters stand for Clearing House Interbank Payments System, and it's located in New York.'

'When was CHIPS started and by whom?'

Passacantando says that CHIPS first came on line in 1970, when nine members of the New York Clearing House Association sought an electronic substitute for the cumbersome method used at that time to settle large-value transactions between banks.

'How were international dollar transactions cleared and settled then?'

'Most inter-bank movements of dollars arising from overseas transactions were achieved by netting big bundles of checks at the New York Clearing House.' Orders from abroad to make payments in dollars would arrive usually by telegraph at the paying bank, which had an office in New York City. If the paying bank were a foreign bank, it would write a check on its dollar account at a New York bank. A foot courier would then carry this check to the New York Clearing House for the next of three daily check exchanges. The receiving bank's courier would take the check, and the officer at the receiving bank would enter the amount in the recipient's account and send a telegraph message to the recipient that the funds had been received on a provisional basis. Then the receiving bank would put the check in a bundle containing all the checks drawn on that same correspondent bank. The bundle, along with bundles for other banks, would be carried back to the clearing house for settlement. At the clearing house the amounts listed on each bundle would be entered manually on a ledger as a positive entry for the receiving bank and a negative entry for the sending bank. After entering, the bundle would go into the bin of the sending bank. After all the amounts for that day's cycle were entered, the New York Clearing House calculated the bilateral net positions for each of the members with each of the others along with the 'net–net positions' with the system. The following morning each of the participants would pick up a preliminary settlement sheet along with the checks drawn on it from the previous day's cycle. Banks then verified the accuracy of the preliminary settlement sheet, adjusted the amounts for inaccuracies and for checks to be returned due to insufficient funds, signed the revisions and sent the revisions along with the bounced checks back to the Clearing House, which prepared a final settlement sheet. Usually by 10:00 a.m. of the next working day after the check was first presented at the Clearing House, a final settlement sheet was delivered to the Federal Reserve Bank of New York, where net–net debits and credits listed on the settlement sheet were manually posted to the settling banks' accounts at the Fed. This last step of final payments was a small fraction of the dollar value of the total payments being processed by the system because of the netting of the check bundles that was done prior to final settlement. After the amounts were posted to the accounts at the Federal Reserve, all of the participants of the New York Clearing House were notified that the previous day's check-clearing cycle had been finally settled.[12]

'Didn't this system have multiple places for human error to occur?'

'Yes.' He points out that everywhere a physical entry was made, there was a chance for human error. Also the physical movement of checks from one location to another, bundling them and unbundling them, increased the operational risks of the system. A good blast of wind between the skyscrapers or the mugging of a courier would be enough to do it. So for human error reasons and transaction cost reasons, the New York Clearing House began looking for ways to automate the process, and CHIPS was born.

'How much dollar volume does CHIPS deliver in a day?'

'More than a trillion dollars a day,' Passacantando says matter-of-factly, pointing out that CHIPS delivers more money in a day than VisaNet, the largest retail payments processor at this time, delivers in a year.

'More than a trillion dollars a day moves through this one computer system? What do all these payments arise from?'

Passacantando reminds me that the dollar is the world's most important currency for making international transactions. Every time a payment is made in dollars, it involves a movement of account money in US banks. CHIPS delivers 95 per cent of this international dollar activity, most of it arising from foreign exchange transactions.

'How does CHIPS work?'

'It's a multilateral netting system much like the old paper check system used by the New York Clearing House, but CHIPS works electronically.'[13] Financial institutions around the world that make dollar payments have accounts at correspondent banks that participate in CHIPS. There are now approximately one hundred CHIPS participants, the great majority of them foreign banks with branch offices in New York City.[14] When an international order for a dollar payment is made, it is usually transmitted electronically to a CHIPS participant through the SWIFT network, not by cable as in the old days. The CHIPS participant in New York stores the SWIFT payment instruction, verifies its authenticity, and then submits this electronic message into the CHIPS network. At CHIPS, the payment instruction is verified, and financial risk controls are applied to it. If the payment doesn't exceed that bank's permissible credit limits, it is entered into the netting process. All day long, the CHIPS computer calculates running balances of each participant's net position with respect to each of the others and with respect to the system as a whole. At a set cut-off point, no new messages are allowed to enter the netting. Participants can continuously monitor how much they owe or are owed by the system.

'How do the foreign banks settle up at the end of the day?'

'They have a "settling participant," one of the big US banks like Citibank, Chase, or Bank of America, that makes final settlements for them at the Federal Reserve Bank of New York.'

'How does final settlement work?'

'The settling banks make sure the banks they're settling for have enough to cover their net-debit positions.' When the settling banks give the go-ahead, CHIPS notifies the Federal Reserve Bank of New York to open up the CHIPS account at Fedwire. First the settling banks who owe to the system will pay out of their own deposit accounts at the Fed into the CHIPS settling account. After all these funds are deposited, which takes only a few moments to arrange, then the amounts owed to the remaining settling banks will be paid to their accounts at the Fed, and the CHIPS account will be closed out at a zero balance. At this point all participants will be informed that the day's payments cycle has been settled with finality. And the next day will begin with no one owing anyone else.

'So CHIPS delivers more than a trillion dollars a day, but it economizes on settlement transactions between banks. How big is the typical end-of-day settlement?'

Passacantando says, 'If there are twenty settling banks, there would be twenty end-of-day transactions at the Fed. About half would be paying in and half would get paid. Through netting, an end-of-day settlement could be done with less than $20 billion, I would think.'

'So a trillion dollars' worth of money deliveries can be accomplished with $20 billion in payments at the Fed? That's a fiftyfold reduction.'

Passacantando corrects me, 'That underestimates the reduction. More than a trillion can be settled with less than $20 billion.'

'CHIPS sounds to me like a giant money funnel.'

An amused look appears on his face. 'Yes, that's about right.'

'But how risky is this – I mean for 95 per cent of the world's dollar payments to be handled by a single private group that extends big credits to each other during the day, and transacting all this activity through a single computer located in Manhattan.'

'It's not risk-free,' Passacantando admits, but he notes the trade-off of risk and costs. We discuss a political dynamic whereby the regulators, whose job it is to prevent system meltdowns, have pressured for safety improvements. Some private-sector interests balk at the intrusion of the regulators at first, but then when a crisis event unfolds, the private clearing houses with support from the regulators find a solution that lowers the risks but in a way that will be seen as cost-conscious by the participants. CHIPS has been innovative in this respect.[15]

'Franco, I'd like to go see this operation in motion and talk with the private-sector side of this. Could you, perhaps, arrange for me to get a tour of CHIPS?'

'I can possibly arrange that.'

'What about someone involved in end-of-day settlement at the Fed?'

'Yes, I think so. When would you like to go?'

'Tomorrow, if possible. If I get a morning train, I could be in New York by early afternoon.'

'OK, I'll get my secretary to work on this. Call in the morning from the train station and she'll let you know the details.'

APPENDIX / diagrammatic notes on currency delivery channels

9.1 / Simplest case delivery: both parties to a deal have accounts at the same bank in both currency systems

London: on Monday, Merrill Lynch sells $10 million to Salomon Brothers in exchange for 15 million Swiss francs. Merrill and Salomon send payment instructions through Citibank London for Wednesday delivery.

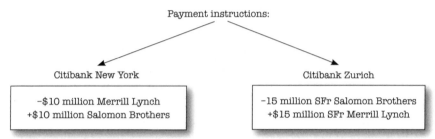

Payment instructions:

Citibank New York

−$10 million Merrill Lynch
+$10 million Salomon Brothers

Citibank Zurich

−15 million SFr Salomon Brothers
+$15 million SFr Merrill Lynch

Result: Safe, simultaneous delivery of currencies is possible when the same bank is used.

9.2 / Safe settlement using the Real Time Gross Settlement systems offered by central banks (parties use different banks in both systems)

London: on Monday, Merrill Lynch sells $10 million to Salomon Brothers in exchange for 15 million Swiss francs. Merrill and Salomon send payment instructions to their banks through SWIFT for Wednesday delivery.

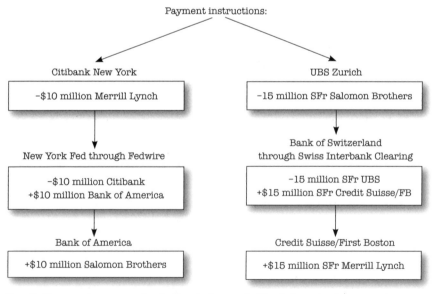

Payment instructions:

Citibank New York

−$10 million Merrill Lynch

New York Fed through Fedwire

−$10 million Citibank
+$10 million Bank of America

Bank of America

+$10 million Salomon Brothers

UBS Zurich

−15 million SFr Salomon Brothers

Bank of Switzerland
through Swiss Interbank Clearing

−15 million SFr UBS
+$15 million SFr Credit Suisse/FB

Credit Suisse/First Boston

+$15 million SFr Merrill Lynch

Result: If payments are consciously timed when central banks' opening hours overlap, final payments in both currencies can be achieved at the same time. Problem: banks have to hold large balances that earn nothing at the central bank.

9.3 / Stylized comparison of Real Time Gross Settlements (RTGS) and a bilateral Deferred Netting System (DNS) for settlement

Time	Bank A		Bank B
9:00	$50 million	⟶	
10:00	$50 million	⟶	
11:00	$60 million	⟶	
12:00		⟵	$120 million

RTGS system   Bank A would have needed $160 million in reserves to cover the morning payments. Bank B would be holding $40 million more reserves than it needed for the 12:00 payment.

DNS system   At the end of the cycle, Bank A owes Bank B the net amount for the cycle: $160 million – $120 million = $40 million.

Result: Netting systems require fewer reserves than central bank systems and are therefore cheaper to use.

9.4 / Stylized picture of multilateral deferred netting cycle

Time	Bank A	Bank B	Bank C
9:00	$50 million ⟶		
9:30		⟵	$60 million
10:00	$50 million ⟶		
10:30		$100 million ⟶	
11:00	$60 million ⟶		
11:30			⟵ $50 million
12:00		⟵ $120 million	

Bilateral net positions (end of cycle)

A owes B $40 million
C owes A $60 million
B owes C $50 million

Net-net positions (end of cycle settlement)

B pays $10 million into system account
C pays $10 million into system account
A gets paid $20 million from system account

Result: Multilateral netting on a net-net basis saves reserves relative to bilateral netting and therefore is cheaper to use. Because fewer reserves are needed to settle, net-net settlement systems are also less likely to run into settlement problems than bilateral netting systems.

9.5 / Large value dollar delivery through CHIPS (late 1990s)

London: On Monday, Merrill Lynch sells $10 million in FX deals to Salomon Brothers for Wednesday delivery. Merrill sends SWIFT message to pay $10 million to Salomon Brothers.

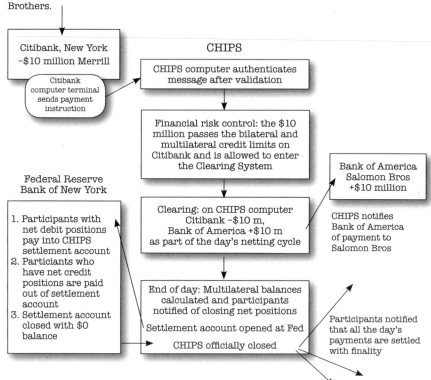

A visit to CHIPS, the world's largest currency delivery system in the 1990s

The last time I was in the Wall Street financial district, the big banks – Morgan, Chase, Citibank, Chemical Bank, Mannie Hannie, and Marine Midland – were clumped within a few city blocks. Starting at Broad Street, where the old New York Clearing House is located, one bank backed up to another all the way to the New York Fed on Liberty Street, their activities blessed by the Episcopal bishop at Trinity Church. The July heatwave drives me into what used to be Chase's headquarters, right across from the Federal Reserve Bank of New York. A friendly receptionist allows me to make some calls. I contact a graduate school classmate who is an economist for the bank. His secretary tells me their new headquarters is in Midtown, on Park Avenue a few blocks from Citicorp Center. Since my last visit, some of the other large banks – Banker's Trust, Union Bank of Switzerland, Sumitomo, and others – have moved from the cramped Financial District up to newer headquarters in Midtown Manhattan. I later asked Passacantando why the banks are moving out of the Wall Street area, and he figured that they must be looking for better restaurants.

I call for Mr Thomas at CHIPS, hoping I can catch him before my meeting at four at the Fed. His secretary puts him on the line.

'George Thomas, Robert Williams. I was hoping to get a chance to meet you this afternoon. I have an interview with Hank Wiener at the New York Fed at four. By chance, could you squeeze me in?'

'Where are you?' he asks.

'I'm in the Chase lobby.'

'Which one?'

'The one across from the Fed in the Financial District.'

'That's too far from here. Maybe we ought to plan for later tomorrow afternoon. I have to go to Washington tomorrow morning and my train won't get back to New York until two.'

I think about the recent problems with the Metroliner.

'How about right now, if that's not too much of an inconvenience for you?'

'Well, you better cancel your meeting at the Fed this afternoon, maybe reschedule with Wiener tomorrow or something.'

I look at my watch. 'It's 2:40, could I just come on over? Where's your office?'

'In the area between Penn Station and Times Square,' he says.

I'm stunned for a second. I'd thought for sure CHIPS would be at the New York Clearing House on Broad Street, a few blocks from here. After all, CHIPS is owned by the New York Clearing House Association, which is owned by some of the most powerful banks in the world. Maybe they could've moved to Midtown, but the Garment District? Not a likely spot for the largest dollar delivery service in the world. I look again at my watch. I wish I had waited in line and called from Penn Station. It had taken forty minutes to get down to Wall Street from Penn Station.

I ask Mr Thomas, 'What's the fastest way to get there?'

He says, 'I believe there's a direct red line that leaves from the basement of the building you're in, but that could be a wait. You'd better catch a cab.'

'OK. I'll try to.' I copy down the directions from his secretary. The route is so strange, I have her repeat it twice. A criss-cross path through an unfamiliar section of town, through the lobby and to the very back of an old building shared with an assortment of businesses and professionals. She gives the street address of the building and recommends, 'If you expect to get here from Wall Street by three, take a cab.'

I look out of the tall windows of the Chase lobby and see a snarl of honking cars and trucks, and wonder where in the world I can catch a cab that will not be stuck forever in traffic. I ask the receptionist where the entry to the red line is and she points to some stairs at the far end of the lobby.

Down the stairs, a blast of hot fumes greets me. Using my briefcase as a rudder, I navigate through the crowd, get to the right dock, tear off my coat, and loosen my tie. Dark patches have formed around my armpits, and another is starting around my neck, which itches from heavy starch and an oppressive tie. I'm in luck. The red line express screeches to a halt. To my relief, the air-conditioning works. I grab an overhead rail to cool my torso. In what seems like minutes, the train stops at 34th Street Station.

With the pushing crowd, I'm spilled into a street of sidewalk vendors. The bazaar atmosphere dizzies me as I'm shoved between rolling garment racks. I look for consecutive numbers on the shops and see I'm headed the wrong way. As I steer into a current flowing the other direction, I glance down at my watch. Two minutes to three.

I've forgotten how long blocks can be in New York. I scramble around slower pedestrians. I follow the directions onto a side street, where walking traffic diminishes. Soon the sidewalks are practically empty. I pass buildings that have been turned into warehouses. A trashed-out parking lot sends up heat waves, giving a mirage effect. In the shade of a boarded-up building, men seated on buckets take turns swigging from a container in a brown bag, a communion of sorts. Across the street is a church with messages and fliers tacked all over the doors, some denomination's urban mission. Could I have gotten the directions wrong?

I look over my shoulder, cross the street and open my briefcase. If I weren't so driven, this heat would make me faint. No. According to the directions and street address I'm headed the right way. I spot in the distance what looks like an office building with some people milling around outside. As I approach, I see it's the correct address.

I pass through the lobby undeterred by security guards. I go all the way to back of the building and up some stairs. In a dark corner is a blank door, no number or name on it, no doorbell, no safety lock. I knock on the door, no answer. I think, this is impossible. If I open this door, I'll find mop buckets. There's space back here for nothing but a janitor's closet. In a state of doubt and confusion, I retrace my steps and ask the security guard where the New York Clearing House is.

He points where I just came from, 'Go all the way to the back, up the stairs and the door's in the corner.'

I return and knock. No answer. I knock loudly, open the door and enter a stale room. Fluorescent tubes hum overhead, casting an unflattering light on linoleum squares, popular in kitchens during the 1950s, yellowed and cracked from decades of Johnson's Wax. Behind a scratched Plexiglas shield stand two guards, who peer at me suspiciously. One focuses on the sweat popping off my forehead, the other asks, 'Whoareyou, and whoareyouheretosee.'

'Robert Williams to see George Thomas.' I take out my handkerchief and dry my palms and forehead.

'Onemomentplease.' He dials on a rotary telephone and checks my story. The other one stares at me. I avoid his eyes; my breathing is too loud for someone who is innocent. I look for some sign to verify if I'm in the right place. There are no letters or an insignia anywhere. On the wall behind the guards is a wooden bin with tiny mail slots that looks as if it was lifted from the check-in of a fleabag hotel.

'Signinplease.' He passes a clipboard through the narrow opening. As I print my name and sign next to the X, I wonder if I'm being inducted into a prison.

I push the clipboard back through the window. The guard pulls in front of him a page of blank stickers with 'Visitor' printed in blue at the top, the kind sold at K-mart. He inscribes my name, leaving off the *s* at the end of Williams, tears the square out of the sheet and pushes it through the hole. My hands are too clammy to pull the sticker off the wax paper, so I ask for help. He starts it for me, pushes it back through, and I stick it on my jacket.

As I wait for Mr Thomas, I notice the decor is unlike that of any bank I have ever seen. Although my legs could use a rest, I decide not to sit on the guest couch lest I slide off the chocolate naugahide. In the corner sits a five-gallon planter, the kind that shrubs are sold in at nurseries. Stuck in it is a large-leafed plastic plant, looking faded and distressed, as if it were retrieved from the hobo parking lot down the street.

George Thomas, Senior Vice-President and Director of Information Systems, enters through the side door and shakes my hand. He's dressed on the casual side for the company of bankers, a blue Oxford shirt with striped tie loosened, no jacket. He looks on call, ready for action at any moment, more like a brain surgeon than a banker. His eyes have a clarity and precision about them, and his movements are cool and under control, as if he's awaiting a rush of adrenaline.

Mr Thomas initials the sign-in sheet. I get my first indication I'm at the right place when Mr Thomas reaches for a small, yet unnoticed gray box, slightly larger than a cigarette package. He punches in some numbers on top and slowly presses his index finger into a soft pad. The door doesn't open; he re-enters the code and more carefully places his fingerprint on the pad. The door buzzes, opens, and we enter an air-conditioned hallway with partitioned offices and a carpeted floor. I think to myself: this is a completely modern building affixed to an old decoy.

Inside his roomy office Mr Thomas takes one look at me and surmises how I got here, commending me on how fast I caught a train and made the hike.

'Before we get started, do you mind if I give Hank Wiener at the Fed a call? I believe it'll be impossible to tour CHIPS and get back down there by four.'

'Sure, here's the phone.'

Hank Wiener is understanding, though I don't mention the cause of my lateness, and he reschedules me for 4:45.

'So what's this book you're working on?' Thomas asks.

'It's a layperson's guide to world currency markets, what goes on behind the scenes. I'm trying to stay as non-technical as possible. ' I deflect the focus from me. 'Franco Passacantando tells me CHIPS delivers most of the dollar payments resulting from foreign currency trades.'

'Yes. That's true.' He explains that CHIPS also processes large-value dollar payments resulting from Eurodollar transactions, international trade flows, and international syndicated loans. 'And as a separate sideline business, we have an automated clearing house for US domestic trans-actions.'[1]

'When did you begin working at CHIPS?'

'Before, I was operations manager for Burroughs, and in 1981 the New York Clearing House hired me when they moved to this location. In the move they upgraded to a Burroughs 7800 system. We're always looking for ways to enhance our system, and since then I've been involved in planning and in charge of implementing all the upgrades. In 1994 we did a big upgrade, replacing the mainframe here with a Unisys A–19 system, and in 1995 we put in a parallel system in our backup over there.' He points toward New Jersey.

'Is the backup in East Rutherford, near Fedwire's processing center?' I ask.

'Something like that.' George Thomas is conspicuously evasive. 'What aspects of our operation are you most interested in?'

I tell him that on the train from Washington, I read the reports on netting systems and systemic risk. 'Franco Passacantando gave me a lesson on payments systems, and I've drawn some pictures of various netting arrangements, but it's still abstract to me. I was hoping a tour would give me a down-to-earth sense of how CHIPS works and what you're doing to reduce settlement risk.'

Thomas responds. 'That's at the heart of what we do here, trying to find efficient ways to get the job done while managing all sorts of risks – not just settlement risk.' He mentions fraud risk and operational risk in addition to the financial risk that a member defaults or has a liquidity problem and can't settle. 'Of course, we always have to weigh the costs of any measure that will lower risk. There's usually a trade-off.'

'I'm aware that banks extend credit to each other all day. Can you show me some ways CHIPS reduces the risk that a bank can't settle at the end of the day?'[2]

Thomas says, 'OK. Let's look at what's happened so far today and I think you'll get a feel for it.' He moves to his computer screen, where numbers in rows and columns constantly change like a slot machine in motion. He points to the bottom of the screen, 'We've already processed $1.2 trillion in payments today, and it's 3:30 so the day's not over. By comparison, the average so far this year is $1.4 trillion per day in 225,000 transactions, making the average payment amount to a little more than $6 million.'

'What can your system handle?'

'Our peak capacity right now is a million transactions a day, more than twice the record number we have ever experienced.'[3] He says that one day earlier in the year (1997) payments volume surged over 400,000 for a value amounting to nearly $2.2 trillion. 'We can process a value of $99 trillion, more than forty times the record surge.'[4]

I point to the top of the screen. 'Can you explain what these other entries are?'

'Look at the first row. That's Chase and the second row is Morgan. This shows that so far today Morgan has sent Chase $80 billion in payments and Chase has sent Morgan $88 billion, but final settlement hasn't happened so Morgan is giving Chase a temporary loan of $8 billion, which is fast approaching the bilateral credit limit for Chase from Morgan.'

'I want to make sure I've got this right. If Chase has sent more funds to Morgan, why would Morgan be lending to Chase?'

He explains it with an example of a merchant who accepts checks from customers. The check is a payment to the merchant, but until the check is deposited and clears the account of the customer, the merchant is extending a credit to the check writer.

'That makes sense. And if you could explain the bilateral credit limit you were speaking of?'

He explains that checks sometimes bounce, so merchants set a limit on the amount of purchases a single customer can make using checks. To guard against a large bounce at CHIPS, each day before opening all of the participant banks set a maximum amount of credit they'll allow each of the others.

'How do they set the limits?'

George Thomas smiles, 'Private banks know long before government regulators if another bank is having trouble. Banks constantly monitor each other on creditworthiness.' He gives the hypothetical example of Chase believing that the fictitious Bank of Moscow might have trouble paying up; Chase could set a bilateral credit limit of zero on the Bank of Moscow. So, during the day, Bank of Moscow will only be able to send payments to Chase if it has already received enough payments from Chase to cover the amount to be sent.

I ask what happens if Bank of Moscow tries to send payments that are over the limit.

'Our computer won't accept the payment instruction.' He says that the computer automatically returns the payment message with an explanation 'rejected due to insufficient funds,' and Bank of Moscow will have to 'self-monitor' and resubmit when it has the funds.

'How does a participant "self-monitor"?'

Thomas describes how each participant watches on a computer screen its ongoing payments flows and credit balances along with its credit limits. The person operating the terminal waits until its credit balance with another bank dips far enough below the bilateral credit limit and then sends the payment. The terminal operator must also watch the net debit cap, which is the overall amount of debt to the system a sending bank is allowed to pile up at any moment, and the operator will postpone payments if the bank is approaching the limit.

'So, what happens if Bank of Moscow goes bankrupt or for some other reason can't pay what it owes?'

George Thomas says that under a 1991 federal law, a bankruptcy court has to permit a netting cycle to go to completion. Before this law, there was the risk that a court-appointed trustee might decide to collect all of the payments made by other participants into the failed institution but refuse to make good on any payments from the failed institution. This law made netting more robust in the US. 'Now the maximum loss for remaining participants has been greatly reduced to the net amounts owed them by the Bank of Moscow at the end of the cycle.'[5]

I ask how CHIPS would deal with an otherwise healthy institution that finds itself short of funds and unable to pay at the end of the day.

He says that if the bank were not insolvent but was just having a liquidity problem, another participant or group of participants might be willing to make a loan for the net amount and the day's cycle could be finalized.

'But what if no bank wants to lend, so a normal settlement can't be achieved?'

Thomas reflects, 'In our old way of doing things, if a participant couldn't make alternative arrangements to settle within one hour of closing, there would be a partial unwind of the system.' He explains that in a partial unwind the Bank of Moscow would be treated as 'failed.' CHIPS would recalculate all the day's transactions but would remove all those involving the Bank of Moscow. The new net–net balances would be settled over Fedwire. 'In all those years when this was the agreed-upon procedure, we never experienced a partial unwind, but we simulated what would happen.'

'What were the results?'

He says that the deletion of a failed bank can radically change the end-of-day positions, turning some banks from net creditors into net debtors. 'More disturbing is that the resetting of positions can be large enough to make others unable to settle. This can lead to further unwinds.'

'What's in place now to prevent this?'

'We now have a loss-sharing agreement.' He explains how all the re-maining participants have to pay in a share of the net amount the failed institution owes. The share is based on each participant's bilateral credit limit set for the failed bank at the beginning of the day. If a rumor gets out that a participant is having liquidity problems, other participants can reduce the bilateral credit cap during the course of the cycle, but loss sharing is based on the maximum bilateral credit extended for the cycle. 'This prevents banks from bailing out of the loss-sharing arrangement during the day.'

'I see, so this makes banks careful about how high they make their bilateral credit caps in the morning. But what happens if a participant decides not to abide by the loss-sharing agreement?'

'I'd sell off its Treasuries and use the proceeds to pay in its share.' He explains that at the beginning of each cycle, all participants have to pledge US Treasury securities as collateral in the CHIPS account at the Fed. Once posted, only CHIPS has the right to sell or transfer the securities. So the loss sharing is mandatory. 'It's not being left up to good will or verbal promises.'

'How much does each bank have to ante up in the morning?'

He explains that the collateral posted is calculated from the two larg-est bilateral credit caps a bank sets at the beginning of the day. 'That's enough collateral to prevent an unwind if the two largest banks in the system were to fail. It would handle the failure of a much larger number of small banks.'

I mention that on the train ride up I read the Lamfalussy Report, which recommended the exact measures he had just described. I ask him, 'Did this report by central bankers prompt you to introduce these safeguards?'

For the first time in the interview, George Thomas gets huffy. 'That's what some people say,' he grumbles, 'but let's see the publication date on your report.' He glances at my briefcase and waits.

I fumble through my briefcase for the publication and pull it out. 'It says here November 1990.'[6]

Impatiently he rattles off the timing of CHIPS' risk control improvements. 'Shortly after I took my job here in 1981, we set up same-day settlement on Fedwire. In 1984 bilateral credit limits were introduced. In 1986 we introduced sender net debit caps, and in October 1990, a month before the Lamfalussy Report was released, we put in action the collaterized loss-sharing scheme. So, before Lamfalussy, CHIPS had all the recommended features in place… and more, I might add. Of course, they closely studied our operation before writing their report. We believe the Lamfalussy Committee used CHIPS as the model for other multilateral netting schemes to follow.' He hits the ball into my court. 'Another question for you. What amount of collateral does the Lamfalussy Report recommend for a loss-sharing arrangement?'

Fortunately, I recall the passage. 'It recommends enough collateral to cover for the failure of the largest participant.'

George Thomas points to the report. 'We can settle if our two largest participants fail the same day.' He lifts two fingers. 'In other words, CHIPS has Lamfalussy Plus One protection. And we'll never stop looking for better ways to manage risks and improve services to our participants.'

'What *could* cause an unwind?'

He smiles. 'We couldn't handle it if the three largest participants, which would be among the largest banks, were *allowed* to fail. When you go over there this afternoon, ask Hank Wiener what it would take for the Fed to let that happen.'

'What about an act of God? You know, a major earthquake or hurricane that knocks out the computers?'

George Thomas rises from the chair, 'Let me show you our system, and you'll see some ways we manage operational risk.'

He leads the way through partitioned offices, punches in the security code and lets the gray box read his fingerprint. We enter a cavernous room that looks like a practically empty warehouse. Toward the end of the room in the center rises a large, impressive board with blinking lights, screens, and digital readouts that looks like the flight control panel at Kennedy Space Center. Two officers in uniform gaze up at the indicators, so we don't bother them.

'With the B-7800s, this room was packed with equipment.' Thomas motions over the empty space.

I point to two units near the far wall, each the size of a dumpster. 'And are those the new computers?'

He laughs, 'No, those are air conditioners. We have to keep the computer rooms at a constant temperature and we monitor the humidity.' Thomas walks toward a row of what look like short filing cabinets. 'Here they are.' He respectfully waves a blessing over six gray units.

In utter disbelief, I ask, '*these* process the world's dollar payments?'

'Not exactly. The first three here do. The other three process our domestic Automated Clearing House operation, which we keep separate.'

'They look so... how do I say it... insignificant. How can they be so small?'

'Microprocessors,' he comments, 'but also this.' George Thomas picks up a rectangular cassette about the size of a stereo tape. 'This disc stores as much information as eleven of those.' He points to a rack along the wall with shelves of magnetic tapes that look like old movie reels. 'A large part of our old units consisted of the drives for the magnetic tapes.'

'And what if one of these first little gray things misfires?' I walk up to one.

'These three are exact replicas of the ones in there.' He points to another security door. 'These receive and store the same information as the primary computers in there, so if one misfires in there, there's an immediate backup.'

'What if Manhattan's electricity supply blacks out again like in 1990?'

'We weren't hit by that one, but some of our participants were. In the event of an outage in this building, the battery system would take over, and dual diesel generators in the basement would crank up automatically, so we wouldn't skip a beat. Each generator is capable of producing enough electricity to run the whole show – lights, air conditioning, everything.'

'What if a bomb or an earthquake knocks out the building?'

'See this phone?' He points to a rather ordinary looking telephone. 'This is a direct line to our backup center in New Jersey. Separate fiberoptic cables alternatively routed from participants' interface terminals carry the same messages this computer receives to the backup site across the river. The backup site has an identical system setup as here, and it's connected to this one with a dedicated fiberoptic cable. In the event of a disaster here, I scramble to that line and in five minutes the backup site becomes the primary center. We test this periodically, and we can have the backup site take over our job in less than five minutes.' He jabs at the competition. 'Be sure to ask Hank how fast he can bring Richmond and Dallas on line.'

'I'm curious about Star Trek central over there.'

We walk to the control panel and Thomas introduces me to the two uniformed technicians. 'This indicates the status of each and every point on the entire system.'

I ask the woman, 'And what happens if you see a misfire somewhere?'

She glances over her shoulder and laughs, 'We just call George. He can handle anything.'

Thomas and I meander back to the line of computers.

I ask him, 'I know this is changing the subject a bit, but with several hundred thousand electronic messages and more than a trillion dollars being pumped through these machines a day, what's to stop someone from jiggling an amount or altering a destination... to, say, an instant retirement account?'

Thomas pauses. 'Secure lines, encryption and authentication.'

'Sounds mystical to me. Can you give me a down-to-earth sense of what's at work?'

He walks over to Gray Unit Number One. 'These are connected to our member banks by fiberoptic cables.' He explains that the cables go under Manhattan streets to the back offices of member banks, where they connect with computer terminals. The cables and computer terminals are dedicated to CHIPS messages only, and he says, 'we keep these secure. If there's any tampering within the CHIPS system, it can happen in two places, at a member bank's dedicated terminal, where we can run a security check and nab the perpetrator, or by someone in this office, and you see how many staff we have here to run security checks on.'

I note to myself how odd it is that I've seen a total of six employees so far, including Thomas and the guards. I prompt him, 'and you mentioned encryption and authentication...'

He explains how payment instructions from all over the world feed into the New York branches of CHIPS member banks through SWIFT or some other message carrier. Before the message is forwarded to CHIPS, the sending bank uses its own in-house procedures to verify its authenticity. When the operator of the CHIPS interface terminal presses the security key to forward the payment instruction to CHIPS, the message is tagged with a unique code for that particular terminal. 'No one at the sending bank, not even the operator of the terminal knows what the code is. We change the code daily here at CHIPS using a random number generator.' He pats the computer. 'When the message is received here, it's edited and stored in this computer,' and a verification copy is relayed back notifying the operator of the contents of the instruction stored in the CHIPS computer. The sender terminal operator checks the verification copy for accuracy with the original message. If it's correct, the operator notifies CHIPS to release the payment message. 'That's encryption and authentication.'

'And then I suppose the computer applies the financial risk controls you told me about earlier?'

'Yes. The payment is screened to see if it can get through the credit and debit caps.' He describes how, if the payment passes the financial risk controls, the computer debits the sending bank's running balance and credits the receiving bank's balance, and the payment is released for delivery to the receiving bank through that bank's dedicated fiberoptic cable.

'What happens if a sending bank's computer terminal misfires?'

Thomas says, 'I'll show you, but to see it we have to go into the main operations room.' He proceeds to yet another security door, punches in the code, and presses down his fingerprint. We enter a much smaller room. Three operators scurry back and forth as another sits, eyes glued to a computer screen.

'See this loudspeaker?' Thomas points to a small black box on top of one of the three mainframes. 'If a sender terminal goes on the blink, the terminal operator has a direct voice line to this speaker and everyone in the room can hear what the problem is in plain English.' He notes that primitive technology is sometimes the most effective. 'In an emergency situation, no electronic message system can outperform the human voice.'

'So if a voice comes over the speaker saying the power is out at the sending bank?' I ask.

'We have a software program that quickly retrieves the last full message from that participant. We report the last message to the participant, and when the power comes back on at the sending terminal, the operator can pick up right where she was interrupted. We've found this combined response system using the human voice and recovery/rollback software to be very effective.'

'How much does CHIPS charge for its services?'

'Participants pay a nominal membership fee per month, it's fifteen hundred dollars now, and then they pay on a transaction-by-transaction basis. As you can see, we hold our staffing costs to a minimum, and we're set up as a cooperative that's owned by the ten banks that own the New York Clearing House Association.[7] If our profit exceeds the amount needed for systems replacement and improvement, we pass those savings on in the way of lower fees to our members.'

'What are the transactions fees and how do they compare with the Fedwire service?'

'We charge less than the Fed, and partly for this reason, our dollar flow is larger than Fedwire.'

'More than Fedwire's total? ... including domestic interbank payments inside the US?'

'Yes. We surpassed Fedwire in dollar volume in 1988. They started charging for transfers in 1980.'

'I'm curious. What exactly are the fees?'

'Right now a Fedwire transfer is 45 cents. The maximum we charge is 40 cents, and that's for a sender or a receiver who's not in our database. We have to manually punch in their account information, and this costs more. Our repeat customers do large volumes using straight-through processing. For them there's no code switching, so they are charged a base rate of 13 cents per transaction, while lower volume customers pay 17 cents per transaction.'

He catches me glancing at my watch and says, 'Speaking of Fedwire. We'd better take you back to my office for your briefcase. Don't want you to miss settlement time at the Fed.'

Through two sets of security doors back to his office, the inner sanctum of CHIPS is so protected I hadn't heard the thunderstorm raging outside. Through Thomas's office window I see the a black sky and water pouring off buildings.

George Thomas hands me the pile of photocopies and pamphlets his secretary has assembled. 'Here's the data you requested and some recent studies of payments system risk I think you might be interested in. Also we have a website that can give you updated information on CHIPS, it's at www.chips.org. Give me a call if you have any further questions.'

He says, 'If you're going to get to the Fed on time, you had better go down to the corner and catch a cab. Hope you don't get drenched.'

As he ushers me back to the reception room I can't refrain from commenting, 'George, I'm curious about the decor in your lobby. Is it part of your cost-containment program? Or is it to throw off would-be saboteurs?'

George Thomas opens the security door and makes a sweeping gesture of appreciation for the floor, the couch, and the pathetic plant. 'At CHIPS, we like to remain low key.' He winks. 'Now I've got to get ready for settlement. Say hello to Hank for me.'

Time to settle up: CHIPS closes the dollar day at the New York Fed

Out of the janitors' closet, down the stairs and through the crowd in the lobby, I hail the first cab, hop the river, and slide into the back seat. Water has filled the floor wells, so I perch my feet on the transmission hump.

The driver, a recent arrival, looks back and asks, 'Where you go?'

'The Federal Reserve on Liberty Street.'

'Where that?'

'The other way,' I point downtown, 'near Wall Street. As fast as you can, please.'

He does a U-turn flips the meter, floors it, and passes a pack of honking cabs. We dart into the safety of a side street, hit a pothole and water from the floor well sloshes up on my socks and pants.

The driver passes back a soggy towel and says, 'Here. To dry.'

I thank him for his thoughtfulness. I'm less worried about appearance than getting there in time for the final settlement. Mr Wiener has been kind to change the appointment, but he did say he had to leave by 5:15 and wouldn't be back tomorrow.

It's whiplash stop-and-go down Ninth Avenue heading for Greenwich Village, where we turn west on a weird little street. He finds the entry to Twelfth, where he steps on it. Soon we're flying past the docks. To heck with wet pants, this guy's doing what I asked. We swerve around a Hertz rental truck, and the driver asks, 'Where we turn?'

I point east. 'Onto Liberty if it goes that way.'

We zoom past the World Trade Center, turn left onto Liberty, go a block and get stuck at Broadway. The other side of the intersection is jammed. 'Better let me out here.'

He protests. 'No. You get wet. I take you to the Federal, sir.'

I scramble out and take an extra five out of my wallet. This should help buy a baling pump.

The New York Federal Reserve building is an urban fortress constructed of massive stones with iron bars on the windows and castle gates for a door. Built in 1924, it occupies a block of prime Manhattan real estate. The architect designed it after the Medici Palace in Florence, where the fifteenth-century bankers could bar the portals and defend their family members – and their reserves of precious metals – against street insurrection and armed attack.

The public entry at 33 Liberty Street faces Chase Plaza, where I called from earlier. The throngs who tour the visitor center on the first floor are already cleared out. The metal detector goes off and the guard confiscates my Swiss army knife.

Mr Wiener's secretary leads the way through a maze of hallways and onto a freight elevator. 'Please excuse our mess,' she says, 'this old place was overdue for a renovation, but now we must suffer for it.'

Hank Wiener introduces himself. 'I'm sorry Robert, but I have an engagement I can't fudge on at 5:15, and I won't be in New York tomorrow morning. In case we don't have enough time to answer all your questions, here's my card.' His card reads: Henry Wiener, Vice-President, Area of Electronic Payment Function.

With George Thomas's hints of competitive rivalry between the privately owned CHIPS and the publicly owned Fedwire, I decide not to explain the reason for my delay. 'What I'm most curious about is how Fedwire works, especially in relation to international payments.'

Mr Wiener looks down at his watch. '4:45. The most important event of the day is happening as we speak.'

'Do you mean the final settlement of CHIPS?'

'Yes.'

'On the way up to New York, I read the publication you and your staff put together on CHIPS, but I'd like to know how final settlement works in practice.'

'Since you're already familiar with CHIPS, I won't go into great detail here about its operations.' He goes on to say that today CHIPS processed a dollar volume of about $1.4 trillion payments between approximately one hundred active participant banks, most of whom are foreign. Because these banks agree to settle at the end of the day for net amounts owed instead of on a payment-by-payment basis, like Fedwire, the final amounts settled for are a tiny fraction of the gross amounts processed during the day. And the foreign banks that are members of CHIPS have seven big US banks that settle for them, 'so there is a further reduction from a hundred payers and receivers to eighteen, all of whom are members of the Federal Reserve System.'

'Are there seven settlement banks or eighteen?'

'OK. Eleven of the eighteen settling banks in CHIPS don't settle for other members, they just settle for what they owe or are owed by the system.'

'So, how is the settlement working today?'

'Today it's simple, because it's a normal settlement.'

'Normal settlement?'

'Yes. All the settling banks agreed to settle for the non-settling banks. So after CHIPS closed at 4:30 and everyone agreed to settle, CHIPS called over here and said, "Open up the CHIPS account," and our operator did so a few minutes ago.'

'Then what happened?'

'Then we took a look at the settlement sheet.'

'What does the settlement sheet look like?'

'It's simple. There's a total of eighteen entries. Today, eight banks owed money into the system and ten are due to receive money. Right now, the eight owing banks are paying out of their own Fedwire accounts into the CHIPS account. When that's accomplished, which should be in a matter of a few minutes, CHIPS will send payments to the Fedwire accounts of the ten banks that are owed. When those funds have been transferred electronically, the CHIPS balance will be zero, and CHIPS will inform us to close the account. At about 5 o'clock CHIPS will notify all the other participants that today's cycle is finally settled.'

'How much is owed today?' I ask.

'The total amount owed by the eight banks in today's settlement is about $9 billion.'

'$9 billion? In eighteen transactions?' I hope to get a rise out of him. 'That sounds trivial compared with the $1.4 trillion CHIPS delivered.'

'Maybe it sounds unimportant,' Mr Wiener calmly muses, 'but that $9 billion is in final money that any financial institution in the world will accept as payment.' He points out that in a netting arrangement like CHIPS, it's the promise to settle up at the end of the cycle in central bank money – and the safeguards to assure that settlement will really happen – that make banks willing to extend credit to each other all day long. 'That $9 billion in eighteen transactions may seem trivial, but it supports all the rest.'

'You mention safeguards. What are some?'

'Well, in addition to the final settlement accounts, we also provide the collateral account for CHIPS in case one of the participants fails before closing.'

'How does this work? Do you move Treasury bonds from a bank's pile into CHIPS pile?'

Mr Wiener laughs. 'Nobody holds paper Treasury bonds anymore; they're all electronic book-entries here at Fedwire.' He describes how every morning CHIPS participants transfer security interests in US Treasuries over to the CHIPS' collateral account. The total amount is enough to cover the top two banks being unable to settle at the end of the day. This Fedwire service is insurance for CHIPS participants that a final settlement in Federal Reserve money will really happen at the end of the day, 'even if there's a snag and somebody says, "this guy doesn't have the funds; I'm not going to settle for him." An abnormal settlement takes longer. It might take till 7:30, but because of this protection, that day's transactions won't unwind.'

'Can you remember when there was a settlement problem?'

Mr Wiener thinks for a moment. 'Well, back in the early 1980s during the LDC [Less Developed Countries] debt crisis, 1982 as I recall, there were periods when CHIPS participants wouldn't allow the Bank of Brazil or the Bank of Mexico to make payments through CHIPS, they could just be sent payments by other parties. There wasn't a settlement crisis but we were afraid of gridlock, so the Fed had to take up the slack.'

'How did you take up the slack?'

He explains that the New York Fed's Central Bank Services Facility holds and electronically transfers dollar deposits and US Treasury securities on behalf of some 140 central banks and other international financial institutions. At that time, he recalls, 'we expanded the collateralized overdraft capabilities of the Bank of Mexico and the Bank of Brazil, and we put in special risk management procedures for those accounts. This allowed the Bank of Mexico and the Bank of Brazil to make payments during the day when the private-sector banks in CHIPS wouldn't extend them intraday credit. And they could make payments through us even when their deposit accounts here at the Federal Reserve didn't have adequate funds. This worked pretty well to keep the loan payments and other international payments flowing at a dangerous time.'

'Do you allow private banks overdraft capabilities?'

'All the time.'

'Can you give some examples?'

'Credit unions, foreign banks, and non-healthy US banks are allowed collateralized daylight overdrafts on Fedwire similar to those we offer central banks. To get the funds, these banks must pledge US Treasury securities, so the Federal Reserve Bank of New York is not exposed to default risk. If they don't pledge the Treasuries, we reject the payments due to insufficient funds.'

'Do you allow healthy banks non-collateralized daylight overdrafts?'

'Yes.'

'Examples?'

He pauses. 'Bank of New York and Chase do substantial clearing and safekeeping operations for Treasury bond dealers and banks. Sometimes big payments imbalances can arise when there are in-transit collateral securities involved. This calls for heavy daylight overdrafts as a normal course of business for these two banks. We know the cause of these overdrafts, and we know we'll get paid, so in order to lubricate the payments machine, we set a relatively high cap for these banks. Chase and other healthy banks generally watch their daylight overdraft caps, but if I see them pushing against the caps, I'll give 'em a call and find out why.' He emphasizes that this interactive practice involving daylight overdrafts and a single risk manager at the Federal Reserve for each member bank is unique in the world of central banking, and it's one of the flexibility features of the system that makes it both efficient and safe. 'The liquidity it brings to Treasury transfers and payments is one of the reasons why the dollar is used so much for international transactions.'

'Do these overdrafts come free of charge to the banks?' I ask.

'Good question. Before April of 1994, we didn't charge banks for daylight overdrafts, so bank managers had no incentive to conserve on the use of this free source of funds. The use of overdrafts by the banks on the system soared to a peak average exceeding $185 billion a day before we began charging. Banks still use the facility but now they monitor the timing of their payments messages so as to conserve on overdrafts. This lowers the Federal Reserve's overall credit risk.'

I ask him what else the Federal Reserve Bank of New York does with respect to foreign exchange markets.

'I'm not the specialist on foreign exchange here, but I can summarize. We conduct all of the open market operations, the buying and selling of US Treasuries, for the entire Federal Reserve System.' He explains that these operations are normally for domestic monetary policy not international purposes, but when US interest rates change as a result of the money policy, a side effect may be a change in the value of the dollar relative to other currencies. 'Also, the Federal Reserve Bank of

New York intervenes directly on foreign exchange markets on our own account and for the US Treasury.'

'Do you intervene to control the value of the dollar?'

'Again, you should speak with our experts on this for greater detail, but I would say in general, no. In today's world it would be foolish for us to try to set a target for the value of the dollar against other currencies. Our reason for intervention is normally to smooth out disorderly market conditions.'

'Disorderly market conditions?'

'For example, if we see a panic brewing that threatens to disrupt the movement of international payments, we might enter a market and sell a currency that traders may be refusing to sell or buy a currency they're refusing to buy. This type of intervention can get two-way trading going again, so the international payments system is not disrupted. On rare occasions, we act in coordination with other central banks when a currency has gotten so far out of line that it's creating unhealthy distortions in the world economy. But when this is done it's not so much to fix a particular exchange rate but to jolt what we believe to be an unhealthy speculative environment.'

'Before you have to leave, I have some questions about recent upgrades in the electronic payments system. Haven't you been working on this?'

'Yes. In March 1997, our new centralized funds transfer system came online, and in February 1998 our security transfer system will be operating.' He describes how previously each of the twelve Federal Reserve District Banks had its own data-processing center with its own software adapted to the needs of its particular region of operations. These twelve processing centers were linked by switch-routing software into a national network. 'This worked OK, especially when there were strong barriers to interstate banking,' but those barriers have been eroding over the years and in June of 1997 barriers to interstate banking were officially eliminated. To handle this transformation in the private sector, 'we developed a single software application for funds transfer and security transfer everywhere in the United States.' What used to be a system of twelve independent processing centers with four backup sites is now consolidated into a single network 'we call FedNet with a single central processing center called EROC in East Rutherford, New Jersey.'

'What happens if there's a power outage at East Rutherford?'

'We have two backup sites, one in Richmond and the other in Dallas.'

'How do these work?'

'Richmond and Dallas have identical mainframes to EROC, and participating banks have alternative lease lines and telephone dial backup lines that can be switched on in the event of a disaster at EROC. Richmond is the first backup, and in the event of a failure there the lines would be switched to Dallas. All of our electronic messages are remote-logged, so we'd have to reconcile with the banks which messages were in transit when the failure occurred at EROC. When this is achieved, the in-transit messages would be resubmitted to the new primary site, and the system would be operating again as normal.'

I see the opportunity to ask George Thomas's question. 'In the event of a failure at EROC, how long would it take to switch to Richmond and have everything running again?'

Mr Wiener thinks for a few seconds. 'The lines could all be switched within thirty minutes, but the reconciliation with the banks regarding the last messages sent might take longer, maybe an hour or so. I think we could be up and operating again within an hour.'

I think to myself, ten points for CHIPS, but I change the subject. 'In this conversion of the domestic payments system, what's been done to interface better with the international payments system?'

'We're modifying our Fedwire electronic message format to be compatible with SWIFT and CHIPS formats. This means less manual intervention by our customers when they send or receive international payments.'

'Is anything being done to reduce Herstatt risk?'

'Absolutely. In December 1997, our Fedwire funds transfer day will expand to eighteen hours. This provides greater overlap with the payment systems in Europe and the Far East, so simultaneous final settlement of foreign exchange transactions can occur, thereby reducing foreign exchange settlement risk, something we've been concerned about for a long time.'

Mr Wiener looks at his watch. 'I've got to catch a train. Here are some articles with more details on the subjects we've been discussing. And be sure to call me if you have any further questions.'

He grabs his umbrella and walks toward the door. 'I have to go out the back way. I hope you don't mind my secretary escorting you down to the security entrance.'

'No problem. I'm delighted to have had this opportunity.' The secretary guides me back through the cluttered halls, down the freight elevator and back to the security guards.

I joke with the guards. 'Can I collect my deadly weapon?'

The guard hands me my pocketknife. 'Don't try to mug nobody.'

Another guard accompanies me carrying a ring of jailer keys. We swerve as the janitor pushes a giant dust mop over the marble floor. The guard unlocks the castle gate and bids me farewell, 'Enjoy the Big Apple.'

APPENDIX/Evolution of currency delivery systems to 2005

Already strong in 1997, pressures from central bank regulators and banking industry groups to reduce Herstatt risk continued to shape payments system innovations and banking practices. Major central banks, which had already moved in the early 1990s to safe, real time gross settlement systems like Fedwire, followed the Fed's 1997 example that Hank Wiener was working on at the time and extended their hours of operation to overlap with each other so that simultaneous settlement of currency transactions in different time zones could be achievable using central bank money. The Bank for International Settlements continued to coordinate efforts of the world's most important central banks, hosting meetings, conducting payments systems studies, and setting standards for 'best practices' that helped regulators encourage private-sector banks to monitor and better manage settlement risk, to create a multi-currency settlement bank, and to make greater use of netting arrangements like CHIPS, which reduce the size of settlement exposures.[1] CHIPS and other private payments processors continued to search for ways to further reduce risk in their systems and to speed settlement finality. The greatest achievement in regard to settlement risk was the creation of Continuous Linked Settlement Bank, a private bank owned by the world's largest foreign exchange dealers, which settles both legs of currency transactions at the same instant in real time using central bank money, thereby eliminating Herstatt risk for currency traders who use the bank's services. Beginning with simultaneous settlement in seven currencies in September 2002, CLS Bank extended its capability to fifteen currencies by 2005, when it was regularly delivering half the world's currency deals by value.[2]

CHIPS upgrades to real time final settlement 2001

With respect to improvements at CHIPS, George Thomas and his team of experts invented a payments procedure that allows CHIPS to deliver final payments all day long at the Fed instead of waiting for the 4:30 p.m. final settlement to occur, as was witnessed in 1997. Patented by Thomas's team in 2000 and brought online 7 February 2001, the 'balanced release payments engine' eliminates settlement risk on the dollar leg of foreign exchange deliveries while maintaining the cost efficiencies of netting.[3] In order to send payments through the new system, all CHIPS participants must deposit pre-funded balances at Fedwire between 9:00 p.m., when CHIPS now opens, and the 9:00 a.m. next-day cutoff. These pre-funded balances are calculated based on actual payments activity of the previous week. Once deposited, they cannot be withdrawn at any time during the day. After depositing its pre-funded balance, a participant can begin sending payments messages to the CHIPS computer. Unlike before when the sending bank operator had to monitor the timing of payments to fit bilateral credit limits and net debit caps, now the 'balanced release engine' does the work of timing the payments relative to a bank's available balances. This makes it possible for an operator to enter a huge stream of payments early in the day without worry about CHIPS denying acceptance of a payment because it exceeds a credit or debit cap. Because every payment is accomplished using pre-funded balances at the Fed, there is no need for participants to post Treasury securities as collateral in the morning; there is no exposure to credit risk by receiving banks during the day; and there is no possibility of an unwind of the day's payments at closing. The software in the CHIPS computer achieves payments finality through its combination of screening, monitoring, ordering, matching, batching, and netting payments in such a way that they are released only when pre-funded balances are there to support the payments. So during the course of the day, the governor on the engine will not allow a bank's pre-funded account balance to drop below zero. To keep the engine running smoothly, a credit 'cap' is set that will not allow a bank's actual account balance to exceed twice the initial pre-funded amount. The credit 'cap' prevents the buildup or 'hoarding' of excess liquidity by receiving banks, so the limited amount of total liquidity in the system – approximately equal to the value of the Treasuries posted as collateral in the system we visited in 1997 – is dynamically spread out to smooth the overall flow of payments. The engine settles with finality approximately 85 per cent of the entire day's payments before noon New York time, though it continues to chug along, receiving and settling payments during the afternoon until 5:00 p.m. when no more payments messages are accepted. After the engine has run the remaining messages, it will have settled on a typical day 99 per cent of the payments by number and approximately 96 per cent of the day's payments by value. The residual of unsettled payments, which could amount to a total value of $30 to $60 billion, will now be processed in a way that resembles the final settlement of the CHIPS system of the late 1990s with participants in net debit positions providing additional pay-ins.[4] If a bank does not provide the additional liquidity for end-of-day settlement, the associated payments are sent back for lack of funds, and the batch is recalculated and settled with the funds that are there. In the new CHIPS system there is no chance of an unwind because all the payments released throughout the day are settled with final central bank money upon release. Even the residual batch will not unwind, because the banks remaining can settle among themselves without the dropout payments. The returned dropout payments can be resubmitted to CHIPS for next-day settlement, or they can be sent through Fedwire before it closes at 6:30 p.m.

CHIPS' new settlement system provides the same safety as Fedwire transfers, but banks save on working capital. On a typical day CHIPS transfers approximately $1.4 trillion worth of payments with only about $2.8 billion in pre-funding, an efficiency ratio of about 500:1. A real time gross settlement system with no netting would require much larger reserve balances; possibly as much as $116 billion would be required to transfer $1.4 trillion in payments, or an efficiency ratio of about 12:1. Using CHIPS for large-value dollar payments, participants do not have to post collateral, they do not have to pay daylight overdrafts at the Fed, and they can make alternative use of the economized reserves. However, neither CHIPS nor Fedwire can eliminate settlement risk from foreign exchange transactions because they can only achieve finality on the dollar leg, which may or may not be timed to coincide precisely with the delivery of the foreign currency leg of a transaction.

Finally, a delivery system safe from foreign exchange settlement risk: Continuous Linked Settlement Bank begins in 2002

As George Thomas and his colleagues at CHIPS worked to achieve all-day settlement finality in dollar deliveries, Continuous Linked Settlement Services was working on a way to eliminate foreign exchange settlement risk altogether. Formed by a group of twenty large banks with a merger of two multilateral netting organizations in 1997, CLS Services created CLS Bank International, whose only function would be the delivery of both sides of a currency trade at the same instant in real time. By 2001, sixty-five commercial banks and investment banks from sixteen countries had invested more than $300 million as shareholders in CLS Bank International (CLS). Working in conjunction with the Bank for International Settlements, central banks, and IBM, CLS prepared a system to settle both legs of currency contracts simultaneously for its membership, which includes virtually every major currency dealer in the world.[5] The degree of participation in CLS by the world's top foreign exchange dealers is even greater than in CHIPS. For example, in the May 2004 *Euromoney* survey, the top thirty currency dealers, who together controlled an estimated 87 per cent of daily currency trading, were all shareholders in CLS Bank, and twenty-eight had settlement accounts at CLS Bank, while only thirteen of the top thirty dealers were listed as direct participants in CHIPS.[6] All totaled, in 2005 CLS bank had 69 shareholder banks, 55 of whom were settling currency trades through accounts held at CLS, and 26 of which were settling for third parties. In essence, CLS is a central bank exclusively devoted to settling currency trades, but the top money changers in the world own it.[7]

How it works is that each CLS settlement member holds a multi-currency settlement account at CLS Bank International, which, in turn, holds settlement accounts at the Federal Reserve and the other central banks. Instead of the traditional method of currency deliveries, depending on the time zone of a currency's payments system, CLS settlement is limited to a five-hour period (between 7:00 a.m. and 12:00 noon Central European Time) when participating central banks' operating hours overlap. All of the day's delivery instructions must be received by CLS by 6:30 a.m. Central European Time (CET). The CLS computer takes the day's delivery orders, matches the two legs of each currency contract, and puts the orders in a queue. It then runs a multilateral netting and calculates for each settlement member a pay-in schedule of the net amounts owed and the net amounts it is due to receive for each currency. All the settlement members are notified of their pay-in schedules, and they have until 7:00 a.m. CET to come up with the initial funding, which they pay into CLS's account at the relevant central banks. Before settlement can begin at 7:00 a.m. Central European Time (1:00 a.m. New York time), all settlement members must have a positive net position at CLS that is in accordance with the pay-in schedule, though the actual currency composition may not exactly match the pay-in schedule.[8] At 7:00 a.m. CET settlement execution begins, during which settlement members with net short positions in certain currencies fund those positions through intra-day swap arrangements with members who have net long posi-tions in those currencies, or they arrange for funding in that currency from outside sources. Only when net funding has been received in the appropriate currencies will the associated payments be settled. If net funding has not been received, the associated payments are cycled again through the queue. Between 7:00 and 9:00 a.m., CLS bank is continu-ously processing, receiving pay-ins, settling payments across its books, distributing pay-outs to its members, and recycling liquidity so that the day's payments have been finalized by 9:00.[9] Between 9:00 and 12:00 noon CET, any settling up between members is undertaken, and by 12:00 CET (6:00 a.m. New York time) all positions at the CLS bank are closed out and the liquidity returned to the members for other uses, for example to pre-fund accounts at CHIPS, which has a pre-funding cut-off three hours after CLS has closed.[10]

Continuous linked settlement speeds up delivery and eliminates settlement risk for currency traders who use it, but CLS creates some new risks in the global payments environment. Moving to a single bank that delivers an ever-larger share of world currency trades concentrates operational risk into a single system that links together fifteen national payments systems. Even if the CLS operating system proves resilient to a shock, an operational problem at one of the central banks or at one of the settlement members could spread liquidity problems through CLS to the other national payment systems. Exacerbating the problem is that CLS requires settlement members to make relatively large pay-ins in multiple currencies that are bunched into a cycle that lasts only five hours, thereby diverting national banking systems' liquidity into the CLS settlement facility for that time period. Netting in CLS reduces liquidity needs relative to most central bank settlement arrangements, but CLS requires far more funding than CHIPS to process large volumes of payments. For comparison, in late 2004 CLS averaged approximately $646 billion in US dollar deliveries per day using average daily pay-ins of $32.6 billion by its settlement members into the CLS account at the New York Fed, or a ratio of almost $20 in payments for every dollar of funding in central bank money. This compares favorably with Federal Reserve turnover of $12 in payments per dollar of reserves achieved without the benefit of netting, but it compares poorly with CHIPS, where $2.8 billion in funding at the Fed accomplished average daily deliveries of $1,377 billion in 2004, or a turnover of $488 in payments for every dollar of reserves used. CLS reserve use efficiency in other currencies is lower than with the dollar, averaging 14.3 : 1 for the top six currencies including the dollar.[11] Fortunately so far, extreme market conditions like those following the 11 September 2001 attack have not tested the resilience of the liquidity arrangements available to settlement members in CLS, but there is some concern in risk management circles of how an extreme scenario would play out and how to prevent a local problem from turning into a global liquidity problem through the CLS connection.[12]

Lessons of September 11th for global payments

The heavy emphasis on emergency backup facilities and operational security at CHIPS and Fedwire that George Thomas and Hank Wiener explained in 1997 paid off for the world financial system following the terrorist attacks on the World Trade Center in September 2001. Fedwire's primary site across the river in New Jersey continued to transfer funds and government securities across the Fed's books throughout the crisis, though thirty banks lost their connections with the Fedwire system. CHIPS' primary site, hidden a safe distance away from all the banks, kept delivering the world's large-value dollar payments, though nineteen of its more than fifty participants temporarily lost connections with CHIPS. Physical destruction of a vital section of lower Manhattan knocked out power and communications for a broader area, disrupting stock, bond, commercial paper, futures and commodity markets for many days. Compound problems in the government securities markets removed a trusted source of dollar funding for all other financial markets at home and abroad and created gridlock in Fedwire, sparking a global shortage of dollar liquidity. Over a two-week period the New York Fed provided massive and timely transfusions into the banking system and the Treasury securities market. The global liquidity crunch induced by the disaster of 9/11 was severe, but the financial fallout would have been a thousand times worse if the CHIPS system with all its backups had failed and a million times worse if the Fedwire system had been taken out. The shock of September 11th brought into broad daylight otherwise hidden or taken-for-granted features of financial markets that keep them flowing during normal times, it displayed financial interconnectedness on a global scale, and it pointed out vulnerabilities in payments and settlement systems, the responses to which have shaped the evolution of those systems ever since the event.

The physical destruction of buildings on approximately 40 acres of Lower Manhattan took with it an estimated 2,795 lives, almost two-thirds of whom worked in the financial services industry. Several of the largest banks active in currency markets had moved their headquarters and currency trading to Midtown Manhattan, but firms at the center of the stock and bond markets had offices and trading rooms in lower Manhattan close to the exchanges and the organizations for clearing and settling securities. Similar to currency markets, securities markets are highly concentrated, with a small number of firms accounting for a large share of the market, and they operate in close proximity to each other. One study found that for the stock market '7 of the top 10 broker-dealers ranked by capital had substantial operations in the World Trade Center or the World Financial Center, across from the World Trade Center,' and for the government securities market, eight of the nine firms that provide brokerage services through which government securities dealers make trades with each other 'had operations that were severely disrupted following the attacks.'[13]

Professional staff that survived had to relocate to makeshift facilities where equipment was scrambled into place, data and voice lines connected, and the new links tested, a process that took days. A former student from years ago, now managing disaster recovery at a major bank headquartered in Midtown Manhattan, relocated his bank's Lower Manhattan back office to New Jersey. He and his team accomplished this task in 36 hours. Somehow he was able to secure a delivery truck and a red blinking light. He talked his way through the blockade at Canal Street, through which access to lower Manhattan was restricted until Friday morning, 14 September. Dodging debris in the streets to get to the bank's back office facility, he loaded up critical equipment to take to the site his team was reconstructing in New Jersey. Some of the equipment included special modems that required hard tokens to be inserted for the back office to be able connect with the clearing house in Brussels. Without that connection, the bank would have been unable to determine its cash position and resume its key role in clearing and settling trades for the commodity, fixed income (including government securities), and derivatives markets. 'If we had not brought that back office online,' he told me three years after the event, 'imagine the disruption to the entire market.' He also recalled many other firms setting up hothouse trading rooms and other facilities in New Jersey.[14] Some firms had primary or backup sites in the financial district that were not physically damaged and were relatively easy to recharge once access to the area was permitted; others had to scurry to get alternative facilities and lines in place. One large broker–dealer rented an entire hotel in Midtown Manhattan where it relocated its center of operations.[15]

Destruction of key telecommunications facilities located at or near Ground Zero spread the challenge of getting the markets going far beyond the 40 acres directly hit. AT&T's transmission facility used to service Lower Manhattan was located in one of the twin towers, and Verizon had three switching facilities in the Trade Center. But the crucial facility used to service much of the financial district of Lower Manhattan was Verizon's central office located at 140 West Street. At 5 p.m. on 11 September the collapse of the 46-story office building at 7 World Trade Center hurled steel girders and other debris into the adjacent Verizon Building, breaching the east wall from seven stories up, damaging digital switching equipment and smashing through a cable vault in the basement that contained lines linking the switching station with customers. Water from broken mains and fire hoses flooded the basement, shorting out the remaining lines that had not been directly cut. Some thirty telecommunications providers had relied on linking equipment in the Verizon Building, and Verizon used the building as a transfer station for some 2.7 million data circuits on its network outside the Lower Manhattan service area. Approximately 4.4 million Verizon data circuits had to be restored, along with 182,000 voice circuits, 112,000 private branch exchange trunks, and 11,000 lines serving Internet providers.[16]

The stock exchanges escaped direct damage, with the exception of the American Exchange, which could not reopen its building near the Trade Center until October. In the interim, American Exchange stock traders were allowed to trade in a section of the New York Stock Exchange, and options traders resumed trading at the Philadelphia Exchange. The closing off of Lower Manhattan for two days, and the difficulties some of the major stock broker–dealers had relocating and testing new lines and equipment, meant that, by Friday 14 September, firms representing only about 60 per cent of typical order flow had been enabled, a portion considered too low to provide enough liquidity to safely resume trading. Stock market organizations and regulators decided to keep the stock and options market closed until Monday 17 September, allowing time over the weekend to test new communications links and to enable more of the big broker–dealers.[17] Because the stock market opens at 9 a.m., very little trading had taken place on the day of the attacks, and the New York Stock Exchange and NASDAQ had not opened at all, meaning there were very few failed trades to reconcile in the coming weeks. Regional stock exchanges and commodity exchanges never opened on September 11th, and regulators and industry groups decided to open in tandem with New York on Monday the 17th, so there was a clean hiatus in those markets and an amazingly orderly resumption of trading the Monday after the attacks, though volatility remained high for weeks.

The commercial paper market suffered more severe disruptions because funds due investors on Tuesday the 11th and Wednesday the 12th were not delivered until Thursday the 13th, forcing firms relying on those payments to seek other sources of liquidity in order to deliver on their own obligations. By far the worst blow was dealt the government securities market, whose failure induced a liquidity disruption worldwide, revealing the critical role of US Treasury securities in the daily functioning of global financial markets.

Virtually every organization that participates in financial markets has US Treasury securities as part of its portfolio. Rarely does the original buyer hold these securities to maturity. Rather, US Treasuries are actively traded on deep and liquid secondary markets as a quick source of dollar funding or a place to park excess cash and earn interest. Considered for half a century as the world's safest and most liquid asset, US Treasuries are the favorite collateral for dollar loans, and Treasury rates constitute the benchmark against which riskier and less liquid assets are measured. Commercial banks suffering unexpected shortfalls in reserve deposits at the Fed can quickly borrow reserves from other banks or directly from the Fed by posting Treasury securities as collateral. Stock and bond dealers, insurance companies, portfolio managers of all sorts, and other financial organizations in the US and abroad who do not have direct access to the Federal Reserve as a source of funding rely heavily on the smooth operation of the US government securities market, whose major trading firms and clearing and settlement facilities are geographically concentrated in Lower Manhattan. Fortunately, the New York Fed's central depository and electronic transfer service for US Treasury securities has its primary site, EROC, in East Rutherford, New Jersey, as Hank Wiener explained. Fedwire remained fully operative the day of September 11 and extended its hours of operation for the remainder of the week to counteract market disruptions.

Because of its importance in funding for the day's stock, bond, and commodity trading, the secondary market for US Treasuries opens before the other markets, 7 a.m. for 'repo'[18] trading and 8 a.m. for straight trades in government securities. By 9 a.m., when the Twin Towers were hit, some $500 billion in repo transactions and some $80 billion in straight Treasury trades had already been conducted. An important way that the numerous dealers in Treasury bonds trade with each other is through nine large broker–dealers, eight of whom were at or near Ground Zero. The largest government securities inter-dealer broker at that time, Cantor Fitzgerald Securities, occupied several of the upper floors of one of the towers and lost 658 employees, or approximately one-third of the civilian casualties of 9/11. Most of the data from the day's trades that were conducted through inter-dealer brokers was lost due to the destruction of their facilities, and communication lines were broken that connected these inter-dealer brokers with the Government Securities Clearing Corporation, the private netting facility for government securities trades. When trade information cannot be reconciled and correct ownership of securities and funds cannot be established at the two private clearing banks for Treasuries, a trade is considered a 'fail.' Failed trades rose from $0.5 billion on 10 September to more than $450 billion on 12 September, falling to $100 billion per day by 17 September, a level of fails sustained for the rest of the month of September. The trades through the failed inter-dealer brokers had to be reconstructed using information from the original dealers who placed the trades, a reconciliation process that took weeks, and in some cases months.[19]

To make matters worse, the Bank of New York, one of the two private clearing and settlement banks for US Treasuries, had its lines of communication with the New York Fed and with its customers cut when Verizon's central office near the Trade Center was knocked out. Bank of New York, whose government securities facility was a block north of the Trade Center at 101 Barclay Street, was unable to restore communications until Friday 14 September, after which it suffered intermittent connectivity problems. The inability of the Bank of New York to recover in a timely manner wreaked havoc for trading in government securities. The Bank of New York's account at the Fed could receive Treasuries and funds, but the Bank of New York could not send instructions to pay out of that account on behalf of its customers. As of 12 September more than $31 billion had been transferred into the Bank of New York's Fedwire account for the Government Securities Clearing Corporation (GSCC), but Bank of New York could not pay out of that account the amounts owed to the bond traders and other clients who were supposed to receive the funds. Nobody who held Treasuries in safekeeping at the Bank of New York had access to those securities or to the funds kept there on deposit for the period when Bank of New York's system was down, in effect freezing a significant portion of the Treasury market's tradable assets. As my former student recalled, 'Because of the Bank of New York, no one on the street knew what their true cash position was... everyone was flying blind. I can't begin to explain the anxiety.'[20] Among the key participants affected were the GSCC (the central netting facility for the market), JPMorgan Chase (the other private custodial clearing and settlement bank), major government securities dealers, and large investment funds that rely on their Treasury holdings for daily funding of operations. Due to the outages at the Bank of New York and damage to the inter-dealer brokers, the treasury repo market collapsed from about $900 billion in transactions on 10 September to $500 billion on the morning before the attacks, to $145 billion per day for the remainder of the week, and the straight Treasury market went from $500 billion in trades on 10 September to $9 billion on 12 September, and did not recover to pre-crash levels until 20 September.[21]

A key reason for owning a financial asset like a stock or a bond over owning physical capital like a machine is that a stock or a bond is more quickly and easily tradable for money. Because of organized secondary markets, where active trading of stocks and bonds occurs, someone who owns those assets and needs money can quickly sell in the active market, though price depends on market conditions at the time of sale. A used piece of equipment, especially one that is not a standard variety, can take a long time to find a buyer. Such a piece of equipment is said to be much less 'liquid' than financial assets that trade in organized markets. Financial assets differ from each other in degrees of liquidity, or how quickly and reliably they can be turned into money. Highly liquid assets provide a convenient exit strategy over less liquid assets, so if the situation changes the investor can turn the liquid asset back into money and move on. For more than half a century the world's most liquid currency has been the US dollar, and the world's most liquid asset next to dollars has been US Treasury securities. Holding Treasuries protects a portfolio of less liquid assets. If an unforeseen circumstance calls for a large outlay of cash, the Treasuries can be sold or used as collateral for a temporary loan, and the less liquid assets don't have to be dumped into an unfavorable market. For the world's most liquid financial asset suddenly to become illiquid placed whole portfolios at risk in the minds of their managers, creating a sense of panic that spread across financial markets.

Not only did the loss of connections between the Bank of New York and the Federal Reserve threaten the liquidity of the world's most relied upon financial asset, but by disrupting the flows of payments between banks it threatened the functioning of account money itself. Because banks that lost connections with the Fed could receive funds into their reserve accounts at the Fed but could not release them, their settlement accounts at the Fed became vessels of hoarding that drained reserves from the active payments stream, creating a gridlock situation in Fedwire. At one point during the week of September 11, the Bank of New York reported being overdue on $100 billion in payments, draining this amount from the reserves available for use by the other banks in the system, a huge hemorrhage when compared with pre-disaster reserve deposits *for the entire banking system* of approximately $13 billion at the end of the day on 10 September.[22] Other banks with good communications responded to the uncertainty by delaying the release of funds, further contributing to payments gridlock.

As lender of last resort, the Federal Reserve acted swiftly using every method at its disposal to keep payments between banks flowing and to revive the market in Treasury securities. To prevent the disaster from turning into a bank panic, the Federal Reserve released clear public statements on September 11th reassuring the public that the Fed was open, operating and ready to lend to banks experiencing payments difficulties. Fed officials stayed in close private contact with individual banks, encouraging them to make payments to other banks and to borrow from the Fed to cover shortfalls. Beginning on 11 September and lasting until 21 September, the Fed waived fees banks had to pay on daylight overdraft credits and waived penalties normally charged on overnight overdrafts. Banks responded by borrowing heavily from the Fed. Daylight overdrafts, which allow banks to make payments when they don't have enough in their reserve accounts at the Fed, far exceeded normal levels, peaking on Friday 14 September at $150 billion, the highest level in history.[23] Normally discouraged by the Fed,[24] overnight borrowing by banks through the discount window surged from an average level of only $200 million before the disaster to $37 billion on 11 September, a record level that increased to $46 billion on Wednesday. Consumers responded to the crisis by withdrawing $4 billion in currency from the banks, thus reducing bank reserves by that amount. The Federal Reserve more than compensated for this withdrawal of cash by allowing deposited checks that were delayed en route to be counted as reserve deposits for the receiving banks without debiting the reserve accounts of paying banks, thus increasing the reserve deposits of the entire system by $23 billion on 12 September, $47 billion on the 13th, and $44 billion on the 14th.

Early Wednesday when troubles in the government securities market became evident, the Fed began emergency measures to revive it, injecting that day $38 billion into the short-term treasury repo market through the few primary dealers that were open. Those dealers' accounts were credited at the only clearing and settlement bank available for Treasuries, JPMorgan Chase, which in turn was credited with reserves of that amount at the New York Fed. With these extra reserves, JPMorgan Chase could make payments and lend reserves to banks and customers short of funds, thus spreading the extra reserves through the banking system. On Thursday 13 September the Fed injected $70 billion of short-term funds in the same manner, followed by $81 billion on Friday and $57 billion on Monday, gradually reducing these amounts as the crisis ebbed the week following the disaster.[25] Additionally the New York Fed responded to securities dealers and allowed them to increase their borrowings of certain US Treasury issues from the Fed's portfolio, thereby enabling the dealers to match customer orders and reduce the number of failed trades.[26] These emergency measures and others kept the government securities markets from imploding and prevented what could easily have turned out to be a string of defaults from a payments system breakdown.[27]

Foreign banks that did not have direct access to the Federal Reserve suffered acute dollar funding problems when their traditional sources of dollars dried up. The Federal Reserve responded by announcing dollar swap facilities with three foreign central banks totaling $90 billion, only a fraction of which was actually used to relieve the stress.[28] With the US Treasury market in disarray, foreign banks with US Treasury securities found what had been considered a reliable source of dollar funding frozen, and foreign banks that relied on non-operative US banks for dollars had to scramble for cash advances and lines of credit at still-operating US banks, whose lending abilities were already strained. Many foreign banks depend on the foreign exchange swap market to switch from local currency, which they have favorable access to, into dollars, switching back after payments and receipts in dollars have been accomplished. The dollar leg of the normally liquid foreign exchange swap market dried up, making payments due in dollars difficult for banks dependent on this source of dollar funding. Faced with uncertainty about receiving dollar payments due them, banks hoarded any dollars they received, further clogging up the international payments stream.[29]

September 11th exposed the uneven state of disaster recovery systems. Some backup facilities were found to be in close proximity to primary sites, rendering them useless following the 9/11 attacks, and backup lines of communication were being channeled through the same central switching station that carried primary lines. Because financial markets are so intricately linked, a disruption in clearing and settlement in one market immediately spreads to others. Most clearing and settlement organizations are privately owned and must bear the costs of backup facilities, but if they skimp too much on reviewing, updating, and testing their backup facilities, the results can put the entire financial system at risk in the event of a disaster. Concerned about systemic risk, regulators and financial industry groups got together, gleaning lessons from 9/11. After considerable consultation and study, three heavy hitters moved to ensure broad private sector compliance. On 7 April 2003, the Federal Reserve, the US Treasury Department, and the Securities and Exchange Commission issued the 'Interagency Paper on Sound Practices to Strengthen the Resilience of the U.S. Financial System,' a joint directive that contained three new business continuity objectives for all financial firms to follow. More directly aimed at the institutions central to the functioning of financial markets, the directive identified four sound practices to be followed by 'core clearing and settlement organizations' and 'private firms that play significant roles in critical financial markets.'[30] In order to avoid the severe dislocations of liquidity experienced in the wake of the 9/11 attacks, the interagency directive called for organizations at the 'center of key financial markets' to set up backup systems in geographically diverse settings that would be capable of settling pending transactions *by the end of the business day on which a disruption occurs*. To be able to achieve settlement by end of day, the directive set the goals of *two hours* to recover and resume activities for 'core clearing and settlement organizations' and *four hours* for private firms playing a 'significant role in a particular critical financial market.' The directive set deadlines on when these systems were to be in place and guidelines for routine testing.[31]

Financial market organizations took this initiative seriously, though some moved out ahead of others. In May 2004, the former student who manages disaster recovery for a bank that plays a significant role in many financial markets told me with some confidence: 'We have the best DRS [disaster recovery system] on the street,'[32] a statement that implied doubts about some of the other major players' progress. The goal his organization had set for him was to be able to recover and resume trading within a two-hour window, half the time set out by the interagency directive. At considerable cost, his organization constructed fully redundant backup trading rooms that can resume trading within two hours. Similarly, CHIPS surpassed the regulatory guidelines and had constructed a third fully redundant backup facility for large-value dollar deliveries. CHIPS had this site up, tested, and running in June 2004, six months ahead of the deadline set by the interagency directive.

The rapid transmission of the liquidity crisis following the events of 9/11 pointed to the reliance of the international payments system on private market solutions to spreading liquidity. When those private markets were shocked, the network of central banks did not have emergency measures in place to provide the type of liquidity needed at the time it was needed. After 9/11 the Federal Reserve bore the lion's share of the adjustment and pumped liquidity through commercial banks operating in the US, but foreign banks could not use collateral they had to gain dollar funding. Similar to Continuous Linked Settlement Bank, many other financial market clearing and settlement systems have been moving toward real-time delivery-versus-payment procedures in order to eliminate settlement risk, but in doing so they have introduced a degree of liquidity risk. One wonders how Continuous Linked Settlement Bank – with greater liquidity needs than CHIPS – would have fared in the face of 9/11, especially considering CLS Bank's reliance on the foreign exchange swap market to reverse liquidity imbalances that arise during its five-hour settlement window.[33] As one group of banking industry leaders and regulators put it, 'A concern is that future, potentially systemic crises could occur in any major market and could have severe liquidity impacts in multiple regions of the world in different time zones. This will require the existence of a well-understood and efficient mechanism for central banks to collaborate in providing real-time access to cross-border liquidity.'[34]

In the City of London after the Russian default: anatomy of currency market storms of the 1990s

In September 1998 global financial markets were still reeling from the Russian default a few weeks earlier, but the contagion had not yet spread to Wall Street, where, in October, it would take out Long Term Capital Management Hedge Fund and threaten a meltdown of the corporate bond market. On my way to a conference at Oxford University, I was able to squeeze in a day of interviews in the City of London. In the morning the chief executive of a German bank's London office spoke with me and arranged a tour of their trading room. Afterwards I had lunch with Avinash Persaud, Global Head of Currency Research at JPMorgan.

In the alley behind the Royal Exchange, jobbers, clerks, bankers, and traders swill coffee before scurrying over the cobblestones to work. Across the walk from the row of coffee shops is Number 1 Royal Exchange, 'our humble address in London,' as the German banker put it in a telephone conversation. The fortress-like Bank of England stands a stone's throw away, just across Threadneedle Street. Inside Number 1 Royal Exchange, boxes clutter the entrance, suggesting a move is under way. A brochure informs me that a week earlier this bank and a regional bank in Germany had merged.

The secretary escorts me to the general manager's suite of offices. She introduces me to a tall, athletic-looking young man, whom I assume to be the chief executive's assistant. It turns out he is the head of the bank.

In the conference room, the German banker explains the merger, which puts him, at age 37, in charge of a combined staff of 300 at three London sites. 'There's room for consolidation here,' he comments.

'How hard were you hit by the Russian default?' I query.

'It hardly touched us,' he says. 'Unlike Deutsche Bank, which has exposures all over the globe, the two banks that merged were really regional Bavarian banks without extensive global exposure.' He explains that the new bank will have to decide whether to concentrate on its national market or whether to extend itself internationally by buying an institution with international expertise. 'This latter move may be smart for us, but it will be expensive. The international banking environment is highly competitive and quite risky, as Russia has reminded us.'

I had expected the banker to be in his fifties or sixties, so I ask him how such a young man had ended up in this position. His career began as a teenager working for a regional bank near his home. Trustworthy and quick with a good sense of humor, he kept earning promotions from within. The trajectory was so steep, university would have been a distraction for him. Even moderately sized regional banks need connections in other financial centers for providing full corporate services and for obtaining funding. A natural diplomat with a talent for languages, he was sent to manage offices abroad: Tokyo, Atlanta, Milan, and now London.

'So, a Bavarian boy is sent to Tokyo in the midst of a speculative bubble?' I ask.

'Yes. It was the late 1980s and I was still in my twenties. I'd never seen anything like it.' Before he arrived, Japan's enormous pool of savings poured into Japanese stocks and real estate, initiating an upward trend in prices. International portfolio managers got in on the boom and increased their holdings in what was touted as the invincible 'Japan, Inc.' In 1988 and 1989 alone, the value of Japanese stocks and real estate doubled. Japanese banks acquired stock, lent on slim margins, and competed with each other to make loans to real estate, feeding the frenzy. 'I could not believe what I saw,' he recalls. 'My Japanese banker colleagues were handing out mortgages for amounts greater than the current value of the property being used as collateral. They were assuming property prices would keep escalating forever at the rates of the recent past, leaving no protection on the downside. This went against everything my elders in Bavaria had taught me about banking.' After he left Japan, the bubble burst. Between December 1989 and August 1992, the Nikkei 225 stock index dropped from its peak at about 39,000 to below 14,000, and Japanese real-estate prices dropped by half. The Japanese banking system hemorrhaged – as he had suspected it would – unable to restructure and get back on its feet even by 2005. Japanese and international portfolio managers down-weighted Japan in their portfolios, and Japanese banks increased their lending to more promising outlets in Asia, Latin America, the United States, and Europe.

The Japanese bubble was the first episode in a series of financial boom-and-bust cycles, one occurring approximately every twenty months for the remainder of the decade. Japan (late 1989–91) to Europe (September 1992) to Mexico (December 1994–January 1995) to South Asia (July–October 1997) to Russia (August 1998) to Brazil (January 1999) to Argentina (December 2001). Each crisis had its own peculiar characteristics, but all of them were triggered by large and amazingly swift flows of portfolio capital, and, except for the Argentine collapse, they were followed by a string of financial crises in other, sometimes unrelated, places.

'That was an interesting fax you sent me on the currency crises of the 1990s.' The young executive rises and shakes my hand. 'I wish my day were not all tied up, so I could discuss this more with you. I gave Paul a copy of your questions. I hope he has had time to prepare some charts for you. Angela will walk you to the trading room down the street. When you come back through London, let's have lunch.'

Angela walks with me through the financial district toward Southwark Bridge. As we approach the river, I see the Vintners' Place symbol on the top of the building. This must have been the old wine merchant's guild with its warehouse on the Thames. We enter a completely modernized interior. As Angela gets security clearance for me, I note the tenants include major international banks and investment houses. I clip the security badge on my suit pocket, and enter an elevator with marble floor and walls framed in mahogany with polished brass rails.

At the entry to the bank's trading room, Paul greets me and we enter the busy dealing room. Two trading modules, composed of four semi-circles facing each other, divide the room in two. Each semi-circle has six computer stations, making a total of forty-eight positions, though only about thirty are being used.

He explains that colleagues will try to cover his calls, but we might get interrupted. 'The head of the bank sent me your letter on currency crisis questions, so I had the charts on those currencies printed out.'[1]

'Great! Do you have the ruble?'

He pulls a chart beginning in early April 1998. 'Lines in the sand,' he says pointing to the steady exchange rate of about six rubles per dollar. 'No one expected a problem in May, June and July, with all the press on market reforms and the IMF supporting the currency.' Interest rates on ruble-denominated government bonds were astronomical, and with the

12.1 / The Russian ruble crisis of 1998 (daily exchange rates, ruble/US$)

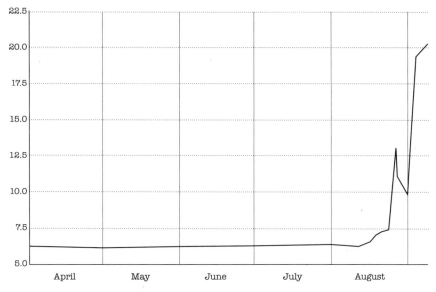

Source: Based on data © 2001 by Prof. Werner Antweiler, University of British Columbia, Vancouver.
Time period shown: 1 April–8 September 1998.

pegged currency providing 'protection,' even some savvy investors were lured into buying these notes.

A colleague overhears our conversation on the way for a coffee break and contributes, 'Few expected the ruble to collapse when it did, but everyone in London knew the IMF was getting taken. For every billion dollars the IMF sent to Russia, a billion got recycled through Switzerland.'

Paul nods affirmatively. 'Then, look at the break. On Monday 17 August the Russian central bank can no longer support the peg, and the ruble loses 15 per cent by Friday. More shuffling of Yeltsin's cabinet, and then the unanticipated default on ruble-denominated government debt, and the ruble goes into free fall. Look at two days ago.' Paul says there were bids ranging from 20 to 25 rubles per dollar, closing at 22. 'And check out the contagion in other markets.' He shows a graph of the Polish zloty, the Czech krone, and the Hungarian forint, all losing ground closely following the ruble, but recovering some in the past week of trading. 'And I hear the Bank of Brazil is doing all it can to keep the real from going. That will be something to watch.'

Paul pulls out a 1997 chart of the Thai baht. 'The recent crisis shows a similar pattern to the Asian crisis last year.' He traces the flat line through April and May. 'Lines in the sand, as the Thai central bank was pegging

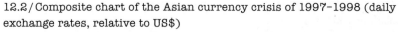

12.2 / Composite chart of the Asian currency crisis of 1997–1998 (daily exchange rates, relative to US$)

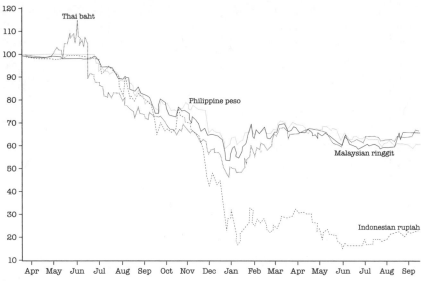

Source: Based on data © 2001 by Prof. Werner Antweiler, University of British Columbia, Vancouver.
Time period shown: 1 April 1997–30 September 1998.

the currency. Then in June the baht rose with higher Thai interest rates and heavy buying by the central bank. Then during the first week of July, the central bank can't withstand the pressure. The dam breaks followed by wild turbulence. By the end of December, the baht had lost half its value. And let's look at the contagion.' He flips to a chart titled MYR=. 'During the second week of July, the Malaysians tried to defend the ringgit. The defense worked for several days, then it collapsed. And the same week, the Phillipine peso, which had strong fundamentals going into this, went the way of the ringgit. Both currencies went into free fall, losing 40 per cent of their pegged values by year end. The third week sent the Singapore dollar into floating mode, though it only lost 25 per cent of its value by the end of December. By the final week of July 1997, the contagion had spread to Indonesia. By December the rupiah had lost 60 per cent of its value, and the country was in flames. Because of massive foreign exchange reserves, the Hong Kong dollar held on, so too did the South Korean won, after promises of a massive bail-out package from the IMF. But in October, the won succumbed to the pressure, and by December it had lost half its formerly pegged value.'

'Do you have a printout on Mexico?' I ask.

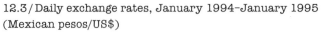

12.3 / Daily exchange rates, January 1994–January 1995
(Mexican pesos/US$)

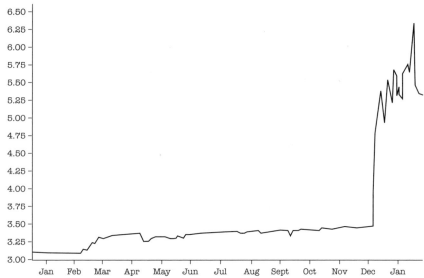

Source: based on data © 2001 by Prof. Werner Antweiler, University of British Columbia, Vancouver.
Time period shown: 1 April 1994–8 February 1995.

A woman in the adjacent semi-circle motions to Paul. 'It's [XYZ].'

'Wait I have to take this call.' Paul puts on his headphones, picks up a pen, scribbles FIM 33.2 m. in a box on his spiral notepad. 'OK, you want to change 33.2 million finnmarks (Finnish markka) into pounds?' He punches the keyboard, looks at cross-currency quotes on his screen, and gives an offer. He quickly writes down 33,284,262.40 8.73 80/90 and circles the 90. 'Done at 873 ninety.'

'Who was that?' I ask.

'[XYZ] Pension Fund.'

'Do you get a lot of requests like that?' I ask.

'Yes.' He shows me the other trades he's done so far today. One includes a trade of 25 million pounds for Greek drachmas, and another involving 50 million German marks. 'London is full of pension funds and money managers. They call us a lot.'

Paul pulls out the chart on the Mexican peso for 1994–95. 'Lines in the sand at 3.1 pesos per dollar until March 1994.' He explains that the fixed rate made Mexican stocks and peso bonds attractive to international mutual funds managers and other portfolio investors. And then there was all the promise of NAFTA. The large inflow meant the Bank of

Mexico built up huge dollar reserves. Then in March 1994, 'there was a political assassination.'

I interject, 'I recall his name was Colosio. I heard the Bank of Mexico's reserves dropped from $26 billion to less than $20 billion within 48 hours after the assassination.'

'Yes,' Paul says, 'and you can see on the chart the Bank of Mexico holds on, but instead of fixing the peso, allows it to gradually depreciate 3.1 to 3.2 to 3.3 to 3.4.'

'As I remember, they replenished their reserves by selling Tesobonos (Mexican government bonds denominated in US dollars) to remove the risk to investors of a peso devaluation. They sold some $26 billion of these before the crash; foreigners picked up some $17 billion worth of Tesobonos.'

Paul continues, 'And every time there was a scare, investors would sell off their peso holdings and collect dollars from the Bank of Mexico.' Then in December 1994, with big losses of reserves and a Zapatista uprising mixed in, the Bank of Mexico widens its band to 4 pesos per dollar. Nobody believes it. There's a panic and on 21 December the Bank of Mexico is forced to float the currency. A week later, the finance minister resigns. Contagion spreads to all of the Latin American stock markets, and Latin currencies come under attack. He points to the surge in the peso-to-dollar exchange rate. 'By March 1995 the peso has lost more than half its previously pegged values.'

'Paul, all the ones we've looked at so far – Russia, South Asia, Mexico – are emerging market booms and busts, which gives the impression it's a matter of "immature" markets, but wasn't the European Exchange Rate Mechanism torn apart by similar movements of capital?'

'Yes. I have those, too.' He pulls out charts for 1992 and 1993, for the Finnish markka, the Portuguese escudo, the Italian lira, the Spanish peseta, the British pound, and the French franc. 'As you can see, all of these were knocked out of their pegs in September 1992, except for the franc, which held on until August 1993.'

The collapse of the European Exchange Rate Mechanism

'A central banker friend told me about this. He was defending the lira at that time.' I say.

'What was his view of what happened?' Paul asks.

'Well, as I remember it, capital controls had been removed several years before, so portfolio managers could move investments quickly from one

12.4 / Daily exchange rates, German marks/Finnish markka

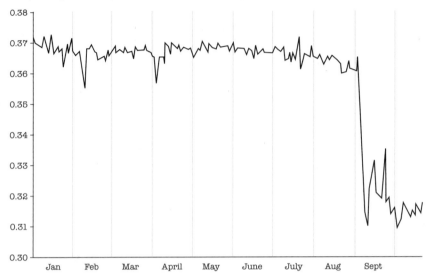

Source: based on data © 2001 by Prof. Werner Antweiler, University of British Columbia, Vancouver.
Time period: 1 January–20 October 1992.

European country to the next. He also said all the central bankers were committed to holding their currencies in a narrow range with the mark.'

'The "snake in the tunnel",' says Paul.

'Yes. When their currency hit the bottom of the tunnel, the central bank would sell currency reserves or raise interest rates, and when their currency approached the top of the tunnel they'd buy up reserves or lower interest rates, or do a bit of both to keep their currency in the tunnel. The problem was, the currencies that were attacked were hitting the bottom of the tunnel more than the top, so they were losing reserves and having to raise interest rates. My friend said a big problem was when the German central bank got freaked about inflation being higher than in France. When the Bundesbank raised rates, the weaker ones had to raise theirs even more to keep their currencies from hitting the bottom of the band. Unemployment rates in 1992 were high, and my friend said the high interest rates were unpopular.'

'So, did the Bank of Italy bend to popular pressure and drop out of the band?'

'No. That's not what he said happened. He told me the Bank of Italy and the other central banks were firmly committed to holding their currencies in the band. He took this very badly when they lost.'

'Well, what did he say made them drop out?'

12.5 / Daily exchange rates 1992: German marks/Italian lira

Source: based on data © 2001 by Prof. Werner Antweiler, University of British Columbia, Vancouver.
Time period: 1 January–20 October 1992.

'He described it like a poker game, where the big fund operators started with smaller central banks like the Bank of Finland and the Bank of Portugal, and, having forced those currencies out of their bands, they took their winnings and went after larger central banks. He said that the tried and true tactics he was accustomed to using to zap the speculators didn't seem to work, and his bank quickly ran down its reserves trying to defend the exchange rate. After taking the winnings from the Bank of Italy, the speculators took on the Bank of England and won another $20 billion.'

The Bank of England loses to the speculators, September 1992

Paul recalls that in London, the rumor was that George Soros made a huge bet against the Bank of England, and many others made smaller bets. When the Bank of England gave in, Soros alone was reported to have collected winnings amounting to a billion pounds.

'Let's look at the French franc,' I suggest.

Paul turns to 1993. 'On this chart it looks like it was the last day of July when the Bank of France lost to the speculators. They saved face

12.6 / Daily exchange rates 1992: German marks/pound sterling

Source: based on data © 2001 by Prof. Werner Antweiler, University of British Columbia, Vancouver.
Time period: 1 January 1992–20 October 1992

and stayed in the Exchange Rate Mechanism by widening the band to ±15 per cent of the central parity with the mark.'

'That means from top to bottom, the franc could rise or fall by 30 per cent. That's hardly a peg!' I remark.

Paul laughs and says something about a long leash. I look down at my watch. 'Paul, this has been instructive. Do you mind if I take these charts with me?'

'No problem. Where's your next meeting?'

I tell him and he points out the window to give me directions to JPMorgan's central headquarters, and then he shows me to the revolving door.

As I walk along the Thames toward Blackfriars Bridge, I reflect on how powerless central banks are to the whims of fund managers. The question remains: what instructs the thinking of this group? I recall the analysis by Guillermo Calvo,[2] who stresses the role of 'specialist clusters,' experts paid to get the inside scoop on a faraway place. They provide the information to the portfolio managers, who decide how to act on this information. For years, I had been impressed by the quality of the international research cluster of JPMorgan. I had followed their *Global*

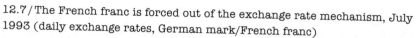

12.7 / The French franc is forced out of the exchange rate mechanism, July 1993 (daily exchange rates, German mark/French franc)

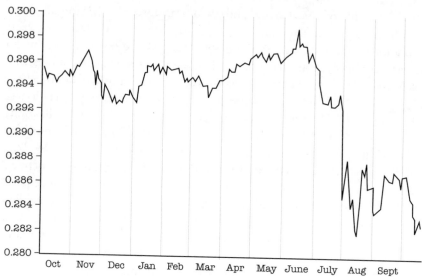

Source: based on data © 2001 by Prof. Werner Antweiler, University of British Columbia, Vancouver.
Time period: 1 October–20 October 1993.

Data Watch for several years, and for a long period it had been one of the best. Now I have the opportunity to have a thirty-minute session with JPMorgan's chief European economist, Bruce Kasman; and their global head of currency research, Avinash Persaud, has accepted my invitation to lunch. I cross under Blackfriars Bridge and on to Victoria Embankment. Number 60 is a building the size of Vintner's Place, but JPMorgan is its only tenant.

Kasman's secretary walks me through the trading room, which is about the size of a football field with straight rows of traders, standing, sitting, leaning, waving their arms, shouting. The noise is deafening. We climb a set of stairs and enter the quiet offices of global research.

Kasman is deluged with telephone calls from clients. He fields questions on currency risks, whether the Fed will lower interest rates at its next meeting, what the chances are of a business upturn in Germany and France. He gives careful analysis to questions from all over the map. My questions, which he answers in between calls, relate to his career, his work as researcher, analyst, economic forecaster, and director of what is regarded as one of the top two or three research teams in the business.

I find out that Kasman received his doctorate in economics from Columbia University. He then took a research position at the Federal Reserve Bank of New York and then was hired by JPMorgan. Now he's a managing director and in charge of the research team of thirty economists stationed around the globe. 'Ten years ago, we made a major investment in computer technology. This allows us to share databases with each other. We hire country specialists, economists mostly who also have a good sense of political culture in the places where they're stationed. Our biggest problem is finding star economists who can also collaborate with others... work in a team.' He describes the process of collecting data, feeding it into the database and writing briefings for *Global Data Watch* and other research reports for JPMorgan's client base. 'Then we have a senior economist who edits drafts, cleaning out the unevenness in the reports, so they read smoothly.' Kasman's day is spent fielding clients' questions and walking through the trading room, talking with traders to get a feeling for market developments. 'I work on Morgan's internal strategy, global position-taking, and risk-control measures, but, as you can see, I also get calls from outside clients.'

'When do you have time to think, to analyze?'

'There's lots of noise out there.' He points through the plate glass to the trading room. 'Sometimes I envy the academic lifestyle you professors have. To filter out the noise, I have to stay late. After 8:00 p.m. it's quiet in here, and I don't get calls. I can think and write. In making forecasts, we're constantly on the line. It keeps us alert.' He says modestly, 'But I'm embarrassed when we miss, like the recent change in the repo rate. We were way off on that.'

'I saw that, but Russia upset *everybody's* forecasts!' I comment that his research team – unlike some forecasting groups – reveals assumptions behind forecasts, and that makes it easier for a thinking person to use *Global Data Watch* than some other research products. Kasman picks up the phone for the conference call he has been waiting for, and his secretary walks me back through the trading room, which has calmed down a bit for lunch. The secretary takes me through a different exit and tells me I'll have to announce myself again at the main entrance for the meeting with Mr Persaud. Outside, I scout around for a restaurant suitable to take Persaud to lunch. The only place nearby is a greasy grill next to a newsstand.

I return to the main entrance. 'Mr Williams?' The woman at the security desk looks up surprised, 'I thought you were still inside. Whom shall I call for this time?'

'Mr Avinash Persaud.'

She contacts Persaud's secretary and explains that he will be a bit late. 'You may wait for him in room number 8.' She points down a dark stairwell.

I have to take care not to trip on the thickly carpeted stairs. A faint light draws me toward an open doorway. A whiff of butter and garlic invites me to glance in. At the far end of the room, a woman, bent over a butcher block, chops herbs with a *mezzaluna*. A broth steams on the stove.

The hostess in the hallway asks if I'm to lunch with Mr Persaud. I answer, 'Well… yes,' thinking still that I am to take *him* to lunch. She motions down a dark corridor. 'This way, please' and opens the door to number 8, a small room with good light streaming in through a full window.

'While you're waiting for Mr. Persaud, would you care for a drink, sir?' She points to the china cabinet running the length of the wall, on top of which a full bar stands at attention. Antique ice bucket, crystal glasses of all sizes and shapes, a selection of mixers, a line-up of bottles: Tanqueray, Stolichnaya, Jack Daniels, Mount Gay, an unpronounceable single malt, a red Bordeaux, and at the end a champagne bucket with a white burgundy peeking through the ice. The single malt tempts me. Yes, this would be a little taste treat, but it might blur my vision. 'Could I have a glass of ice water, please?'

'Sparkling or still, sir?'

'Sparkling, please.'

With silver tongs, she plunks ice cubes in a tumbler and pours the bubbling water over it. 'Mr Persaud should be here shortly.'

At the center of the cozy room is a round dining table that seats four, but only two places are set on opposite sides. Festively folded napkins rise like fountains from Wedgwood plates, which are framed by complete settings of silver and a pair of wine glasses. A vase with a yellow rose is placed on a doily in the middle of the table. Facing each setting is an engraved menu.

I walk around to check out the artwork. An etching of the great fire in New York with frenzied activity and flames is signed by a French printmaker. Another print shows the Wall Street headquarters of JPMorgan, probably produced shortly after the building was constructed. In a small frame next to the door is a letter. Touch-typed with a worn-out ribbon is a letter addressed to JPMorgan and Company, confirming a $100 million revolving credit, signed by Winston Churchill.

I hear footsteps in the hallway, and Persaud walks in. He excuses himself for being waylaid by a meeting. Medium height, shiny black hair, alert dark eyes and youthful face, he shows a politeness and diplomacy that suggests an education in elite schools in Britain.

'Would you like an aperitif of some sort before lunch,' he asks.

'What are you having?' If he were to pour a malt for himself, I might risk matching him.

'I'm having a grapefruit juice... when I interviewed here five years ago, grapefruit juice and water were the only two choices.' He looks down the row of bottles and smiles.

I think to myself, maybe the turbulent 1990s drove them to expand the selection. 'I'll have some more water, please.' I hand the hostess my empty glass. I turn to Persaud, 'Have you lived in England all your life?'

'My father, an entrepreneur, brought us all to London from the West Indies when I was seven.' He says that both sides of his family were originally from India. They migrated to Guyana and Trinidad in the 1880s and 1890s. When they came to London from Barbados, he was enrolled in a public school established long ago by a London guild. Its purpose was to provide a first-class education for enterprising children of the poor, for whom there were generous scholarships. 'Wouldn't be able to afford it any more; it now costs something like ten thousand pounds a year.'

After Persaud finished graduate training at the London School of Economics in 1987, he went to work researching bond markets and then currency markets at Phillips Drew, which was soon acquired by Union Bank of Switzerland. Very early on Persaud saw that asset and currency prices didn't follow very closely the economic fundamentals of models he had worked with in graduate school. 'If currency prices do finally return to some fundamental economic equilibrium, it was unlikely to happen within a time frame relevant for the fund managers I was advising.' He explains that fund managers come under quarterly and annual performance reviews. By the time it would take for currency and asset markets to arrive at the values predicted by these models, the fund manager already would have been made 'redundant.' Aware of the importance of global capital flows in the movements of currencies and asset prices, Persaud began looking for a rigorous way to analyze and detect major shifts in investors' appetite for risk.[3]

'Shall we see what's on the menu today?' Persaud motions for me to sit down.

I unwrap the origami napkin and look at 'Starters.'

I order the roasted red pepper stuffed with poached salmon, and he orders hearts of palm.

'Sir, if you would like to decide on the first few courses, I won't need to disturb you.' The waitress prompts.

I look at 'Soups.' 'How's the vichyssoise?' I ask Persaud.

'The soups here are all very good, but the French onion soup is a meal in itself.' His eye catches my intent, and he orders. 'Two vichyssoises, served hot, please.'

Under the 'Main Course,' I request monkfish in light cream sauce, and he asks for chicken with wild mushroom sauce.

'Then we'll have a salad of greens,' he says, 'and you should have a dessert. It's their specialty.'

Thinking of the forthcoming feast, I say, 'May I postpone that decision till later?'

When the waitress turns, Persaud asks, 'So, tell me about the book you mentioned in the email.'

'It's a lay reader's introduction to world currency markets. Everyone's influenced by them, but most of the writing about foreign exchange becomes so technical, so mysterious, so abstract. I thought it might be more down to earth to visit the places and meet the people who move the world's money, and write about what they do and how they think.'

'How far along are you?' Persaud asks.

The waitress quietly slides a plate in front me. The grilled red pepper is stuffed with salmon flakes. On top is a dollop of hollandaise sauce with a sprig of dill.

'There are two chapter drafts to go, one on the currency crises of the 1990s, and the other on whether the euro will replace the dollar as the world's favorite currency.'

'A good way to end such a book.' He pulls a tape recorder from his pocket and before placing it next to the rose, he asks, 'Do you mind if I take notes?'

'Not at all.' I reach into my briefcase for a legal pad. 'If you don't mind me scribbling while we dine.'

I hear a cork pop. The waitress displays the label to Persaud, who draws a line at the bottom of his glass, just enough for a taste. After splashing a few drops in his glass, she approaches me. I pray silently, "Oh Satan, get thee hence." I've got to stay clear, and this looks too good to turn down. Then I remember the saying: "White wine quickens the mind, red wine dulls." I draw a line one third up the glass. We both sniff of the golden liquid, and I roll a few drops around my tongue. The taste goes on and on. After letting it linger, I remark, 'Yum, yum, as we say where I come from.' Persaud nods in complete agreement as we clink glasses.

'So, Avinash, you've been advising managers of funds long enough to see them through the crisis episodes of the 1990s. I've never understood how their logic can shift so fast. Can you explain this to me?'

'Are you most interested in the contagion that spreads into other markets after one currency crashes – like what's happening now in Venezuela and Brazil following the collapse of the ruble?'

The waitress removes our starter plates and places cups of steaming white soup with chives sprinkled on top. The smell of broth, potatoes, and cream are heavenly. I taste it, and she offers to grind some white pepper.

'Yes, I do want to understand how the contagion spreads, but that's just one phase. I'd really like you to walk me through all the phases from the beginning, when fund managers begin to be attracted to a place.' I turn to a new sheet and draw a wave.

'How to start...?' Persaud rests his spoon on the saucer. 'Let's say a few fund managers have experimented in small amounts in a place they've researched, and their investments begin paying noticeably high returns.' He explains that news of this circulates among the group that sits on the boards of funds. At the board meeting of a fund that has not yet dabbled in this new area, 'a board member asks the fund manager, "What do we have invested in this place?" The manager answers, "We don't have a position there." The board member says, "Well, I hear so and so is making 40 per cent returns there." A second board member chimes in, "Yes, and I hear fund Y is making 45 per cent returns there." The board members all look at each other and at the fund manager. A third board member asks, "Could we be overlooking some opportunities here?"' Persaud explains that after the meeting with the board, the fund manager starts doing research on investments in this place. 'He finds something he doesn't feel too uncomfortable with, and invests a small amount there. At this point managers of other funds are doing the same.'

I put down my pen. 'And so the asset prices in this newly discovered haven begin to be bid up.'

'Yes, but the capital won't be widely dispersed.' He explains that fund managers will tend to buy a few of the most actively traded stocks in that country. Some of these stocks may be commercial real-estate companies in the capital city. Because of this concentration on a few issues, prices can be bid up quickly. He gives examples of local banks borrowing abroad in foreign currency and lending in local currency to the high-growth sectors on the collateral of the rising assets. 'This credit activity feeds the bubble.'

'And if the currency is pegged in some way,' I ask, 'won't the influx of capital boost the foreign currency reserves of the money authority and give the appearance of safety in terms of currency risk?'

'Yes, and this confidence may lead to some uncovered currency exposures, often by the local banking system, which can borrow at lower interest rates abroad and lend at very high rates in the local currency.'

'A smart move,' I catch where he's going, 'so long as the currency remains fixed and the loans perform.'

The waitress serves the main course. The monkfish is sliced into scallop-sized bites, and the cream sauce has a sprig of parsley on top. They call this poor man's lobster, I think to myself. She tops my wine up.

'Because the capital is so concentrated,' Persaud places his hand over the top of his glass, 'ultimately there will be diminishing returns, but the asset prices continue to climb.'

'And who gets out first?'

His eyes brighten, as if preparing for a debate. 'There's all this talk of "hot money" versus the long-term direct investor. But I've found the ones to get out first are the ones most directly connected with the underlying assets, the direct investors and local businesses in the know.'

'Can you give an example?'

'Who will be the first to see the low occupancy rates in an overbuilt situation?' He waits to answer the question himself. 'The ones directly managing the commercial buildings.' He says that those in the know 'will begin switching out to hedge their local exposures.'

I think aloud. 'So they might borrow more in local currency using their inflated assets as collateral and then buy dollars with the local currency at the fixed exchange rate? Or they might sell some more shares to a fund manager, and switch the proceeds into dollars?'

'There are numerous ways to do this.' He goes on to explain that if the central bank raises local interest rates to recover some of the drain of foreign exchange reserves, it may not burst the bubble yet. 'It could even serve for a while to attract short-term investors seeking higher interest rates.'

'So, what pops the bubble?'

'It could be anything. A major political or economic event could at this stage set off a scramble to sell local assets and move capital out.' He explains that fund managers attempt to hedge their currency exposures, which places a strain on central bank reserves. He paints one scenario of the central bank attempting to prop up the currency with even higher interest rates. But at this stage, the higher rates may burst the bubble on interest-sensitive assets like real estate. Officials may make public statements that they will never devalue, and they may line up help from the IMF or other central banks. 'This invites hedge funds and others who see an opportunity to win on some short-term bets. Those who have been unable to get out in time suffer big losses when the currency and asset markets collapse.'

'And now, the contagion,' I prompt.

'There are two phases of contagion with regard to global portfolio managers. The immediate reaction is involuntary on their part.'

'Involuntary. How so?'

'Well, they've taken a hit in one part of their portfolio, which means they must sell off some other assets to build up cash reserves. Their impulse will be to sell off the next-riskiest assets in their portfolio. These may be in the next country over.'

'And the voluntary phase of contagion?'

The waitress quietly serves the salad.

'The manager of the fund is called before a special session of the board.' Persaud skewers a spinach leaf with his fork. He explains that whereas before the board members were talking 'missed opportunities,' with no consideration for the longer history, now they're quizzing him on 'why he took on so much exposure' given previous bubble episodes. 'Our fund manager discovers that the board's appetite for risk has changed. The message is now "get out of places like this and come home."'

'How fast does this happen?'

'The involuntary phase is immediate, same day.' He says that the voluntary phase takes longer, depending on how long it takes the board to get its bearings. The voluntary phase can happen within a week, and it involves much larger movements of capital. With a directive from the board, fund managers sell off assets in places that resemble in any way the trigger spot. 'These assets may have good value and the economic fundamentals of the place may be solid, but the thinking is: "if one place devalues, it could just as easily happen in another," so currency exposures are hedged.' He says that this situation attracts hedge fund managers and purely speculative investors, who make leveraged bets on which asset class and currency will be the next to go. 'The wave is so strong, central banks in places viewed as similar to the initial trouble spot can't withstand the pressure and are forced to let their currencies float or devalue.'

'So, how do you use this knowledge in advising clients?'

'The issue is timing. Hedges are costly, so if one could detect when investor appetite for risk is beginning to shift, one can more optimally time the purchase of protection.'

'How do you go about measuring something so psychological as a change of appetite of a group of portfolio managers?'

Persaud explains that one of the first places a change in appetite by portfolio managers will appear is in markets for derivatives. The fund managers need protection fast. It may take some time actually to sell off assets they hold and transfer the proceeds into strong currencies. But they can buy immediate protection, for example, on the options markets. If a currency is under suspicion by portfolio managers, you'd see a rise in the ratio of puts (options to cover the event of a currency falling) to calls (options to cover for the rise of the value of the currency). The put-to-call ratio would rise before a general sell-off of assets takes place. Based on this idea, Persaud and his colleagues developed a global event-risk indicator on twenty-six markets for four regions. The indicator places a number from 0 to 100 on the likelihood of a currency crash, based on derivatives trading in those currencies. 'You can look up our site and watch the indicators change in real time. Our clients can use the indicator in managing risk in their portfolios.'[4]

I comment, 'If too many fund managers use your event-risk indicator, it would remove the timing advantage for your clients, and hasten the breaking of the wave.'

The waitress asks if we would like dessert or coffee. I ask for tea and Persaud orders espresso. 'And,' he winks so the waitress can see, 'they will be disappointed in the kitchen if you don't try one of the desserts.'

'Which one would you recommend?'

'I can't afford to have this every day at lunch,' he pats his tummy, 'but you should try the trifle, even if you only have room to taste it.'

I think to myself, why not? 'The trifle then.' The waitress leaves, and I clear my palate with a sip of water. 'But there's a development issue here. How healthy is it for these so-called "emerging market" economies to be so open to short-term flows of capital? The influx, as you say, is so concentrated in a few areas that a bubble forms and a few people prosper. Then when the investors bail out, the banking system and economy can be left in ruins, and many people suffer. From what you're describing, all this happens due to the changing appetites of portfolio managers sitting in their offices in London, New York, Boston, and Tokyo.'

The tea is strong and the trifle has been doused with sherry. We discuss issues of accounting standards and transparency, and the legal and regulatory institutions needed to reduce negative consequences. We discuss the wisdom of slowly phasing in capital market liberalization to allow time for regulatory institutions to develop. But a place that has been opened for some time to capital flows might find it difficult to clamp down on them later.

Persaud points out the many kinds of distortions that occur when governments try to contain capital flows. He points out that central banks need to become more sophisticated with their own reserve management.

'Portfolio managers have all sorts of instruments at their disposal to manage risk. Why is it that central banks in these countries use only one or two types of intervention, when there's an arsenal out there?'

'Can you give an example?'

'Well, for example, when capital is flowing in and the central bank is flush with reserves, why shouldn't it buy insurance against the event of the currency crashing? In that situation hedging would be very cheap.' He points out that if portfolio investors were to move out suddenly, the central bank wins back reserves through the exercise of its derivative contracts, and the impact of the outflow won't be so devastating on the system.

That's a fresh angle, I think to myself, the central bank moving ahead of the system instead of getting caught in the backwash.

Persaud looks at his watch. 'I wish we had time to talk about the euro, but I must be off to a two o'clock meeting.'

As we leave the dining room, and enter the dark hallway, I think how much could be learned if I were to spend a whole week in the City talking with people like this, who are on the cutting edge of world finance.

The euro in its infancy

Prologue

The footage in the following two chapters was taken during the summer of 1999 when the euro was in its infancy, a mere six months old. On New Year's Day 1999 eleven European currencies were merged into one by permanently fixing their exchange rates in relation to the new single currency.[1] That day all the stocks, bonds, currency contracts, derivatives and other financial market instruments that had been denominated in those eleven currencies were converted into euro at officially decided rates. For Europeans uninvolved in financial markets, not much noticeably changed. The national currencies Europeans were accustomed to using continued to circulate for another three years until January 2002, when the first euro notes and coins were introduced and the old currencies began to be withdrawn from circulation. For financial market participants, however, the birth of the euro was a monumental event that forever altered the landscape of global finance. For six months leading up to the launch of the euro, professionals in major financial centers around the world prepared for the event. Official preparations centered in Frankfurt, the future home of the European Central Bank. Private-sector preparations centered in London, the city predestined to become world headquarters for trading in euro-denominated financial instruments,[2] though the United Kingdom did not adopt the euro. For months ahead of the launch, financial experts from around the world met in London to decide on the conventions that would be used to trade, clear, and settle financial contracts denominated in euro. Going to London six months after the launch of the euro was like entering a scientific laboratory in the midst of a great experiment. Excitement filled the air as results streamed in on the capital market revolution set in motion by the single currency. Simultaneously a sense of gloom spread over the City, as doubts about the new central bank and about the euro's role as world money sent it sliding downward against the dollar. My research partner and I found a City as divided as we were on the euro's future.

In the build-up to New Year's Day 1999, the conventional wisdom of financial experts in London and New York was that the euro would be a 'strong' currency, more like the German mark than the Italian lira or the Spanish peseta. The financial press circulated the story of a strong euro. Optimism did not last long. Back at school in North Carolina, my students and I watch the new currency slide in value from an early January 1999 high of $1.18 per euro to $1.06 as graduation approached in May. Their questions about why a currency with such potential would suffer such a lack of confidence could be only partially answered from our reading of the US financial press. At an awards luncheon the idea arises to cross the Atlantic to see the capital market revolution in process, to view the real economic transition in its infancy, and to find answers to the troubling slide of the new currency on foreign exchange markets.

A voice thunders from across the dining hall, 'Professor Williams, come sit with us.' It is the unmistakable Walter Blass, former director of strategic planning at AT&T, an outspoken member of Guilford College's board of trustees. A tall Germanic-sounding character with an Abraham Lincoln beard, Blass points to the empty chair across the table. On both sides of him are board members, an insurance company executive, a pharmaceuticals manufacturer, and next to me a senior in economics.

After introductions, Blass, who keeps up with the intellectual life of the college, asks, 'Well Robert, how's your book on world money coming along?'

'Fine, I need interviews on the euro for some of the later chapters.'

He needles me, 'Why end on such a depressing note?'

The board members know Blass as a cantankerous sort, and they chuckle politely, awaiting my response.

'Walter, come on, this is an incredible economic experiment – the merger of eleven money systems. The euro has already changed the traffic patterns of global finance. Over time the balance of power in the world monetary system will shift, and the dollar could be in for a ride.'

'Fat chance,' he booms. 'People in Europe don't even want to use euros. A few weeks ago I went to my bank in Grenoble to pick up the euro checks I ordered months ago, and the clerk hands me a new French franc checkbook. I quietly say, "I requested one in euro." He says, "It'll be here Saturday." The other clerk breaks in, "No, not that soon." My clerk looks puzzled and the other one says, "well so few people want the checks, we just let the requests accumulate and print them once a month!"'

Everyone laughs, as Blass continues. 'At a seminar I gave last week in Chambéry, the President of the Banque Populaire complained he could not allow customers to use funds for eight days if they deposited checks written on Spanish banks. He claims it takes forever for the Spanish system to clear. And he said his bank had to charge extra fees on euro-checks from certain countries because of check-clearing charges in those countries.'

I think for a few seconds. 'I'm not surprised by the slow acceptance by the public of euro checking accounts. Why confuse themselves with two ways of counting? After all, people are still paying for things in the old, familiar currencies. They won't even fold a euro note or toss a euro coin for another two and a half years.' I turn to Blass, 'But I *am* surprised by the delay in cross-border payments. Last New Year's Day, TARGET, the official payments system like our Fedwire, went on line to speed cross-border transactions between banks. That's weird, Walter. Cross-border checks should be clearing faster than you say. Maybe TARGET has some glitches we're not privy to.'

The insurance company executive leans in my direction. 'What's the word on the conversion to euro for stocks and bonds?'

'The research reports from international banks claim technical trading systems were up to speed within a week. But the euro set off a revolution in capital markets we are only beginning to see the results of. Their reports picture the Big Plunge as if it were a catalyst dropped into a test tube of reactive chemicals.'

The pharmaceuticals executive asks, 'If the Big Plunge was a success, why has the euro been performing so poorly on currency markets? I've watched it lose 10 per cent of its value since January.'

Blass clinks his knife and fork on his plate. 'The Big Plunge may have worked, but the euro has done a belly flop. The simple reason is: No one trusts the new currency.'

'That's what I suspected.' The pharmaceuticals executive squints in Blass's direction. 'What are the doubts based on, Walter?'

'Well for one, there's no clear lender of last resort. There are the same eleven national bank supervisors as before, but now there's a European

Central Bank, supposedly at the top but with almost no staff. What would happen if some big bank with operations all over Europe were to fail? Who would be in charge?' Blass points around the table, 'While they're all pointing fingers at each other, a panic could rage out of control. Imagine if a Long-Term Capital Management Hedge Fund type of insolvency were to hit Europe now.'

After several moments of silence, the economics major looks my way. 'Won't money policy be hard to coordinate with this unbalanced central banking structure?'

'Good point.' I respond. 'As I understand it, the new European Central Bank is legally set up to be politically independent of the eleven governments. But because this arrangement is so new, there are doubts about how politics will influence the setting of monetary policy in practice. I've noticed whenever an ECB official leaks something to the press, financial markets react negatively, sending the euro lower.'

Walter aims his fork at me. 'It sounds like you're changing your tune on the euro, professor.'

'Not really. My position is that anything new like this has bugs in it. I find these interesting. They reveal how money works in ways you can't see in a mature system like ours. Walter, you've mentioned some snags I hadn't thought about. But once they're worked out, the dollar will have a rival that wasn't there before.'

'I'm not convinced,' Blass says. 'Why don't we get the inside scoop this summer? I have to go to Germany in July. Want to do some interviews together?'

I think to myself: with Blass's energy, the interviews won't be dull. 'We could get interviews at the ECB (European Central Bank) in Frankfurt, but wouldn't the continent be too much on *my* turf, Walter? I'm afraid we wouldn't find enough euro pessimists there to give your position a chance.'

'I could stop in London on my way,' says Blass coyly. 'There are some cheap flights now into London.'

'Well, I hear London is a hotbed of euro-pessimists.' I hesitate.

'Scared are you?' Blass prods.

'I'm game, Walter. I just need to think logistics.'

Over the next months we book our tickets and make contacts for interviews. The luckiest connection turns out to be a colleague of my Italian central banker friend who is the Italian financial attaché in London. It doesn't take me long to find out that Signor Luigi Marini knows everyone in the City. I fax him a detailed list of questions, and his staff goes to work arranging interviews with the right people to answer each one. In

May and June 1999 the euro keeps sliding. A week before we leave for London, Blass emails me,

> Robert, Your euro isn't doing so hot. Did you watch it crash yesterday after Prodi's speech? Here's an article, from London, attached... By the way, has Mr Marini set up the interviews? We're getting down to the wire. Send me the itinerary when you get it. Walter

I read the attachment and search through the Internet news reports. It appears that Romano Prodi, president-designate of the European Commission, warned a group of Italian industrialists of the painful adjustments they would have to make in the new euro setting. Prodi's words were open to misinterpretation, and in a matter of minutes out came the soundbite: 'Prodi says, "It could become difficult for Italy to remain in the euro."' Within seconds the euro plummets against other major currencies. Prodi hastily amends his comments with a counter-soundbite, 'There is no chance of Italy leaving the euro.' Prodi's initial remarks make the front pages in London.[3]

> Walter, Thanks for alerting me to the Prodi speech. It's curious how the London papers built it up. Really, for the new chief of the European Commission to be promoting the breakdown of the European Monetary Union! I had a terrible time finding it in the Wall Street Journal. Finally there it was on page C15 tucked away in the middle of the foreign exchange column. My guess is Prodi's remarks will be a mere stumble in the near random walk of foreign exchange markets. But for a misinterpretation to cause such a market reaction tells me there are some deep, underlying doubts about the euro. Points for you. Check out the attached list of euro experts Signor Marini is contacting. Robert

> Robert. I'm amazed at how well connected Marini is. His list of experts looks like the gatekeepers between the City and the continent! See you in London. Walter

The potential of the euro as a world currency

At 9:00 a.m. behind the Royal Exchange, Blass sports a Bavarian felt hat with a small feather tucked in the band. 'Breakfast?' He points to a quiet coffee shop.

Blass slaps down the *Financial Times* on the marble counter. 'Did you see the euro hit $1.02 yesterday?'

'I did, Walter, and I read that some traders are saying it could test parity with the dollar this week... while we're in London.'

'That would be a 14 per cent loss since this "strong" currency was introduced in January. Not so good for your rival-to-the-dollar theory!'

'Give me a break, Walter, did I ever say the euro would rival the dollar the same year it was launched?'

'No, but before January that was how it was advertised. Has its pitiful showing gotten to you?'

'Not really. I'm as interested as you are in finding out the source of the doubts about the euro, and we're here at a good time. All I've read and heard since I arrived is how unworkable the monetary union is.'

'Convince me of its grand future, professor.'

'I think I'll leave that to Christopher Johnson. From his credentials, he may be the only one who could get you to see the euro's potential.'

Blass says, 'I saw on the itinerary that Johnson is Adviser from the United Kingdom for the Association for the Monetary Union of Europe. I checked out their website.'

'What did you find out?'

'It was founded to promote monetary union back in the 1980s by the heads of the largest industrial and banking enterprises in Europe. Agnelli from Fiat is on the board, and so is the chairman of the board of Deutsche Bank, and the list of board members goes on like that for the rest of Europe. Did Signor Marini tell you anything else about Christopher Johnson?'

'Yes. Signor Marini gave me some press clippings – interviews with Johnson where he's arguing for Britain to join the monetary union. Marini said Johnson has been working with the Association for the Monetary Union of Europe since it began in 1987. Johnson has published widely on the issue of monetary integration. In the early 1990s Johnson was the chief economist for Lloyds Bank. In passing, Signor Marini mentioned that Johnson's father-in-law is the celebrated British economist Lionel Robbins.'

Blass's eyes widen as he takes a sip of coffee. 'We should get ready for this one.'

On our way to the Italian financial attaché's office, I comment: 'I've looked at Johnson's publications. He's a world money man with a long view. He'll have insights into the euro as world money versus the dollar. Let's draw him out on the economic backing for the euro.'

Christopher Johnson, a tall, lean gentleman with bushy eyebrows and fine, chiseled features enters the meeting room, takes off his coat and sits at the head of the long table. He pulls some papers from his briefcase.

13.1 / Daily foreign exchange turnover (April 1998, %)

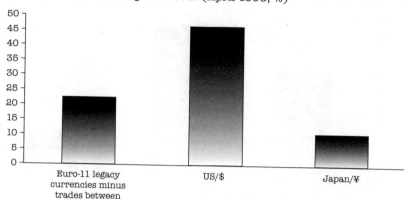

'Mr. Marini sent me a copy of your questions. Very interesting. I've pulled together some figures for you in response to them. In our discussion, shall we follow the order of your questions on the economic backing for the euro?'

'Good idea.' I turn a new page on my legal pad.

'First, let me make it clear. The purpose of monetary union is *not* to create a rival to the dollar as a world currency. It's to make Europe more competitive and efficient within, and thereby promote healthier conditions for growth over the next few decades. But the enlarged currency area will have unintended side effects as your questions suggest.'

Johnson passes us copies of his prepared tables.[4] 'Don't be misled by its recent slide on foreign exchange markets. The euro has force behind it.'

Johnson first demonstrates the euro's potential by looking at how actively traded the eleven currencies were before they merged. His calculations subtract out the trades between each other to give an estimate of their combined importance in currency trades outside the Eurozone. He argues, 'As you can see, the block of currencies that formed the euro were twice as important in currency trading as the Japanese yen.'

Blass comments, 'and about half the importance of the dollar.'

'Right, Walter, but over time,' I turn to Johnson, 'don't you think the euro will be used much more for transactions outside of Europe than the mark was ever used?'

Johnson agrees but argues that to see the euro's potential, you have to look at the separate reasons for using a currency and then ask why international actors would be inclined to use the euro instead of the

13.2 / Internal market size (% of world GDP in 1998 at 1990 PPPs)

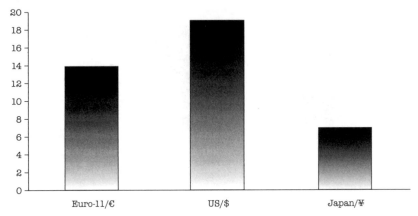

dollar or the yen to achieve that particular end. He begins by asking why the euro would be used as a currency to pay for real goods and services traded internationally.

'One can see its long-run potential as a transactions currency in world trade by looking at a few basic facts. First, there's a large internal market. Last year the euro-eleven's GDP was twice Japan's and about two-thirds the total market activity recorded in the United States.[5] And with a population exceeding that of the United States, the euro-eleven has great potential for a growing internal market. If one projects Britain, Sweden, Denmark, and Greece joining later, the internal market would be larger than that of the United States.'

'In addition to a large internal market,' Johnson continues, 'the euro-eleven has the largest share of world trade of any single economy, larger than the US share, and about four times larger than Japan's.'[6]

Blass says, 'But companies involved in international trade all have dollar accounts. They'll continue to use those accounts for their international transactions.'

'Yes,' I begin a line of questions, 'but isn't the currency used in international contracts open to negotiation?' Companies may continue to use their dollar accounts, but over time 'won't there be a power shift in favor of euro-based companies?' With the size of their internal market, European companies could simplify things by having all of their business conducted in euro. Because of the massive volume of business they do with the rest of the world, 'won't euro-based companies be able to pressure their international suppliers and customers to do business with them in euro instead of dollars?' Once the international suppliers and customers

13.3 / Importance in international trade (% share of total world trade, 1997)

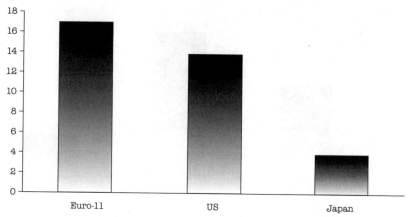

set up euro accounts, they can use those accounts to transact business unrelated to Europe. 'So won't the dollar's turf in international trade be encroached upon?' I turn to Johnson. 'Have you seen any evidence yet of pressure on outsiders to switch to the euro?'

Johnson says, 'It's early yet to see this effect, but because Europe is such a large buyer of raw materials, there has been talk recently of oil and other raw materials pricing to shift to the euro from the dollar. For example, after British Petroleum has converted its systems to the euro for its European sales, it will be simple to extend the euro payment option to customers outside the Eurozone.'

Blass points out, 'But the pressure won't come until companies within Europe switch their invoicing and payments systems to the euro. To my knowledge, that hasn't happened. Until then, European companies might as well continue using their dollar accounts for external transactions.'

Johnson agrees with Blass that companies within Europe will first have to switch their systems to the euro before they will apply any pressure on outsiders to do so. The long-run potential is great, but its use as a currency for moving real goods and services internationally will be delayed.

'And as an international investment currency?' I ask Johnson.

Johnson's eyes brighten. 'We're already seeing results.' He explains that before, financial markets were divided by exchange rate risk. Over New Year's weekend that barrier was removed, so there's no currency risk between holding Italian or Portuguese bonds versus German bonds. Without currency risk the securities markets of the eleven are quickly integrating. This allows for larger issues, more liquid secondary markets,

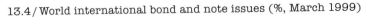

13.4 / World international bond and note issues (%, March 1999)

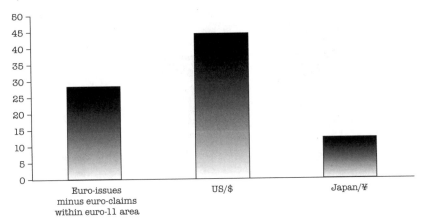

and a much wider choice of investments than before. 'All of this will attract international fund managers.'

I point out that international portfolio managers favor US Treasury securities as a parking place for cash. The market is so huge and liquid, one can always move money in and out of US Treasuries with no problem, and they earn interest while they hold them. 'How does the euro change this scenario?'

'Overnight,' Johnson pauses for emphasis, 'euro-denominated government securities surpassed US Treasuries to become the largest bloc of government securities in the world.'

'So,' I interject, 'over time the euro will be seen as an alternative to the dollar as an investment currency.'

'But,' Blass interjects, 'for that to happen euro interest rates would have to rise relative to dollar interest rates, and international money managers would have to trust the euro.'

'Right,' I respond, 'but before the euro, there was no currency that came close to the dollar in terms of securities backing. Now there is.'

Johnson moves on to point out the significance of the euro as a currency for international borrowing. To show the potential he calculates the total of loans in legacy currencies to borrowers outside the euro-11. These were converted to euro over New Year. This baseline level of international loans in euro amounts to one-fifth of the world total, about twice those denominated in yen, but approximately half the level of international dollar loans. He argues that as euro-denominated hedging tools develop – like interest rate swaps and options – the euro will

13.5 / International loans (% of world total, end of 1998)

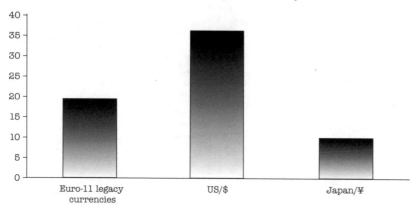

become much more attractive for borrowers and lenders than the eleven previous currencies combined.

'And,' Johnson moves on, 'we've seen a surge in euro-denominated international bond issues since January (1999). The first quarter surge astonished us, but the number and size of new issues in April, May and June should make the second quarter figures larger than the first.'

Blass comments, 'it looks like the euro is a great currency to borrow in, but no one wants to hold it!'

Johnson acknowledges that many borrowers in euro are swapping into dollars. But borrowers will need to make payments to banks or bond-holders, and so they'll have to acquire euro to make those payments, and this will mean a future demand for euro.

'And what about central banks?' I ask, 'What's the potential for the euro to become an international reserve currency?'

Johnson says that because of the dollar's dominance as world trans-actions and lending currency, in 1998 central banks held about 70 per cent of their foreign exchange reserves in dollars. Before monetary union, the currencies of the charter eleven already comprised the second largest share of foreign exchange reserves held by outside central banks, more than twice the share of reserves held in Japanese yen.[7] 'Over time, central banks will need to build up their foreign exchange reserves in euro.'

I mention a rule of thumb that central banks try to cover their foreign exchange needs for so many months. 'If most of a country's imports, debt payments, and other international obligations are in dollars, the central bank will hold a larger share of its reserves in dollars. As the euro

13.6 / Use as a reserve currency by central banks (% of FX reserves, end of 1998)

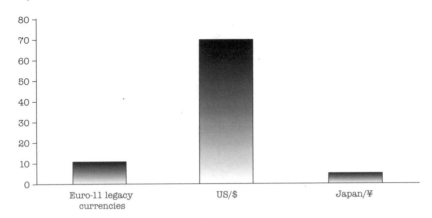

becomes used as an international transactions currency and as countries' debts become denominated in euro, central banks will naturally increase their euro holdings.'

'That's the logic,' Johnson says, 'and it will happen first for countries whose trade and capital flows are most integrated with Western Europe.' He gives Eastern Europe as an example.

I observe that once the euro becomes used more in international trade, international investment, international lending, and as an official reserve currency, it could easily become a vehicle currency in foreign exchange trading. 'I noticed last fall when I was in London that foreign exchange traders were using the German mark as a vehicle instead of the dollar when a customer would request a transfer, say, between pounds and Finnish markka. They said the mark "crossed" faster and there were "thinner spreads" using it as the vehicle. Won't the same happen with the euro?'

'Yes,' Johnson affirms, 'this will happen, and it will happen first for the currencies of countries most integrated with the Eurozone.'

Blass, who has been tapping his pen on his notepad for some time, asks, 'If the euro is so attractive as a vehicle currency, why has the Swiss franc taken over the currency trades that the mark was being used for before January?'

Johnson quickly replies, 'UBS and Credit Suisse. They're big actors in these trades, and they've found it more convenient to switch through the Swiss franc.'

Blass follows up, 'And with all its attractiveness as an investment currency, why has the euro lost 15 per cent of its value since January?'

Johnson replies, 'Relative interest rates,' and he mentions some technical reasons for the decline.

Blass picks up his pen and draws an imaginary target around Johnson's torso. 'Could there be some doubts about how the new European system of central banks will handle a chaotic situation like the Russian default? With eleven lenders of last resort, what's the plan for dealing with a financial crisis?'

Christopher Johnson grins in amusement and closes the session. 'With all the talent there, I'm sure there's a plan in place at the level of the European Central Bank.' With a twinkle in his eye he asks, 'But is it prudent to publicize a bailout plan before the event? Won't the private sector be kept on its toes if it's unsure about being rescued?'

The euro revolution in stocks and bonds

'Walter, I hope we're not late for this one.' We jaywalk to the entrance to the Underground.

'Robert, I'm running out of steam. Can we stop and get a sandwich?'

I speed up the pace. 'Walter, *you* out of steam? We have a 30-minute slot with the main guy in London on euro-securities. Marini said Bishop is booked solid for all next week. We'll be lucky to get there. It's all the way to Victoria Station.' I unzip my satchel and pull out a Power Bar. 'Will this hold you till lunch?'

Walter reads the nutritional contents while walking. 'This ought to do it. Thanks.'

A voice calls out over the loudspeaker. '**MIND THE GAP.**' We jump on the Circle Line and get the last two seats.

'Johnson got us ready for next week. Fine executive briefing.' I say.

'He's sure sold on the euro. Hope we hear the other side while we're here.'

'I think Signor Marini has that in the plan. But *not* for today. With all the securities underwriting business Johnson was talking about, my hunch is that Graham Bishop is more of a euro-optimist than Johnson. Salomon Brothers must be raking it in right now.'

'Who is this Graham Bishop?' Walter takes a bite of chocolate jerky. 'Jeez, this stuff will pull my fillings out.'

'He's Salomon/Smith Barney's Adviser for European Affairs. What I gather from the news-clippings Marini gave me is that Bishop was one of the leaders from the private sector who worked with the Bank of England to prepare the London capital markets for the Big Plunge. And he's apparently active negotiating Salomon Brothers' new euro-issues. He writes the quarterly research report called *Delivering the Benefits of EMU* for Salomon/Smith Barney's client base. I've seen the first two. They're good. He's quoted all the time in the financial press. Four contacts in London pointed me to Bishop as the one to see on the capital market revolution under way. Here's our stop.'

The crowd around Victoria Station is dense, and the entrance to Salomon Brothers is hard to find. 'Walter, we're ten minutes late.' We sign in at security and climb a set of marble stairs. The receptionist contacts Bishop's office.

A man with a neatly trimmed beard, who probably runs marathons at weekends, greets us at the top of the stairs. Graham Bishop shakes his head as he looks down at his watch. 'We're going to get cut short. I have an appointment in twenty minutes, gentlemen.' Catching my breath as he rushes us down a Persian-carpeted corridor, I say to Bishop, 'For an international securities adviser, the past six months must have been exciting.'

Bishop replies, 'The past six months *and* the six before that.' He opens the door to a small, wood-paneled room. At the end is a green felt-covered table that seats five. As we pull out our chairs, I think to myself, all we need now are cards and poker chips.

A knock on the door and a secretary peaks her head in. 'Coffee or tea, gentlemen?'

'Could we have a glass of water please?' I ask, aware that Walter's Power Bar may explode without some dilution.

'Two ice waters,' Bishop says to the young woman.

'And the lead-up to New Year? What was it like?' I ask.

'Intense…' Bishop pauses. 'Many meetings.' He says they first had to agree conceptually on the harmonized conventions that would be used, then they went to work on the information technology conversions for trading and settlement systems. 'It is perhaps surprising to those unfamiliar with the City that an "out central bank" would pursue such an activist role in the preparations.'

'Are you speaking of the Bank of England?' I ask.

Bishop nods affirmatively. 'From the beginning, the Bank of England worked with us to ensure that the City of London was ready for the birth of the euro, a huge event for the world financial system. The scale of the preparations went unreported in the media. Our intention is to turn the European Union's capital markets into a simple, transparent, harmonized market.'

'Were you surprised at how smoothly New Year's weekend went?'

'With all the time we spent last year... the thought, the meetings, the fire drills, the dress rehearsals?' Bishop shrugs, 'I wasn't surprised at all.'

'What snags did you experience?'

'The only snags were a few minor payments system problems...'

'Like?'

'Like payments being delivered to the wrong branch of a bank. By the way, those mostly originated on the Continent, not in London.'

I shift the focus. 'I'm told the euro government securities market is now somewhat larger than the market for US Treasuries.'

'*Somewhat* larger? 'Bishop looks at me as if I'm a rube from the sticks. He quickly cites figures that the euro-11 government bond market is 22 per cent larger than the US Treasury counterpart. He estimates that when the UK, Sweden, Denmark, and Greece are eventually included, the total market size could be more than 40 per cent larger than the US Treasury securities market. 'Even without them there will be growth in euro-government bonds versus Treasuries.'[8]

Bishop explains that the euro has allowed governments that previously relied on short-term borrowing at high interest rates to issue longer-term bonds at much lower rates, a huge benefit to government budgets. 'If European governments converted three-quarters of their current debt into bonds, their government bond market would be twice the size of the US Treasury market.'

'And what patterns are you seeing in this rush of new bond offerings by governments?'

Bishop becomes more animated. 'European governments are intentionally competing – and successfully so, I might add – with the US Treasury in terms of size of new issues.' He quotes figures on benchmark bond issues since January that were larger than typical US Treasury issues. 'This size of issue would have been impossible before the euro, when the market was divided by exchange rate risk.'

'Why is there such a fixation on size of a bond issue?' I ask.

Bishop explains that a large issue will be sold off to lots of fund managers. This wide dispersion of the same bond reassures investors, because they know a secondary or 'used bond market' will develop in that issue, and they'll be able to sell it if they need cash. 'The extra liquidity provided by a large issue makes it more attractive to portfolio managers.'

I ask, 'What will this mean for the euro as a world currency?'

Bishop argues that the size of the euro-denominated government securities market, their trading as a distinct "bloc", the liquidity of the issues, and the increasing availability of hedging instruments, will make them attractive as an investment for international portfolios. 'This will hasten the emergence of the euro as an international investment and reserve currency.'

Blass asks, 'If the euro is such an investment currency, why are investors shying away from it?'

Looking impatient, Bishop snaps at Blass. 'Don't confuse short-term exchange rates – where the euro has been weak – with capital markets, where monetary union has been successful. Euro securities issues have been snapped up by investors.'

I knee Walter under the table and move to a sympathetic tack. 'How about corporate securities? How has monetary union affected this market?'

Graham Bishop pauses to consider where to begin. 'It's here that the most profound changes are taking place.' He describes how capital markets in the US were transformed in the 1980s and 1990s as savings moved out of banks and into investment funds, which hold stocks, bonds, and other traded securities instead of traditional bank loans. The same pressures for 'securitization' that swept through the US more than a decade ago are converging on Europe. And the single currency allows fund managers to move money around the Eurozone seeking higher returns without having to worry about currency risk. So corporations now don't have to go to banks as they did in the past to borrow. They can go to the bond market or issue stocks and get financing now. 'Europe is ripe for securitization. The technology has been thoroughly tried and tested in the United States. This technology and expertise can be transplanted quickly into Europe.'[9]

'So,' I rib him, 'besides big bucks pouring into the London office of a certain Wall Street investment bank, what implications do you see from this revolution sweeping European capital markets?'

Barely amused, Bishop answers: 'Pressure from the owners of securities will stimulate a bottom-up restructuring of European industry. This bodes well for the future competitiveness of the European Union.'

'And politically?' I ask.

'Financial markets of this scale are independent of individual governments. They act as a rolling referendum on the views of savers about government policies.' He explains that as large investment funds exercise their new freedom to invest in securities other than those of their own governments, a government viewed as breaking fiscal discipline will be penalized by the bond market. And investment funds will pressure for removing barriers to capital flows and other impediments to efficiency. As portfolio investment flows into areas that embrace liberalization, legislators and regulators will be pushed along. He looks at his watch and rises. 'In the long run, the euro securities market will attract even more international investors. This will increase the use of the euro as a world currency.'

As we exit the room, I hand him my business card. 'Would you mind putting me on your publications list? I want to keep up on this.'

He turns his head as he rushes off. 'I won't flood you with publications, just the important ones.'[10]

Outside, Walter vents, 'My God, what an optimist!'

'I wouldn't mind having Salomon Brothers' underwriting fees this quarter. Can you go with me to the *Financial Times*?'

'Sorry Robert, I have a business matter to take care of this afternoon. When's your interview over?'

'4:30.'

'Let's meet at 5:30 for a pint.' Blass suggests.

'How about the Sherlock Holmes near Trafalgar Square? '

'Good. By the way, who is this you're seeing at the *Financial Times*?' Blass asks.

'His name is Hugo Dixon. He's the editor of the Lex column.'

Blass says, 'Yes, I read his column from time to time. Of course, the *Financial Times* is the *Wall Street Journal* for Europe. Sorry I'll miss this. His column is widely read.'

'Mr. Marini said Dixon is writing a textbook titled *The Penguin Guide to Finance*. He says Dixon has been following the merger movement and European stocks since the euro. Bishop was great on bonds. I'm hoping to get a lesson now on European stocks.'

'Good luck. See you at 5:30.'

I catch a cab to the *Financial Times* building across Southwark Bridge from the financial district. Hugo Dixon greets me and invites me up for tea. Full of cigarette smoke and reporters, the cafeteria looks down on the Thames and over to the skyline of the City. We find a table as far from the noise as possible.

'When's your book coming out?' I ask.

'Should be this autumn if I finish the draft and Penguin moves along on it.'

I hand Dixon my card and ask him to put me on the course adoption list. 'I notice from the Lex column you've been following corporate developments since the euro was launched. How has the euro changed things?'

'Before the euro, separate currencies protected national rigidities in labor markets, in the government sector and in capital markets.'

'How did that work?'

He mentions the political difficulty of laying off workers and cutting government programs. 'Before, governments could postpone the pain of restructuring by allowing their currencies to depreciate with respect to their neighbors.[11] Now the currency play is no longer an option within the Eurozone. It will take some time to see the results, but the outcomes will be of great benefit to the European economy.'

'What drawbacks do you see?'

'The greatest problem is if the pace of structural change moves too fast and provokes a political counter-reaction.'

'What adjustments are taking place in equity markets?'

Dixon brightens up. 'That's the silver lining of currency unification. For some time the US, the UK, and the Netherlands have enjoyed relatively efficient equity markets. But before monetary union, traditional stock markets on the continent were much smaller, and they remained trapped in national circuits controlled by clubby networks.'

'What kinds of clubby networks?'

'In some cases, key industries were government-owned or with large government stakes. Union representatives sat on boards. "House banks" held controlling interest and provided loans to the same companies they controlled. Government regulations impeded cross-border flows and movements of capital between sectors.'

'And the consequences?'

'In this setting capital could not flow efficiently into areas of lowest risk relative to reward... with serious consequences for improvements in productivity and economic growth. That "management should consider the interest of the stockholders in making decisions' was viewed on the continent as' – Dixon mimics the accent of a British lord – '"crude and too American." And there was similar disdain for hostile takeovers.'

'So how do you see the corporate culture changing with the euro?'

'Changes began creeping in years ago, but with the euro it's almost like night and day. Stock markets are merging across borders, regulations that impeded cross-border investment are being dismantled, government stakes in industry are being sold off in public stock offerings, hostile bids and takeovers are becoming commonplace, and for the first time the general public is beginning to participate in stock ownership.'

'Can you give some examples of these changes?'

A journalist with a mind for details, Dixon rattles off a list of particular cases to back up each point.

He concludes the interview with an illustration. 'If I were to show you a chart of the number of stock mutual funds in Italy for the past twenty-five weeks, you would probably mistake it for the price actions of a technology stock.[12] The pressure is on; there is the glint of steel in the market. Over time European management will change attitudes and behavior. Capital will be used more efficiently. And, finally, the interest of the stockholder will enter the mindset of corporate executives.'

Geraniums in hanging baskets cascade over the entrance to the Sherlock Holmes. It's Friday and the place is packed. From a dark booth, Walter Blass waves to me through a cloud of smoke. Good thing he got here early. I point to the bar and he shouts 'Ale.' I catch the bartender's eye. 'Two pints of your best, please.' He slowly pulls a lever that reads Sherlock Holmes Ale.

'Thanks Professor.' Blass beams as I set down his brew.

'Walter. I'm curious. Deep down, why are you so pessimistic about the euro?'

Walter takes a long sip of ale as he thinks out an answer. 'Well, Robert, Europe has structural rigidities. Management can't do anything without organized labor or government sabotaging it. In seminars I give, I hear executives from France, Germany, Belgium, and other countries complain. Case after case.'

'So, Walter, in the face of competition, would you see companies and governments freezing up instead of flexibly responding with greater efficiencies as Christopher Johnson sees it?'

'Yes, and the result will be pockets of high unemployment, and central banks can't do anything about it. I fear there will be a huge political backlash that could disrupt the monetary union. There's already a right-wing resurgence in France.'

'OK Walter, let me accept your point about structural rigidities. But what about the capital market revolution? Johnson in the morning, Bishop at midday, and Hugo Dixon this afternoon – all point to this revolution as forcing flexibility on management. Dixon and Bishop see an emerging "discipline" over governments, labor, and management by bond and stock markets. Of course they see this as a move to greater efficiency and therefore "good." I can see harm coming from it.'

'What harm could there be?' he looks incredulous.

'I see the monetary union as inviting Ronald Reagan and Margaret Thatcher in through the back door.'

'An example, Professor?'

I take a gulp of ale. 'For example, one place in the Eurozone may have achieved environmental gains through years of struggle. Now capital will move out of the areas where those environmental laws have driven up costs, and capital will move into areas where the laws are lax, and political pressure will come to bear to loosen environmental restrictions in the places with the high standards.'

Blass interjects. 'That didn't happen on the Mexican border. I saw an article arguing environmental standards improved when US investors put in factories down there.'

'That's not the story I hear. Also worker health and safety standards may be higher in some places than others. The "discipline" of the markets will be to lower these standards. It simply costs less to the companies to go to a place that's lax. The outcome may be "efficient" – a code word for "profitable" – to the company in the short run, but I don't see that as necessarily good for people in the long run.'

'Yeah, yeah, yeah. Deny the inevitable, Professor.'

'But ethical values aside, Walter, How can the structural rigidities in Europe be at the bottom of the doubts about the euro in the financial markets? If anything, the monetary union has been a catalyst to dissolve what you call "structural rigidities."'

'The political backlash could cause major disruptions.' Walter gives examples of political polarization on the continent.

I confirm. 'Dixon was concerned about this. But the question is, is the monetary union reversible? Political backlash may slow down adjustments, but could a government drop out without triggering a financial meltdown? I think not. So the force of capital market discipline will continue.'

Blass comes back at me. 'So, Professor, why are the financial markets so pessimistic about the euro?'

'I believe the doubts may have to do with your lender-of-last-resort issue and the completely untried central bank setup. Maybe there are problems in TARGET that we haven't gotten wind of yet. Next week I hope we'll get the answers. But there's something going on at a gut level I'm trying to put my finger on.' I take another swig.

'What's that?'

'Maybe there's a "Doubting Thomas" syndrome going on here.'

'Doubting Thomas? I've heard the term, but what do you mean?'

I continue. 'If I remember correctly from Sunday School, the disciple Thomas wouldn't believe Christ had risen from the dead until he touched the nail holes in Jesus' hands and feet.'

'OK. So where are you going?'

'Well maybe people are going to have to feel the currency in their hands and see that it physically works before they'll believe in it.'

'Yes,' he says, 'there could be a schizophrenia in this transition period. Electronic payments in euro for stocks and bonds during the day, and then, on the way home from work, our financial manager goes shopping and uses the same old marks or francs to buy bread, cheese, and wine.'

'And, back to the point you made this morning. Until companies involved in the real economy of Europe switch their systems to euro, there will be no pressure on the rest of the world to do so. Next week let's find out when companies in Europe are going to switch to the euro.'

Blass drains his glass and rises. 'I've got to catch the train to Richmond. Have a great fourth with your friends.'

'I don't expect fireworks. The Brits aren't too keen on American Independence.'

The transition of the real economy to the euro

Monday morning, 5 July, I greet Walter Blass outside Citibank House, an island of plate glass on the busy Strand.

'Did you see any fireworks?' he asks.

'Actually yes. Some drunk Texans in a flat across the park were shooting them off from their balcony. I thought it was a good show, but the British at our dinner party thought it rude when a rocket clipped one of the Queen's swans.'

While waiting for security clearance, I pick up a slick blue brochure with a euro coin pictured at the center. 'The Citibank Euro Account' it reads in bold white letters, and below in lighter print 'When in Europe, make sure your money speaks the language.' Below the euro coin in small letters it reads 'The Citi Never Sleeps.'

'Robert. Tell me a bit more about John Atkin.'

'I believe he's Citibank's main adviser to corporations on monetary union. I subscribe to several banks' global research products. In my view, Atkin did the best job preparing briefings on the lead-up to the euro and its first six months. His series is called *EMU Watch*.[13] He's written a book on monetary union I want to pick up while we're here in London. My hunch is that Atkin is busy now advising Citibank's corporate clients on switching their systems to the euro.'

John Atkin's assistant introduces herself and leads us up a stairwell, then through a hallway that smells stale, archival, like the inner sanctum of a research library. Floor-to-ceiling shelves hold neat, labeled stacks of publications.

Light streams in from the window behind Atkin, who sits behind an enormous desk that more resembles a professor's than a banker's. Piles of documents line its perimeter. A computer, a telephone, and a writing pad are within Atkin's reach. Behind him, traffic moves along the Strand.

Blass pops the question: 'Why with such success in the securities markets has the euro done so poorly on foreign exchange markets?'

Atkin slides some charts across his desk. 'Most currency watchers now are looking for the euro to be friendless during the rest of the year unless growth prospects improve in Europe and short-term interest rates tighten relative to dollar rates.' He quietly chuckles. 'Of course, the press looks for the "sexy" – that is, political – reasons behind currency changes.'

Atkin points to a chart showing his estimates of the price of the euro that would bring about purchasing power parity with the dollar. 'We find that at \$1.02 the euro is considerably undervalued for commodity trade purposes. It would take an appreciation to around \$1.23 to get to purchasing power parity with the dollar. This calculation shouldn't surprise you. It's about one cent higher than the average price during the 1990s of the basket of currencies that combined to form the euro, and it's roughly what the old dollar-mark exchange rate was when trade between the US and Germany was more in balance.'

Blass points out, 'And if these numbers are close to the truth, shouldn't the weak euro make Europe's trade surplus with the US continue to widen?'

'Correct,' says Atkin, 'not a bad situation for a slow economy. All this gloom and doom over the weak currency is misplaced, in my view.'

I place the blue brochure advertising the Citibank Euro Account on the desk. 'Have you gotten many takers on this yet?'

Atkin leans back in his chair. 'Enquiries mainly. Corporations haven't moved to convert their systems yet. Of course you hear members of the European Commission complain about legacy currencies still being used so widely by corporations.' Without cracking a smile, he says 'But last month when I was in Brussels, I tried to use a euro check to buy a book in the European Commission's bookstore. The cashier refused to accept my check, so I had to pay in Belgian francs!'

'How are you working with corporations on the switchover?'

'I advise individual clients and I give workshops like this.' He takes a packet from a stack near him and slides it across the desk. It's a PowerPoint presentation entitled 'Outlook for Sterling and the Euro' with Citibank's logo on each slide.

I thumb through the packet and pass it to Blass. 'Why have companies been so slow to move to the new currency?'

'It takes about two years for a big company to become fully euro-compliant, and some payments, like wages, will be postponed to January

2002, when euro notes and coins will first become available. Social security benefits won't convert to euro until the end of 2001 because of the time it will take to make their information technology systems euro-compliant, and smaller companies that are more connected to the cash economy will try to delay switching to the euro until the last minute. For the bulk of the 290 million inhabitants of the EMU area, the euro will make little impression on their lives until they begin using euro notes and coins in 2002.'[14]

I ask a concluding question, 'Do you think companies inside Europe will have to switch to the euro before it gains acceptance outside Europe?'

Atkin rises from his chair. Like a professor ending a lecture, he announces: 'It is said,' his voice lowers to a whisper, '"Money is by acclamation not proclamation."'

Atkin leads us through the archives, out the door and into the spacious elevator room. On the other side of the elevators is a glass wall. Inside are rows of computers and overhead screens, a room that extends to the far end of the building.

'When your assistant showed us up the stairs, I didn't notice you were on the same floor as the trading room.'

Atkin says, 'You don't notice it now. It's so quiet. If you'd been here last fall after the Russian default, we wouldn't be able to hear ourselves speak. It sounded like a street brawl in there. Some days it was so loud that I couldn't think all the way back in the far reaches of my office. Now with the euro, and the removal of so many currency pairs, there's much less trading. We've had to greatly reduce our trading staff, by 15 or 20 per cent I would guess.'

Outside the building, Walter comments: 'Atkin had some of your answers. Who are you seeing this afternoon?'

'Signor Mario Cotto, director of the London branch of Banco IMI, a big Italian bank. I'm hoping he'll tell me some more about personal bank accounts in euro. Too bad you won't be able to attend this one, Walter.'

'I'll meet you at 2:00 at the Italian office on King Street.'

I take a cab to Saint Paul's Cathedral. The bells sound eleven o'clock as I walk across the street to Banco IMI.

Upstairs, Signor Cotto, a gentleman with a white beard and many years of banking experience, recalls: 'I was in France more than two years after the conversion of 100 old francs to one new franc. Shopkeepers were still quoting prices in old francs! Two decimals off more than two years later.' He points to his brain. 'That's how deep the mental habits of money are ingrained.'

'And now with the conversion to the euro?' I ask.

'I'm the first to admit I still think in lire when I'm comparing prices of household items. But I've bought stocks in euro, and I don't need to convert back to lire mentally to check on how they're doing. But I'm a banker, accustomed to numbers. The general public is not. It will take a long time for them to get used to the new currency.'

'What is Banco IMI doing in this regard?' I ask.

'Our bank is committed to helping people climb the learning curve.'

'How are you doing that?'

'The trick is to begin quoting two-way prices as soon as we can.' He pulls out a bank statement and shows how they've provided a euro column next to the lira column. 'The customer gets used to seeing them next to each other, so they get the feeling of a euro being worth almost 2,000 lire.'

Below the final balance in lire and euro is a statement that reads, 'This is an itemized statement in lire. The right column expressed in euro does not have any effect on the balance in your account, the only purpose is to help instill confidence in the new money.'[15] Below is the signature of the general manager of the bank.

'In Italy, public utilities are expressing rates in euro now, and shoppers who go to stores in tourist areas get an early feeling for price comparisons in the new money. We're hoping that with this early start, there will be less public confusion when 2002 approaches.'

'With the move to the euro, what's been happening in capital markets in Italy?'

'This is the biggest change going on right now. In order to see it you have to understand that Italians save a lot. First they put their savings in a house. After the home is taken care of, they build up their savings deposits at the Post Office.'

'The Post Office?'

'Yes. In Italy, the Post Office is the largest bank, but Italians also have accounts at private banks, or they invest in Italian government securities.' He says that all of these were relatively safe places to save, and before the euro they earned relatively high returns. With the euro, interest rates have fallen on all these traditional savings instruments. At the same time, the government is selling off its holdings in oil, electrical energy, telecommunications, and is moving to privatize the postal bank. 'So there are all these new public offerings of stocks that then get traded in Milan. And the government is making it clear that the old state pension system will be unable to take care of people as it once did, and it's giving tax incentives like in the US for people to set up private accounts like your IRAs [individual retirement accounts] .'

'How has your bank been involved in this revolution?' I ask.

'We are at the forefront of setting up mutual funds and retirement accounts for people, and educating them about the risks. I'm afraid that is not the general case in Italy, where regulation hasn't caught up with the changes.' Worries cross his forehead. 'There are thousands of get-rich-quick products being offered to savers now. Most of them are rubbish. People are going to get burned. But our bank is looking long-term, making sound investments, and advising our clients on the ups and downs of stock funds, something the average Italian is not aware of yet.'

'I read all these negative reports on the euro and the new central bank here in London. How does the view from London differ from Italy?'

Signor Cotto smiles. 'In Italy, it's not a matter of whether we like it or not. Monetary union is a reality. So we are looking for ways to make it work. Here in Britain, they're asking, "Do we really want to be part of this? Do we really want to give up control to something that hasn't proven itself? This opens up room for doubts.'

Doubts about the euro and the new central bank

'How did your interview with the Italian banker go?' Blass asks.

'Interesting on how Signor Cotto's bank is educating the public, trying to get them prepared for the euro. Also his bank is busy creating retirement accounts and mutual funds, and they're selling like lottery tickets in Italy. But Walter, you would have been antsy.'

'How so?'

'He was as high on monetary union as Bishop and Johnson. '

'The cards are stacked in your favor, Professor.'

'I have a feeling that won't last.'

'Who are Marjorie Deane and William Clarke?'

'Marjorie Deane worked as editor for *The Economist* for years. Now she's an economic consultant. Four years ago, she and Robert Pringle published a book titled *The Central Banks*, a history of central banking.'

'And William Clarke?'

'He was director of British Invisibles for many years, a government-sponsored organization that works closely with the financial services industry to promote London as a financial center. Back in the early 1980s he wrote a book, *Inside the City: A Guide to London as Financial Centre.* Mr Marini says he's updating it into a book with the title *How the City Works.* I checked last night on the Internet and found Clarke published a book in 1990 titled *Planning for Europe 1992: Britain and the Common Internal Market*, so he's no stranger to the European Union.'

The elevator door creaks open, and voices spill through the cloakroom. They enter the conference room, and Signor Marini introduces us. I pull out the chair at the head of the conference table for Marjorie Deane, who lets me seat her.

'What about this new central bank?' I start off.

Marjorie Deane, with silver-white hair and sharp eyes, nods to William Clarke to begin. Clarke leans back in his chair and says slowly and soundly, 'They're putting the cart before the horse.' He pauses for this to sink in. 'You need a state first, then a central bank. Never before in the history of central banking has the order been reversed. Am I not right Marjorie?'

He turns to Deane, the authority on central banking, who says, 'Indeed this is true, and there will be confusions and negative consequences from this, I am afraid.' Her eyes express concern as she looks to Clarke, who picks up the thread.

He explains that monetary union in Europe was pushed by politicians, who saw it as a way to keep the "united Europe" movement alive at a time when it appeared to be losing steam. Now they have achieved a single central bank with a "one size fits all monetary policy," covering eleven separate states, each with its own political pressure groups, structural rigidities, phase of economic cycle, and fiscal policy.

Deane looks to Walter and me. 'Am I not correct that in your country Greenspan has to deal with one Treasury chief, not the governors of fifty states?'

I ask, 'Are you questioning whether it's possible for a central bank to rule over a confederacy?'

William Clarke responds, 'Indeed, that is the structural question.' He goes on to say that if all of the regions covered by the single currency were in the same phase of the business cycle, or if labor were mobile 'as in your country,' the new setup might have a chance to work. 'But labor is not mobile in Europe, and our cycles are badly out of sync.'

'Yes.' Marjorie Deane reinforces the point that the 'core of Europe' – Germany, France, and Italy – is experiencing very high, and politically charged, unemployment rates, and the 'peripheral countries' – Spain, Portugal, and Ireland – are experiencing inflationary booms. 'The peripheral economies could use some monetary tightening right now, while the center needs lower interest rates.'

Clarke asks rhetorically, 'And who has the power in setting the single monetary policy? The core, and Ireland gets dictated to.' He argues that if growth in the core does not pick up soon, political pressures in France could lead to a European summit. 'The big boys, France and Germany – who don't want to get in a fight again – would meet ahead of time to decide what course to take, and together they could push to amend the Maastricht Treaty rules.'

'And what would be the repercussions?' I ask.

'Well,' Clarke says, 'we've already had a glimpse of what's to come. Whenever there is mention of bending the monetary rules, the big funds move against the euro.' I catch Walter's eye to register the point.

Deane reflects, 'As I see it, one of the most serious problems with the European Central Bank is lack of transparency. This is quite different from your Fed, which makes clear hints on direction of the Open Market Committee's leanings well ahead of time, and quickly publishes minutes of meetings. The president of the European Central Bank, Wim Duisenberg, will not utter a whisper about direction of policy. Minutes of Governing Council meetings cannot be published for sixteen years,' she lowers her voice to a whisper, 'supposedly to shield National Central Bank governors from local political pressures when they decide on monetary policy for Europe.' Her voice strengthens, 'In the United States, if a financial crisis were brewing, Greenspan would meet with your treasury secretary to coordinate a course of action. Greenspan would check in with the Open Market Committee, announce the action at a news conference, and quickly restore confidence in the markets. I am afraid the shroud of secrecy surrounding the European Central Bank will increase market turbulence instead of calming the waters.'

Blass asks, 'And how is the system set up to deal with a major bank failure? Who will be called on to act as lender of last resort?'

'Precisely the question!' As Marjorie Deane pauses, I think to myself, if this woman had been born a half century earlier, she would have been in the Bloomsbury Group with Keynes. She explains that the details for crisis response had not been spelled out, and the same regulatory and supervisory groups as before continue to operate. These national groups, not the European Central Bank in Frankfurt, 'have the best credit information on banks operating in their borders. In the event of a local crisis, presumably the same machinery as before would be called on to deal with illiquid or insolvent institutions.'

I ask, 'and what if the crisis spills over?'

She responds, 'We're all asking these questions. How will decentralized credit information be shared with higher authorities? Who will be ultimately responsible in the event of a general liquidity crisis in TARGET? Or one involving a pan-European bank with no clear home base? Might this not create an awkward situation?'

Blass interjects, 'And the timing issue!'

'Exactly,' she continues. 'How long would it take to decide which institutions are illiquid but solvent and which ones are insolvent? Would the Governing Council of the ECB have to meet to decide on extending the range of assets that would serve as collateral for ECB credit? Wouldn't the secrecy cult of the European Central Bank make the problem worse?'

Walter glances my way and chalks up points for himself on an imaginary scoreboard. 'It seems from what you're saying that Britain, Sweden, and Denmark have been wise to sit it out on the sidelines and wait for the crises to unfold on the Continent.'

William Clarke turns serious. 'I cannot speak for Sweden and Denmark, but from a British perspective, the central banking culture here prides itself on openness and transparency. And our political institutions are democratic and responsive. Many of us are reluctant to hand over political sovereignty to Brussels or monetary sovereignty to Frankfurt.' He pauses uncomfortably. 'Thank God we're not in this. We could destroy it without intending to.'

'What do you envision happening over the next year or so?'

William Clarke explains that the eleven national governments in the monetary union remain subject to their own local political pressures. In today's world of global investment funds, political events quickly move markets. Combine this with the unsettled lender-of-last-resort problem, the awkward policy implementation structure, and the secrecy issue and vulnerability is compounded. 'I do not know the particular political or economic event that will trigger it, but *within the next twelve months, the euro will be tested.*'[1]

As Marjorie Deane and William Clarke leave for their next meeting, Walter turns to me as he waits for the elevator to return, 'See what I've been talking about?'

'Yes. Points for you Walter. They're on to something, and I hope to follow up with more details on the new central bank this afternoon.'

'Who are you seeing?'

'I'm going to Central Banking Publications, a think-tank that keeps tabs on the world's central banks. Neil Courtis edits a journal called *The Financial Regulator*, and Benedict Weller is completing a book with Robert Pringle on how central bankers around the world view the euro. Courtis and Weller have just conducted a survey of central bank reserve managers and their plans to use the euro.'

'Fill me in on that after we see the central banker tomorrow morning.'

'I'm hoping we'll get something on TARGET from him. But please, Walter, let's avoid the word 'crisis' tomorrow morning. If he says the C-word, fine, but remember, he's a central banker and is probably gun-shy. Is that a deal?'

194/ The Money Changers

'I'll try.' Blass shakes on it. 'And be sure to thank Signor Marini for me. He has set us up right.'

I touch up my notes from the interviews outside Signor Marini's office. When he has finished up work with his staff members, Marini calls me in.

'Professor Williams. How are things going?'

'Intense. It seems you've found the best person in London to answer each of the questions I sent you.'

'I warned you I would put you to work.'

'You have. Walter Blass and I have hardly had a chance to catch our breath.'

'My staff helped with the logistics, which weren't easy. These people are very busy. But I did let you off for the 4th of July weekend. So you're fresh for this week. Which questions have not been answered yet?'

'I need a few more details on the new central bank structure, and the new euro payments systems, especially TARGET.'

He looks at the computer printout of the schedule. 'This afternoon, you'll get details on the new central bank, and I see tomorrow morning you're meeting with the central banker who took charge of his country's link-up with TARGET. We were lucky to get you in there. When you confirmed with him, what did he say about Walter Blass attending?'

'He sounded reluctant, but agreed on the condition of no recordings or identification of him or his central bank leaked to the press.'

'Of course. A single comment from one of the four "out" central bankers[2] could be taken wrong by the financial markets.'

I comment about how Prodi's remarks were distorted a few weeks before.

'Ridiculous, no?' He gestures with palms up. 'The future president of the European Commission saying his own country could drop out of the monetary union! I clipped some of the press articles for you.' He pushes me photocopies of newspaper clippings. 'Do you see any gaps, any other contacts I might be able to arrange for you while you're here?' Signor Marini asks.

'The only other contact I would like is at CHAPS-euro.' I tell him about my visit to CHIPS in New York and I'd like to see how London banks deliver large euro payments. 'The expert I'd like to see there is Michael Lewis, who helped design and install CHAPS-euro.'

'I cannot promise a tour, there may be security problems. But Michael Lewis *is* the man to see. Give me a call tomorrow morning, and I'll let you know if it's arranged.'

A European central banker waits on the sidelines

Walter Blass greets me outside the meeting place. 'How did your interview at Central Banking Publications go?'

'Terrific, I'll fill you in on some of the details tomorrow at lunch. I'm in at CHAPS-euro this afternoon and tomorrow morning I'll meet with John Stevens, a political activist for monetary union who used to trade currency in the City.'

'Too bad I have business to take care of. Take good notes for tomorrow's lunch.'

The meeting room is dimly lit from amber wall sconces. Heavy drapes block all but one bright stream of light from the window. Seated across the conference table from us, the central banker describes the massive collaborative effort leading up to the financial market conversion. Now he's designing the procedures to be followed in the event that his country decides to join the monetary union.

'It's not up to us but to our politicians. If they and the voters decide to join the monetary union, then it will be our job to make the merger work.'

I ask, 'Can you give us a little background on the connections between your payments system and the euro system now that financial markets have converted to the euro?'

He explains that all fifteen of the national central banks in the European System of Central Banks are linked into the TARGET system, not just the eleven first-wave central banks. This allows cross-border payments in euro to be settled with finality using euro accounts at national central banks or at the ECB [European Central Bank]. The safety of having a euro settlement system in real time using central bank deposits is important because it is the safety net for the five private-sector euro payments systems,[3] which all rely on TARGET for finality.

'And how smoothly does TARGET run?' Blass inquires.

The central banker continues, 'As might be expected in any new system, there were "teething problems" during the first months of TARGET.'

Blass probes like a dentist. '*Teething* problems?'

He explains that sometimes payments would end up at the wrong branch of a bank, but as participants identified the problems they corrected them.[4] 'After the first few months of operation, we have seen reductions every month in errors of this sort.'

'Have you experienced any other sorts of problems?' I ask.

'There have been some technical problems with the system.' He mentions a safety feature that notifies other central banks to stop sending payments if a problem arises in one national payments system. 'This prevents liquidity from the well-functioning systems from being tied up in the frozen system.'

Blass asks, 'And how often have you experienced these stop-sends?'

He replies, 'In the first five months of the euro, there were a hundred stop-send messages, or approximately one per business day.'

I ask, 'Where have most of the problems arisen?'

The central banker's lips curl in guarded amusement. 'That information is unavailable. But let's say a very large volume payments system is more likely to encounter problems than a smaller one.'

I write down: 'Biggest payments snags – Germany?'

He reminds us of the size of the task, creating a system like Fedwire in the States but one that operates across eleven national payments systems with link-ups to the four 'out' payments systems. He reassures us, 'One comforting discovery from the first six months of TARGET is that when a problem arises in one national system, it does not spread to others, but remains isolated until it is solved.'

I think to myself, dead-end on TARGET, so I shift to monetary policy. 'I'm curious about monetary policy intervention. Will this take place in one financial center, like New York in the US case, or will there be decentralized intervention?'

'At present, it is intended to be done in a few major centers, Frankfurt and Paris, primarily, but also perhaps Milan.'

'And might there not be confusion from this?' I ask.

'Perhaps, at first, but this will all be worked out and understood by the financial markets in time.'

Blass asks, 'And what are the action plans in place in the event of a major financial panic like happened after the Russian default?' I lightly knee Walter under the table to remind him of our deal.

'The arrangement is for the existing regulatory bodies and national lenders of last resort to step in and deal with problem banks.'

'What if there is a general liquidity cri—' I stomp Blass's foot 'general liquidity problem?'

The central banker disguises his annoyance. 'Look,' he says, 'all the policy procedures and details worked out over years of trial and error in your country and mine have not been worked out for this new central bank. I'm not sure you fully appreciate the effort expended to meet "Le Weekend" deadline. Since New Year, the fifteen central banks have been working full-time to streamline TARGET so it can operate under normal conditions as well as during unanticipated surges like those following the Russian default. Then there is preparation for Y2K.' He explains that he and his colleagues at the European Central Bank have not had time to work out all the procedural details for every possible event. 'Even if the strategic details were already worked out for responding to a general liquidity *crisis*, as you were referring to' – he looks Blass in the eye – 'should we broadcast these?'

'So are you saying the new central bank is so busy working on more immediate problems that it will take an emergency to move their attention to the unresolved procedure?' I ask.

'I might not phrase it that way, but basically, yes. Policies will be created when there is a need.'

'Isn't this a bit risky?' Blass asks.

The central banker counters that there are also risks in creating procedures and announcing the details. Any overt move by the European Central Bank invites the scrutiny of politicians. So for some procedures it may be wiser to wait until the moment of need, then decide the course, instead of igniting a public debate, increasing doubts, and provoking divisions within the new governance structure. 'Furthermore,' he adds, 'the announcement of procedures to deal with extreme events can itself unsettle markets by focusing public attention on the possibility of those events occurring.'

'Practically speaking, how do you envision the new central bank deciding a procedure in a "moment of need" as you put it?' I ask.

'At such a point, the Executive Board will be in close consultation with the eleven national central bank governors and whoever else is needed, depending on the nature of the disturbance. We and the other three "out" central banks would certainly be advised and possibly consulted. This group of central bankers has a history of working together, so I'm sure responses will be quick. In this way, policy implementation details will be decided out of situations that call for them.'

We exchange business cards, and he reiterates, 'feel free to call me for any questions you might have, but please do not identify me or my organization when you write this up.'

'Don't worry. I'll be discreet.'

The doorman bows as we leave the quiet sanctuary into the noisy streets.

Out of earshot, I comment, 'Well our central banker was as open as he could be, and I'll be careful not to disclose his nationality when I write this up, but there's more I'd like to know about TARGET.'

Blass replies, 'Me too. And I'm not so sure this policy evolution will take place as smoothly as he thinks. Get the goods on TARGET this afternoon. I want to know at lunch tomorrow.'

Doubts about TARGET, the official euro payments system

Triton Court stands like a huge wedding cake at the end of Finsbury Square. It must have been built at the height of the British Empire with its Victorian turrets and central tower. I pass archways quaintly inscribed Neptune House, Jupiter House, and then I find the address I'm looking for: Mercury House. As I walk through the entrance I can't imagine this place being wired to service the City's official payments link to Europe. Once inside there is no sign of the nineteenth century. It appears as if the filling was thoroughly removed and replaced by the same architect who designed Citibank House. Modern lines, brass, polished marble, large panes of glass. The guards at the security partition are chatting and pay no attention to me or to what might be inside my briefcase. The list of tenants beside the elevator assures me of fiberoptic connections. Asset managers, public relations firms, management consultants, a stock brokerage interface, a Canadian bank, an insurance company, a shipping company, a computer services company, and APACS (Association for Payment Clearing Services), the company that runs CHAPS-euro. Despite the nineteenth-century icing, this cake is on the grid.

Michael Lewis, who appears to be in his early forties, has worked on payments systems for much of his career. He recalls that when European Monetary Union began to look like a reality, central bankers and payments systems experts from all over Europe met in Basle. 'At lunch one day, we were puzzling over what to name the electronic network that would link the national payments systems of the new monetary union. Some of the names they were coming up with were horrendous, like the "European Electronic Payments System."' 'He looks disdainful, 'Now EEPS would really inspire confidence.'

He waits for me to finish laughing and continues. 'To push the absurd, I tossed out the name 'Trans-European Automated Real-time Gross-settlement Express Transfer-system'. I told them that since no-one would be able to remember all that, they would have to use the acronym TARGET.'

Amused, I ask, 'How did they respond? I mean, isn't sabotage the recurring nightmare of this group?'

'I admit, there *was* a moment of anxiety around the table, followed by nervous laughter. Of course, they joked about it in the hallways and the elevators. What astonished me was that by the end of the conference, of all the names offered up, TARGET was the one that stuck.' He lowers his voice to a whisper, 'Not all of my naming suggestions have shared TARGET's fate.'

'Tell me one that missed.'

'When the Bank of England was looking to name its electronic settlement facility, you know, our equivalent of your Fedwire – I suggested they call it Threadwire.'

'And how was this received by the gray gentlemen of Threadneedle Street?'

'The suggestion was greeted with the politest of chuckles… and never mentioned again.'

'Speaking of the Bank of England, I saw a curious statistic in their June 1999 edition of *Practical Issues Arising from the Euro*. It reported that during the first five months of operations, TARGET experienced more than a hundred official "stop-send" disruptions – or about one per business day – and that only 3 per cent of these had originated in CHAPS-euro.[5] Can you interpret this for me?'

Lewis's mood turns serious. 'The frequent "stop-sends" are just one indicator of some deeper payments system problems on the continent. Another is that on half of the mornings since TARGET has been in operation, one or more national central banks in the system has been unreachable. So if a payments system problem arises, there is no official information available to the participants on the exact nature of the problem.'

The worry departs from his face. 'Operational problems aside, the basis of TARGET is secure.' He explains how a bank must have enough in its account at the central bank to send a payment through TARGET. Unlike the private netting systems which have to wait for the end of a batch for final settlement, when a payment is made through TARGET it's final, so there's no chance of a system unwind if a bank that's made a lot of payments fails.

'So TARGET is set up like Fedwire, not CHIPS.'[6]

'Yes. TARGET is set up to be as safe as Fedwire.'

'So, why are you so concerned about TARGET?'

Lewis explains that for this kind of system to work well, the banks with settlement accounts must have a collective goal of keeping the traffic moving. When they receive funds into their settlement accounts, they should quickly release the funds if they have a backlog of payments to be made. 'Unfortunately,' he says, 'on the continent there is a different payments culture than here in Britain. Instead of quickly releasing funds received, some participants on the continent hoard liquidity by delaying payments.' He explains that the bunching of payments causes traffic jams, especially late in the day. 'Did you realize that under normal conditions it can take five to ten minutes to complete a cross-border payment through TARGET?'

'And under difficult conditions?' I ask.

Lewis looks chagrined. 'Using TARGET, a cross-border payment can take twenty minutes or more depending on the circumstances.' He adds that after half a year of operating, TARGET has no electronic time-stamping of payments to locate accurately where the traffic jams are and no information center to announce the reason for a delay. 'So it's hard for banks to manage their liquidity during the day. A bank may receive a message directly from another bank that funds have been sent, but it's unpredictable how long it will take for those funds to arrive so they can be used.'

'Isn't the European Central Bank working on these problems? Aren't they trying to introduce some discipline?' I ask.

'Yes. We have called these issues to their attention, but they have a huge structural problem.'

'What's the problem?'

'In TARGET, every bank, no matter what the size, can have a settlement account in the system, and there are some 5,000 such credit institutions. This makes it very difficult to see who is hoarding liquidity and who is not. And then there is the issue of how to enforce discipline on such a large diverse group.'

'How about CHAPS-euro?' I ask.

With thinly veiled pride, Lewis says, 'CHAPS-euro is much faster and more predictable. Where it may take TARGET five to twenty minutes between when a payment is sent and it is received, the typical cross-border payment through CHAPS-euro takes thirty seconds end-to-end.'

'I thought CHAPS-euro was just the London link to TARGET. All the statistics show CHAPS-euro payments volumes as the UK part of the TARGET totals. Am I missing something?' I ask.

Lewis smiles ironically. 'That's the outward impression given by the statistics. Maybe they lump us together because we work on the same, safe legal basis as TARGET. Or perhaps because we have a link that allows our participants access to all of the banks on the TARGET system. But not everyone knows that the bulk of CHAPS-euro payments bypass TARGET altogether.' He looks amused by my astonishment, and says quietly, 'We set it up that way.'

'Who are "we"?' I probe.

'The shareholders of CHAPS-euro.'

'And who are the shareholders?'

'There are nineteen now: eighteen private banks and the Bank of England. We are looking for this number to rise modestly over the next few years.'

'Are these big British banks?'

'Here's the list. It's public information.' He opens a slick brochure and passes it across the table.

I look at the list and comment, 'Of the eighteen I see only seven British banks and two Scottish. So only half the membership is from the UK.'

Lewis explains, 'In 1986, we opened up CHAPS-sterling to foreign participants. Citibank was the first, followed by some European-based banks and a large Japanese bank. We don't discriminate by nationality. Now Citibank is the chair of CHAPS. When Bank of America applied for membership last year, it was a doddle.'

I point out Deutsche Bank, the largest German bank, ABN-AMRO the largest Dutch bank, Bank of Tokyo–Mitsubishi, Den Norske Bank, and National Australia Bank. 'I know these are large banks with global reach, but how does CHAPS-euro handle such a volume of business with so few members?'

Lewis explains that the eighteen members constitute the first tier, the heart of the system. They settle with each other across euro accounts at the Bank of England. They are the *only* ones allowed to settle, so it is very easy to monitor the payment flows, to see where there are slowdowns, to communicate the reasons, and to manage the traffic. 'Also this small group has a culture that keeps the system moving. When they receive funds into their accounts, they quickly release payments. They realize "the sooner I release a payment to others, the quicker I will receive payments later in the day." So there is no bunching of payments at the end of the day.'

'What if there is a huge payment that exceeds a member bank's account at the Bank of England? Would that clog the system?' I ask.

'No. To lubricate the system, the Bank of England has a 3 billion euro account at the European Central Bank. This account finances intraday overdrafts by members of CHAPS-euro, who repay the Bank of England before the end of the day. While only eighteen banks participate in the final settlement facility, there is broad access to using CHAPS-euro.'

I ask him to explain how other banks pay through CHAPS-euro.

He says there is a large second tier of indirect members, numbering around four hundred, including most of the major banks in the world. They hold euro accounts in London with the eighteen direct settlement members. These indirect members have technological remote access to the direct members in London, so they do not have to have offices in London to send payments through CHAPS-euro. The system allows euro-payments to be made between accounts at some ten thousand branch offices in 120 countries around the world. 'This can be accomplished in a matter of seconds, without having to go through TARGET. And the number of branch destinations could double in a few years.'

'But I'm still curious. How can this happen so fast?'

'Our settlement process is at the heart of it, but also we use straight-through electronic processing.'

'And what if the destination is not to one of your participants. Let's say a payment is sent to some little savings bank in an Alpine village?'

'Then the payment would have to be routed through TARGET, which has practically every bank in the European Union on its grid. CHAPS-euro's link with TARGET more than triples the number of branches we can send payments to. That is one of the virtues of TARGET. However, the payment through TARGET will take longer to reach its destination, and it will cost more. Because of the efficiency of straight-through processing, CHAPS-euro charges participants very little for payments to other participants. In fact, the charge is the same as for a domestic CHAPS-sterling payment.'

'So, in addition to CHAPS-euro, what alternatives to TARGET are out there?'

He says some banks still use correspondent banking relationships to achieve payments across national boundaries, but these bilateral agreements should 'wither away over time because they cost more to use than CHAPS-euro and the five private sector systems now operating.'

'How do these five private alternatives compare to CHAPS-euro?'

He explains that similar to CHAPS-euro, the five private systems are fast. But unlike CHAPS-euro these other systems use some form of netting arrangement between the members. Then at the end of a payment cycle the members settle in central bank money for the net amounts owed.[7] 'At this time, the total value of cross-border payments processed by the private netting systems is larger than those processed by TARGET.'[8]

'With these private netting systems, what would happen if a big bank were to fail before a netting cycle was finally settled in central bank money?'

'That could lead to problems,' Lewis admits.

Walter is not here, so I ask his question. 'And I am curious: what do *you* think of not having a central authority that acts as lender of last resort in the event of a bank panic in Europe?'

Lewis looks undisturbed. 'I sleep better at night knowing that national central banks and their established regulatory bodies are in charge. They are known entities, quite capable of responding.'

I ask him, 'What policy-response scenario do you envision in the event that highly chaotic conditions were to appear in euro financial markets?'

Lewis responds, 'I cannot imagine such a problem would be so isolated.' He leans back confidently. 'The governors of the Group of Ten central banks have a long history of cooperating with each other, and they keep in touch. They would be in close contact with each other, especially Greenspan and Duisenberg. All of them could quickly get on a plane, meet in Basle, and arrive at a solution. Afterwards, they would tell everyone "this is what we've done," everyone would say "what a good job they've done," and that would be it.'

It is getting late, so I pop the question. 'While I'm here at Triton Court, might we be able to drop in and see the CHAPS-euro computer?'

'Which one?' Lewis asks.

'The one where all the euro transactions are cleared and settled?'

Lewis laughs. 'There isn't *one computer*.'

I look up toward Mars and hum.

Lewis responds, 'No really, I mean it, there is no single computer. I could show you the computer in this building, but it just monitors the flows. There is no intervention possible from this site. They could send a rocket through this window, blow up Triton Court, and it wouldn't faze the system.'

'How *is* the CHAPS-euro network set up, then?'

'Members have terminals in secure sites around the UK.'

'In garages?' I ask.

'Some might use that cover. Two have remote-access terminals outside the UK. All terminals have direct, secure connections with each other and with the Bank of England's terminal, through which payments are made. Each of the members, including the Bank of England, has a fall-back terminal, in a separate location, with parallel connections that continuously operate in the event that the primary terminal has a technical problem.'

'What about the four hundred participants?'

'All non-settling participants have secure terminals that feed instructions into their clearing member's computer, where the message is automatically forwarded into the primary terminal – if the payment passes the credit limits on the participant's account.'

I ask, 'What would happen if something took out the Bank of England's primary and backup computers?'

Michael Lewis answers calmly, 'The system would shift into "by-pass mode." A multilateral netting agreement between the eighteen would come into play so payments would continue undisturbed. On 20 June when demonstrators assaulted the Bank of England on Threadneedle Street, there was not the slightest chance it would disturb the CHAPS X-25 network.'

Reflections on the future of the world monetary system

In the London home of John Stevens, a political activist for monetary union, I pose the question: 'Someone I interviewed the other day predicted, "Within the next twelve months the big funds will test the euro." Do you believe this is a possibility?'

Stevens worked as a trader in the City for ten years before moving on to devote the next ten years of his life 'to bring about the monetary union of Europe.' For several of those years, Stevens served as a British representative to the European Parliament in Brussels. Now he's active in British politics to favor the UK's entry into the monetary union.

In his living room surrounded by portraits of ancestors, Stevens answers, 'Sure the new currency will be tested. I wouldn't be surprised if the euro were to drop to ninety cents or lower. The only problem this might present would be if finance ministers lost their nerve and pressured for a "strong euro." The Germans, in particular, haven't got their heads around this "strong currency" issue yet. They might be provoked to intervene if there is a loss of investor confidence. With the core European economy dead, I am concerned that tight money to defend the euro might lead to a sense of humor failure in Paris.'

'And how will monetary union affect economic performance in Europe?' I ask.

'I expect the European economy to underperform the United States for some time. Europe has great rigidities that need to be dealt with, and these are going to take some cultural adjustments that may take time. In the medium and long term, however, I am quite bullish on European growth; the upside is much greater than in the United States.' Stevens warns: 'But don't expect all of the adjustments you have available in America to appear in the single currency area of Europe. There has always been labor mobility in the United States. It's what your country was built on. But Europeans are quite happy to stay at home. That is not going to change. So if you're looking for labor mobility to become the adjustment for regional growth differences, forget it. That will *not* happen in Europe.'

'How will adjustment take place,' I ask, 'when there's one monetary policy for highly diverse regions?'

'Capital mobility will play a greater role than in the United States. Already we can see it happening in Europe. Euro-skeptics before monetary union said "what a bloody good idea this will be for France and Germany, but what about poor Portugal?" Now we're seeing the opposite. The periphery – Spain, Portugal, Finland and Ireland – is booming and core

Europe – Germany, France, and Italy – dead. And now the skeptics are saying, "how will Ireland cope with the inflationary pressures of low unemployment and a racing economy, when they cannot raise interest rates?" But perhaps we're observing the adjustment process, Ireland's low wage structure and more flexible economy gets pulled up while regions that resist restructuring lose capital to the more flexible regions.'

'And do you think it's possible for a central bank to rule over a confederacy?' I ask.

'Euro-skeptics use the US example to question this. My question is: Is it really necessary to have a large central government to run a monetary union? I mean, what has been happening in the US? Hasn't the federal government been cutting its obligations and shoving them onto the states? Has this undermined the role of the Federal Reserve?' He warns again, 'So, don't expect the experiment in Europe to copy in every way the American. In some areas there will be powerful parallels to America. For example, financial markets in Europe are quickly moving in the direction of those in the United States.'

I pose a scenario. 'Let's say the euro weathers the storms of international investor uncertainty over the next few years. Let's say the European Central Bank doesn't lose its nerve and gains some respectability. And let's say some of the structural rigidities in Europe are shaken up and the continent enters a period of sustained growth. Do you believe over time the euro will replace the dollar as the world's favorite currency?'

'Replace? No, not replace. But the architecture of the world financial system will be fundamentally different.'

'What will be its shape?' I ask.

'Instead of a single dominant currency at the center, the world I envision will be divided into currency blocs, the euro and the dollar. Even with all the doubts about the euro in its infancy, we're seeing blocs beginning to form. Estonia and Bulgaria have currency boards based on the euro, and some Latin American economies are moving that way with the dollar. Eastern Europe and other big trading partners are beginning to hold euro reserves. After the new system has been tested a few times and fine-tuned, when growth resumes, the euro will become a very attractive alternative to the dollar for international investors.' Stevens pauses. 'But the dollar will not be replaced, as you say, by the euro. Perhaps a third bloc in Asia will form around the yen, but I doubt it. I see two blocs at the center with some countries attached firmly to one bloc, while others will balance between the two. And, who knows, we may even see some negotiated exchange rate structure between the dollar and the euro, something like the Bretton Woods system.'

'And what will these mean for your friends still trading currency in the City?'

'With the first six months of the euro, we've already seen a dramatic reduction in foreign exchange turnover.' Stevens leans forward intently, 'when the new architecture is finally unveiled, the heyday of foreign exchange could be over.'

Wrap-up session with Walter Blass

Blass meets me at a garden cafeteria, where we get a table with an umbrella. 'What was the scoop on TARGET at CHAPS-euro?' he asks.

'As we suspected, there have been problems integrating the national payments systems, poor communications, and delays in TARGET, but the amazing thing is how the big banks have bypassed TARGET's sluggishness by setting up CHAPS-euro in London and five private netting schemes similar to CHIPS on the continent.'

'So, Professor, have you changed your mind on the euro?'

'Not on its long-run potential. I see it as practically inevitable that over time the euro will threaten the dollar's hegemony as a world currency.'

'Yah, yah. Long run, Long run. What is it Keynes said about the long run?' he chides.

'The quotation you're trying to whip me with is "In the long run we're all dead."' I put down my sandwich. 'But, I *will* concede some ground to you, Walter.'

'I'm all ears.'

'It has to do with timing. This visit to London has made me see it will take a lot longer than I first thought for the euro to become used and trusted internationally.'

'What changed your view on this?'

'A couple of things. When John Atkin told us how long it would take for companies inside Europe to become euro-compliant, I realized businesses hooked on cash won't convert their accounting and payments systems until the last minute. So it won't be until 2002 that companies inside Europe will be able to pressure international suppliers and customers to pay and receive payments in euro. Until then, companies will continue using their dollar accounts for international trade. So the commodity backing behind the euro – which is substantial, as Christopher Johnson explained – won't come into play until 2002.'

'And what else?'

'Before coming to London I didn't realize how deep-seated the doubts were in the financial community about the new central bank. Marjorie

Deane and William Clarke were so clear on the political-structural reasons behind the doubts. These doubts will delay the build up of euro positions in financial portfolios despite the capital market revolution we see in full swing.'

'So, it took bringing you to London to see this?'

'I believe so. If you think about it, Walter, London is the rest of the world's outpost for watching what's up on the Continent. The specialists hired by the major financial houses to watchdog Europe are clustered here in London. We've seen they have differences of opinion, but the intelligence-gathering process is tarnished by the debate raging over sterling. You have to admit, the British pundits are scrutinizing every fine detail of the monetary experiment underway on the other side of the channel.'

'Yes, and for good reason,' Blass says.

'Even if not for good reason, I'm convinced the "big funds" as William Clarke says, will "test" every move the European Central Bank makes. Duisenberg and his successor will be compared unfavorably with Greenspan. How will he face up to political pressures? Will he try to manipulate the exchange rate? Will he be able to calm a financial crisis? Walter, without a track record, the new central bank is going to face greater financial mood swings than those faced by the Fed. And the doubts are not just from the financial community. Two days ago I heard more about central bankers' doubts.'

'What were the findings from that central bankers' survey?'

'Weller at Central Banking Publications said that the most frequently checked off categories were 'lack of a track record on money policy' and 'lack of unified capital markets.'[9] Reserve managers expressed doubts about how the European Central Bank would be able to coordinate money policy. Some of the concerns I discussed with Courtis and Weller had to do with the unwieldy make-up of the Governing Council[10] and poor staffing at the ECB.'

'What are some of the details you learned?'

'The European Central Bank is reported to have 620 employees while national central banks have more than 50,000 employees. And there's an unconfirmed rumor going around that the ECB has more lawyers and translators on its staff than it has economists. So when the Governing Council meets, the eleven national bank governors are said to come better prepared to money policy meetings than the six members of the Executive Board.'

Blass asks, 'And what did they say about bank supervision?'

'Just as bad. For a while, there were rumored to be only two people at the ECB level involved in prudential supervision of banks. Some central bankers outside of Europe are wondering whether the Executive Board in Frankfurt will be hobbled when it tries to coordinate policy actions between the eleven national central banks. Additionally, Weller said that 90 per cent of the respondents believe the euro will not develop into a full-fledged international currency for a number of years.'[11]

'So,' Blass chalks up his points, 'the euro will be avoided as a currency for international trade and international portfolio management, and there goes your euro as a reserve currency for central bankers! Well, now I can leave. I've won the debate.' Walter takes a bite of chocolate cake.

'Don't finish your dessert so quickly. Let's think historical time here – rise and decline of world currencies instead of fund managers' time. On the longer time horizon, you're going to lose the debate.'

'Are you talking centuries here, Professor?'

'Maybe decades, considering the doubts we've encountered. I think John Stevens, whom I met with this morning, is on the right track. He believes that over time there will emerge two competing currency blocs, the dollar and the euro. But I cannot imagine his idea of a fixed exchange rate between the two blocs happening any time soon – that is, without some gigantic crisis. I envision a long period of instability as the dollar's turf is systematically eroded.'

'So are you busy buying euro, Professor?' Blass smirks.

'That's a personal question, Walter, but I am thinking it might be smart to wait for the "testing episodes" William Clarke was referring to and get some.'

'I wish you good fortune on this risky venture.'

APPENDIX / Euro developments after the 1999 London interviews

William Clarke's prediction about euro-testing and John Atkin's view that the euro would remain 'friendless' proved correct as doubts about the new central bank expressed in the July 1999 interviews surfaced for a period lasting approximately three years. As Figure 14.1, charting the euro price in dollars, shows, the euro was pushed below the psychologically important $1 level in January 2000 and suffered repeated bouts of weakness thereafter, breaking through the 90 cents level in May 2000. Each 'testing' period carried with it market stories casting doubts on the mettle of the new central bank.

The most spectacular episode came in September and October 2000, when the European Central Bank first tried its hand intervening on currency markets to prop up the euro. The intervention was widely perceived

14.1 / Daily exchange rates, US$/euro

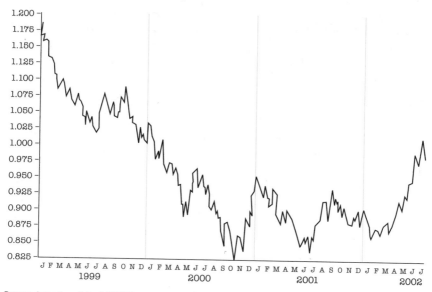

Source: based on data © 2002 by Prof. Werner Antweiler, University of British Columbia, Vancouver.
Time period: 1 January 1999–2 August 2002.

by financial analysts as the work of amateurs. The actors broke so many rules of conduct that the episode may go down in history as a landmark case of how not to conduct an intervention.

Rule no. 1   Don't go it alone. On 22 September the ECB was able to coax the central banks of the US, Japan, and Britain to join the ECB in buying euros. This was in anticipation of the Danish referendum on 28 September 2000, when 53.1 per cent of the Danish electorate rejected a bid to merge the krone with the euro.[12] The intervention worked for about a week, but press leaks gave the impression of lackluster support from the US. The big funds questioned the resolve of the intervention after Treasury Secretary Lawrence Summers was quoted reaffirming his belief in the benefits of a strong dollar and admitting reluctance in going along with the intervention. The financial press interpretation was that the Americans went along because the Europeans had begged for help.

Rule no. 2   Be ready to intervene repeatedly and in large amounts. Only $3 to $5 billion was spent by the four central banks during the first week, enough to send the euro up briefly to 90 cents. When market participants tested resolve in early October, it appeared that no other central bank was in the market supporting the euro.

Rule no. 3 Show resolve, speak with actions, and keep your mouth shut. The day of the announcement of the intervention the head of the ECB, Wim Duisenberg, released a statement saying European monetary policy had not changed, giving the impression that interest rates would not be used as a tool to support the euro. Then on 16 October 2000, Duisenberg granted a newspaper interview, during which a reporter questioned whether central banks would be prone to intervene in currency markets if unrest in the Middle East unsettled the markets. Duisenberg was quoted, 'I wouldn't think so.' Within an hour the euro dropped below 85 cents. Then central bank governors of Germany and Belgium made public remarks critical of Duisenberg's statement, giving the impression of an extremely weak central bank president and a divided Governing Council, a confirmation of the structural vulnerability that Marjorie Deane and William Clarke pointed out in July 1999. Stories circulated about Duisenberg's resignation, a scandal involving the governor of the Bank of France, and the unwieldy structure of the seventeen-member Governing Council. The euro was pushed to a closing low of 82 cents on 26 October 2000, about 5 cents below the month before when the intervention began and 30 per cent below its value at launch in January 1999. The financial press in London had a field day.[13]

After this harsh lesson from financial markets, the European Central Bank refrained from interventions to prop up the euro and concentrated efforts on scheduled tasks, some of which were formidable. On 1 January 2001, Greece entered the union with the big plunge conversion of financial market transactions to euro, bringing the total number of countries in the euro to twelve. This gave Greece only one year of transition to educate the public, implement the conversion of retail bank accounts to the euro, and prepare for distributing euro notes and coins. John Atkin was correct that businesses and private citizens would wait until late in the transition period to convert their bank accounts and invoicing systems to euro. The mass conversion of account money did not begin in earnest until July 2001. Belgium and France, at one extreme, converted gradually over the last six months of the transition period, while Ireland and Austria postponed the conversion until the last minute, midnight on 31 December 2001, when all bank accounts were successfully switched into the euro at once.[14] On 1 January 2002 euro notes and coins were introduced, and legacy currencies began to be withdrawn from circulation. During the three-year transition period some 50 billion coins were minted and 14.5 billion notes were printed. A portion of this was front-loaded to

ATM machines, banks, and post offices leading up to New Year's Day, when distribution to the public began. Distributing the new currency and withdrawing the old was an enormous job for authorities, banks, businesses, and the general public, and it was carried out with fewer hitches than expected. On 28 February 2002 legacy currencies ceased to be legal tender, though national central banks continued to exchange outstanding legacy notes and coins.[15]

The financial market revolution that we witnessed in its early stages in 1999 continued to sweep through the Eurozone. Euro-denominated international bond issues continued to rival US dollar issues both in total volume of issues and in size of issue, and US investment banks, operating primarily out of London, continued to be the leading underwriters of new euro-denominated bond issues.[16] Corporate borrowing through the bond market continued its feverish pace, and, just as Graham Bishop predicted in 1999, companies with lower credit ratings were increasingly able to borrow in the bond market instead of having to rely on traditional bank loans.[17] The progress toward financial market integration was highly uneven. Wholesale money markets and government bond markets were already well integrated by July 1999, but, with thirty-two stock exchanges, eleven different legal and regulatory frameworks, and fragmented clearing and settlement systems, the equity and corporate bond markets were more difficult to harmonize and integrate. In March 2000, the Paris, Brussels, and Amsterdam stock exchanges merged to form Euronext, which adopted the Paris Bourse trading engine as a common platform. In the summer of 2000, the European Commission set up a committee to investigate the best ways to speed the Eurozone toward a single capital market, and the following year a Financial Services Action Plan was put in place. By early 2002, an electronic exchange called Virt-X, formed by the merger of the Swiss stock exchange and a London-based electronic exchange (Tradepoint), was listing UK and European blue-chip stocks, but despite these efforts and those by Europe's largest exchanges to list stocks from other exchanges, cross-border trading was inhibited by the fragmented regulatory and clearing and settlement services, a problem that also inhibited cross-border trading in corporate bonds.[18]

The late shifting of corporate payments systems within the Eurozone delayed pressure for companies outside of Europe to begin invoicing in euro or to set up euro accounts for international trade purposes, and it took some time after euro notes were introduced for Eastern Europeans to begin using them as a substitute for dollar bills. Furthermore, central banks continued to be reluctant to shift reserve holdings into euro. By the April 2001 foreign exchange survey, the euro's importance in global currency markets was approximately the same as that of the German mark during the 1990s.[19] Doubts about the new central bank and Eurozone economic performance kept the euro trading at around 90 cents during 2001 and early 2002, when financial market players began shifting their doubts toward the dollar.

Testing the dollar's hegemony: will the adjustment be smooth?

Dollar strengthening that began in the summer of 1995 lasted until the spring of 2002, when doubts about the dollar began haunting currency markets. In successive episodes, speculative runs on the dollar pushed the euro, the world's second most important currency, through key thresholds, first through the $1 mark in July 2002, then through $1.10 in March and $1.15 in May 2003, through $1.20 in December 2003, and in the latest episode to date through the $1.30 mark following the November 2004 elections. Following each period of turbulence, the dollar recovered some from the damages, and currently as I write (July 2005), the euro is trading at around $1.20, or about 30 per cent higher in dollar terms than in early 2002 when the period of dollar weakening began. What is behind the dollar doubts? Are the storms over, or should we be prepared for more? Will the structural imbalances that triggered bouts of dollar weakness be smoothly reduced, or will they continue to build up toward a greater storm? What are some possible adjustment scenarios, and what will be the political and economic ramifications for people living in the United States?

How long will foreigners finance US overspending?

All four episodes of dollar doubting between 2002 and 2005 were associated with market stories questioning foreigners' willingness to continue

15.1 / Speculative moves against the dollar push the euro through key
resistance levels, 2002–05 (daily exchange rates, US$ per €)

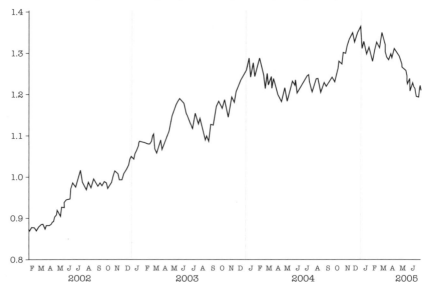

Source: based on data © 2005 by Prof. Werner Antweiler, University of British Columbia,
Vancouver.

financing US overspending. During the preceding period of dollar strength,
1995–2002, little attention was paid to this issue. To understand why this
story became important all of a sudden, how it evolved and escalated into
speculative storms in 2003 and 2004, and what the implications are for
the global financial system in the future, it's necessary first to understand
how national overspending is measured and how US overspending has
been financed.

The best measure of whether a nation is overspending or saving with
respect to the rest of the world is the 'current account balance,' which
takes all the nation's current income and earnings from abroad in a given
year and subtracts all its current expenditures.[1] When income exceeds
expenditure, the nation will run a 'current account surplus,' which represents national saving that year in relation to the rest of the world, a
move towards improvement in that country's net wealth position with
respect to foreigners. When spending exceeds income, the 'current account
deficit' calculates the amount of dissaving or overspending relative to the
rest of the world, a move that reduces that country's net wealth position
with respect to foreigners. For the three decades following World War II,
the US ran current account surpluses for most years, building up a huge

stash of net claims on foreigners. Since then, overspending by the US has whittled away at the stockpile, and some time in the mid-1980s the US net wealth position went from being positive to negative, meaning foreigners had more claims on the US than the US had on foreigners. This was no particular cause for alarm, because the US credit-rating was excellent. The US was the world's greatest military power, which gave confidence in its ability to protect assets over the long haul, and the US currency was world money, meaning that payments to foreigners could be made by printing more dollars and foreigners would hold them without cashing them in.[2] Furthermore, US financial markets were by far the deepest and most liquid in the world, meaning foreigners could store their accumulated savings in a broad array of US assets and those assets could be exchanged quickly for money and moved at any time, allaying fears of being stuck in a dangerous position at any point in the uncertain future. So long as foreigners remained confident that the US was the best place to store their savings, the US could continue overspending and running current account deficits.

The longest expansion in US history from March 1991 through March 2001 was extended in its last three years by a massive influx of foreign savings that was invested in US corporate bonds, stocks, and government-sponsored agency securities.[3] Without foreign savings, US interest rates would have risen much sooner, stock prices would have fallen sooner, and the technology-driven investment boom would have been held in check. With foreign savings channeled as they were, US securities prices were bid up so investment banks had an easy time floating new corporate stock and bond issues, supporting – among other things – real investment in new technology. Similarly, with foreign buyers in the market, government sponsored agencies like Fannie-Mae found it easier to float mortgage-backed securities, supporting the US housing market and consumer spending. Also helpful in extending the investment boom was that the US government was not crowding out private-sector borrowers by issuing Treasury bonds; 1998 through 2001 the federal government ran significant fiscal surpluses, which allowed the US Treasury to buy back its own debt, allowing more room for private-sector borrowers and government-sponsored agencies to sell securities to investors. Foreign investors enabled American corporations and consumers to spend way beyond their means, and the US current account deficit, which hovered around $100 billion a year in the mid-1990s, zoomed over $200 billion in 1998, $300 billion in 1999, and $400 billion a year in 2000 and 2001. Normally such an excess supply of dollars generated by US overspending would depress the dollar on global currency markets, but foreigners'

15.2 / Balance on current account (US$ billion)

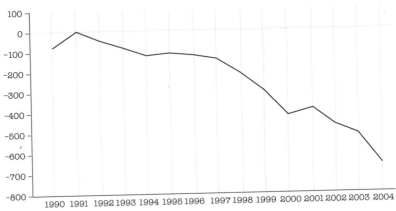

Source: Bureau of Economic Analysis, *U.S. International Transactions Accounts Data*, 17 June 2005.

aggressive buying of US securities overcompensated. Currency strategists who bet that current-account deficits would weaken the dollar lost money between 1995 and 2001, so the current-account story lost credence in the action/reaction process of the currency markets.

Doubts first surfaced in March 2002, regarding foreigners' willingness to continue to finance US overspending. With each successive bout of dollar weakness, market stories focused on the precise sources of US overspending at the time and analyzed the structural imbalances and political choices that appeared to be fueling it, and market analysts began comparing US overspending with foreigners' appetite for US securities. Extreme bouts of turbulence came to be connected with stories that some large holders of US-denominated assets were beginning to dump them and switch to assets denominated in euros or some other currency. During the late 1990s' boom, currency market participants hardly paid attention when US current account statistics were released. At the time of writing everyone in the foreign exchange market prepares for US current account and trade balance data, they anxiously await the Treasury department's releases on foreign purchases of US securities, and they have their terminals tuned into the websites of the Asian central banks for any news of a change in holdings of dollar-denominated securities. As an economic adviser to a large currency dealer put it following a sudden drop in the dollar, 'The fall in the dollar is a purely psychological phenomenon based on traders paying attention to the current-account deficit for the first time in years.'[4] How did this story evolve to become so important in the action/reaction process of world currency markets?

Dollar testing episodes and the evolution of market stories

Episode 1: spring and summer 2002 From March to late June 2002, the dollar lost 15 per cent of its value against the euro, and on 15 July 2002 the euro burst through the $1 resistance threshold for the first time in two and a half years. Financial news that spring was dominated by investigations of schemes that had misled investors during the stock market craze of the late 1990s. Connected with a record number of securities fraud cases and bankruptcy proceedings, investigations revealed that as regulators had napped, executives from some of the most reputable Wall Street accounting firms, investment banks, and brokerage houses were colluding in various ways with Main Street corporations to help them raise cash through the issuance of securities. Charges and some convictions involved executives from major success stories of the previous investment boom, including energy-trading giant Enron and technology firms Qwest, Tyco, WorldCom, Adelphia, and Global Crossing. Each release of evidence on corporate foul play weighed down on stock prices, and news that foreign investors had lost their appetite for US securities weighed heavily on the dollar. On 26 June, when the WorldCom accounting fraud[5] was reported, the dollar lost 1.5 per cent of its value against the euro, 1.4 per cent of its value against sterling and 2 per cent of its value against the yen. That day the euro hit an intraday high of 99.45 US cents, just short of the psychologically significant $1 mark.[6]

On 15 July 2002, when the euro finally broke through the $1 mark, a currency market story with a fresh angle was introduced. Instead of corporate fraud cases diminishing foreigners' appetite for US corporate securities, the financial news story that morning reported that Asian central banks, which together held more than $1 trillion in foreign exchange reserves, might begin switching them into euros. Although the first line seemed like alarmist reading, 'Foreign central banks may well have access to the trigger that could spark a much more swift slide in the dollar,' the text of the report was not, arguing that analysts believed 'any shift by those central banks would be extremely gradual and only carried out in a manner that wouldn't spark a run on the dollar.' Nevertheless, the story pointed out that the prospect of those central banks beginning to shift into euros 'gains more likelihood as the common European currency approaches the elusive bar of parity with the dollar.'[7] That afternoon, the elusive bar was breached. Although the currency order flows that pushed the euro over the $1 mark that day may have been caused by numerous factors other than the number of currency traders who may have reacted to the morning news, the coincidence of the dollar dropping through a key threshold on the day the story was printed gave credence to the story line, and more currency strategists began following the actions of Asian central banks.

Episode 2: the buildup to war   Over the next few years attention turned away from corporate excess spending to overspending by the US government. Corporations that had overextended themselves in the 1990s' investment boom became extremely cautious after the crash. Even when profits surged during the second half of 2003, US corporations hoarded their bulging cash flow instead of repeating the mistake of the 1990s. US corporations withdrew from the borrowing trough and became net savers, a position maintained into 2005. Choices by the federal government went the other way. The Bush tax cuts of 2001 combined with loose spending bills turned fiscal surpluses into deficits beginning in June 2001, so that by July 2002 federal spending exceeded revenues by more than $150 billion on an annualized basis. During the fall of 2002, the Bush administration's drive for war in Iraq was meeting resistance from European allies, and by January 2003 currency analysts negatively compared the likely effects of this war with the Persian Gulf War of 1991, when allies paid the United States government $50 billion for ousting Saddam Hussein's troops from Kuwait.[8] Currency market analysts noted that income from foreigners in 1991 had pushed the US current account into surplus for the first time in ten years, a situation that quickly reverted to current account deficits after the payments ceased. Without allied support, the story read, the 'lion's share of the bill' for George W. Bush's war in Iraq would mostly likely be footed by the US government, which would soon be spewing dollars into the Middle East and increasing the already swollen US current account deficit. The analysts argued that instead of sparking a dollar rally, as occurred in 1991, a war this time around would depress the dollar. From December 2002 through February 2003, news that raised the likelihood of an invasion weighed on the dollar, while news that lowered the prospects of war supported dollar strengthening.

In early March 2003, a fresh character was added to the script when newly appointed Treasury Secretary John Snow made his debut on global currency markets. Ever since December 2002 when Treasury Secretary Paul O'Neill was replaced by Snow and White House economic adviser Lawrence Lindsey, a vocal advocate of a strong dollar policy, resigned after he estimated the costs of an Iraq War at $200 billion, reporters had been questioning if the new economic team represented a shift on the official policy of a 'strong' dollar. Reporters got their chance late on Tuesday 4 March, when Treasury Secretary Snow talked with them following testimony before the House Ways and Means Committee. According to the report, Mr Snow's 'off-the-cuff remarks... sparked a wave of [dollar] selling that pushed the Swiss franc – and briefly the euro – to fresh four-year highs... Earlier in the global session [on 5 March 2003, the next day] the euro shot up on Mr Snow's comments, briefly flirting with the $1.10 level, an area not seen in four years.'

All the treasury secretary was reported to have said was 'that the dollar [was] trading within a normal range and that he did not "see anything troubling" about recent declines against major currencies.' But, the reporter explained, 'traders viewed the remarks as tacit approval for a softer dollar, a marked departure from the strong dollar policy in place since Robert Rubin was Treasury chief during the Clinton administration.' The following day at a signing ceremony for new paper money, Snow softened his previous day's remarks by saying, 'Let me reiterate my support for the strong dollar,'[9] but his previous day's remarks, which were followed by a sudden shift in currency values, would be the words that would be remembered, worked over and analyzed for months. Perhaps reassured that the US Treasury would not intervene to slow the dollar's slide, on Friday 7 March 2003, when Secretary of State Colin Powell took the Bush administration's case for war to the United Nations, the euro finally broke through the $1.10 mark.

Mr Snow's debut tainted his credibility in the currency markets for the coming years. From an economic textbook perspective, however, the treasury secretary's analysis made good sense: an orderly depreciation of the dollar should enhance the international competitiveness of US industry, improve the US trade balance, speed up the US economy, and slow down the loss of jobs due to import competition. After Mr Snow's debut in March, analysts connected his position on the dollar with his 'real economy' credentials as the previous chief executive officer of a large railroad company, and they linked him with fellow Main Street 'real economy' executives who had suffered from a strong dollar. John Snow was frequently contrasted with President Clinton's treasury secretary, Robert Rubin, whose political constituency had been composed of Wall Street 'financial economy' executives.[10] Rubin had earned respect from financial market participants having masterminded the Clinton administration's fiscal conservatism that produced federal budget surpluses, and having helped calm financial markets during major chaotic episodes like the Mexican peso crisis in 1994–95.

Currency analysts quickly pointed out financial market repercussions that might make Mr Snow's 'real economy' textbook scenario backfire. One report explained:

Currency markets 'are notoriously hard to predict – and control. One danger in Mr Snow's strategy is that a sell-off could drive the dollar down more than Mr Snow might want. In that scenario, the foreign capital flows that have propped up the US economy over the past decade could slow, since the dollar-denominated value of portfolios held by foreign investors would fall. The loss of such capital could force up US interest rates, undercut the US stock market and crimp the nascent recovery.[11]

A *Wall Street Journal* editorial was more caustic. Pointing to the high concentration of foreign ownership of US bonds and stocks, the editorial said that foreign investors'

confidence in those U.S. dollar assets isn't helped if they think the Treasury Secretary is trashing the value of what they own in order to squeeze out more export growth. The last Treasury chief who tried this was Michael Blumenthal in the unlamented Carter Presidency, and his trash-talking turned into a dollar rout. The markets yesterday gave Mr Snow a little taste of what can happen…. Someone in the White House should tell Mr Snow he is playing with fire.[12]

Episode 3: fall of 2003   In early September 2003, Treasury Secretary Snow visited China to negotiate, among other things, a more flexible Chinese exchange rate policy. While the euro had risen dramatically against the dollar, giving US manufacturers some relief, the Chinese yuan was pegged to the dollar at a low rate that US manufacturers complained subsidized Chinese exports to the US. Other Asian central banks had been intervening to hold their currencies in line with the Chinese yuan, lest their export markets be taken by the Chinese. Similarly, for several years Japanese authorities had intervened in currency markets to slow the yen's rise against the dollar, thereby supporting Japanese exports in US markets. In a meeting of the Group of Seven (G7) industrialized country financial authorities in late September 2003, Snow helped craft a joint statement that read: 'We emphasize that more flexibility in exchange rates is desirable for major countries or economic areas to promote smooth and widespread adjustments in the international financial system, based on market mechanisms.' Mr Snow said publicly that the 'the G7 wasn't singling out any nation,' but members of Snow's staff told reporters in private that 'it was obvious that China and Japan were the main targets.' On Monday 22 September, the *Wall Street Journal* reporter who covered the G7 conference in Dubai underscored the political motivations behind the end-of-weekend communiqué.

The seemingly innocuous statement, backed by US Treasury Secretary John Snow, is loaded with meaning at a time when many American workers, manufacturing executives and presidential hopefuls are making an election-season political issue out of the unwillingness of China and Japan to let their currencies float freely against the dollar.[13]

The paradox of the statement was not lost on global financial markets. During Asian and European trading on Monday 22 September 2003, there was a steep sell-off of US Treasury securities that reporters attributed to the G7 statement, and the dollar fell to 112.13 yen from 114.30 on Friday, its sharpest one-day percentage decline in more than eighteen months, while the euro rose to its highest finish against the dollar in eight weeks. The market story explained the connection between the G7 statement and the sell off of US Treasury securities.

> Asian central banks, notably the Bank of Japan and the People's Bank of China, have managed the valuations of their nations' currencies through covert market interventions... Bank of Japan interventions have involved buying dollars against yen, and many of the dollars accumulated through such purchases have been channeled into the US Treasurys market. Investors now fear that if the central banks were to refrain from buying dollars to keep their currencies weak, they would need to purchase fewer US Treasurys.

By encouraging China and Japan to let their currencies rise against the dollar to help out US manufacturing interests, Treasury Secretary Snow was unwittingly advising the Chinese and Japanese to stop buying US Treasury securities. As one bond trader in New York put it, "The implications are really not good" for Treasuries. "There will probably be less intervention money coming into the U.S. market." And with ballooning federal budget deficits assuring a swell in issuance of Treasuries, "there will probably be an upward bias in interest rates."[14] A *Wall Street Journal* editorial that day put it less diplomatically:

> It's always possible that things aren't yet this bad, and that we are merely witnessing the hard currency education of one more rookie Treasury secretary. Mr. [John Snow] ran a railroad in private life and perhaps he wasn't paying attention to the global currency crises of the past 70 or so years.[15]

After the steep sell-off of Treasuries following the Dubai conference, currency strategists began to watch US Treasury auctions closely for any hints that foreign central banks were reducing their purchases, and they compared trade and current account deficit numbers with statistical releases relating to foreign purchases of US securities. In November

2003, the day after the dollar hit a new low against the euro, the financial press explained the drop as currency market reactions to the release of Treasury Department statistics showing a slowdown in net inflows from foreign purchases of securities to their lowest level since October 1998. A study from one of the largest currency dealers was quoted as concluding that 'because the Bank of Japan is believed to invest the bulk of its proceeds from currency interventions in U.S. government securities, the drop in net purchases of treasurys to $5.6 billion "raises concern that some central banks are net sellers of bonds".'[16] Two weeks later, on 2 December 2003, the euro shot through the $1.20 mark for the first time since it was launched.

Episode 4: 2004 presidential election and its aftermath Fears that foreigners would stop financing the US current account and fiscal deficits sparked another run on the dollar during the election campaign in the fall of 2004. Trade balance and current account numbers dramatically worsened despite the dollar's two-year slide, and the 2004 current account numbers were headed for a deficit approaching $700 billion, up from $500 billion in 2003. In September, estimates of the current account deficit were running at 5 per cent of US gross domestic product, and fiscal deficits were approaching 4 per cent of GDP, clearly unsustainable imbalances, but the Bush campaign was promising to make the 2001 and 2003 tax cuts permanent and to eliminate the estate tax altogether. President Bush's address to the Republican convention in late August promised a grab bag of new spending initiatives from job training to children's health to college aid, and the Kerry campaign was doing the same. All of this came on top of an expensive prescription drug benefit that was tacked on to Medicare. In George W. Bush's first term, every spending bill Congress sent to him the president signed.

Paradoxically, the fears that foreigners would stop buying US securities did not pan out. Not only were foreigners buying up US Treasury securities in record amounts, but they continued supporting the US housing market by buying up mortgage-backed securities issued by government-sponsored agencies. From June when the Fed started tightening and election day, ten-year Treasury yields fell by half a percentage point, reinforcing the fiscal euphoria gripping Washington, and conventional mortgage rates fell from 6.3 per cent to 5.75 per cent, making home buyers and the housing industry happy.

From the time of the Republican Convention in late August to election eve, currency market stories were dominated by the prospects of ever-increasing federal and US current account deficits, and the euro rose

15.3 / Net foreign purchases of US securities (US$ billion)

Source: US Treasury Department, *Transactions with Foreigners in Long-term Domestic and Foreign Securities, by Type and Country*, July 2005.

from $1.20 to $1.27.[17] After the election, the dollar slid further. As one reporter put it, 'the catalyst for its [the dollar's] most recent decline was President George W. Bush's re-election last Tuesday. Investors perceive his policies as likely to aggravate the steep U.S. budget deficit.'[18]

Before Thanksgiving 2004, the news turned to Treasury Secretary Snow's visit to Europe. European finance ministers meeting in Brussels 'stepped up calls on the U.S. to bolster the dollar by curbing the country's budget and trade deficits.' Snow responded by pointing 'to Europe's responsibility for its own problems. "The euro zone is growing below its potential," Mr Snow told British Broadcasting Corp. "When a major part of the global economy is below potential, there are negative consequences for their trading partners." He said inflexibility in the German labor market and the French pension system, not exchange rates, are Europe's main barriers to economic growth.'[19] Following further comments by Snow on

17 November 2004, the euro burst through the $1.30 mark for the first time in its five-year history.[20]

Alan Greenspan was sent in two days later to mop up. At a European banking conference in Frankfurt, Greenspan spoke to what was most on their minds, the disturbing loss of confidence in the dollar. Greenspan directly engaged the problem of US current account deficit, noting that it had risen to more than 5 per cent of GDP.

> The question now confronting us is how large a current account deficit in the United States can be financed before resistance to acquiring new claims against U.S. residents leads to adjustment. Even considering heavy purchases by central banks of US Treasury and agency issues, we see only limited indications that the large U.S. current account deficit is meeting financing resistance. Yet, net claims against residents of the United States cannot continue to increase forever in international portfolios at their recent pace... Reducing the federal budget deficit (or preferably moving it to surplus) appears to be the most effective action that could be taken to augment domestic saving.

He admitted that such efforts might fall short, but he underscored the 'flexibility of the American economy,' evidenced in its recent responses to 'the bursting of the technology bubble, the terrorist attack of September 2001, and the corporate governance scandals.' Greenspan reiterated his faith that 'market forces should over time restore, without crises, a sustainable U.S. balance of payments.' 'At least,' he added, referring to a recent study by a Federal Reserve economist, 'this is the experience of developed countries, which since 1980, have managed and eliminated large current account deficits, some in double digits, without major disruption.'[21]

The dollar's slide continued and pressures mounted for the Bush administration to do something. A bond market scare on November 29th reinforced the 'jitters that foreign investors might cut back on their purchases of U.S. government securities.'[22] Rumors began circulating around Washington that Treasury Secretary Snow would be fired.[23] On 6 December European finance ministers made a joint declaration saying that recent currency moves were 'unwelcome and not conducive to orderly adjustments of external imbalances,' and on 15 December the European Central Bank, in its 'Financial Stability Review,' called the US current account deficit one of the biggest risks to the global economy, and the challenge of financing it raised 'the possibility of severe downward pressure on the U.S. dollar.' The ECB pinpointed the 'progressive easing of US fiscal policy after 2000' as the primary reason behind the 'ballooning of the US current account deficit,' and it said that the 'fiscal deficit is unlikely to contract significantly in the foreseeable future.'[24] President Bush was quoted as saying, 'People can buy more United States products if they're worried about the trade deficit,' but on 16 December Mr Bush appeared to be feeling the pressure from the currency markets when he told the Italian prime minister that he would try to bring about 'the conditions such that a strong dollar will emerge' by doing 'everything we can in the upcoming legislative session to send a signal to the markets that we'll deal with our deficits, which hopefully will cause people to want to buy dollars.'[25] President Bush later announced budget cuts for the first time, calling his fiscal 2005 budget 'a tough budget, no question about it, and it's a budget that I think will send the right signal to the financial markets and those concerned about our short-term deficits.'

The budget cut announcements did not seem to convince currency market participants. On 30 December 2004 the euro hit $1.36 and traded over $1.30 for most of the first three months of 2005. Dollar sentiment was not helped by President Bush's emergency supplemental defense spending request of $80 billion, or by a survey released in late January showing that central bank 'diversification from dollar-denominated to euro-denominated assets appears to be taking place more rapidly than had been anticipated' from the previous survey taken in 2002.[26]

Trading during the first few months of 2005 remained orderly relative to the hectic days following the election in the fall, except on 21 February 2005, when the 'dollar registered its worst daily decline in two months, 1.4% against both the euro and the yen, handing the Dow Jones Industrial Average its biggest point loss in two years.' The catalyst cited was 'media coverage of plans by South Korea's central bank to diversify its foreign-exchange reserves.' The report explained that '"diversification" has become a buzz word that the currency and stock traders tend to read as "dumping dollars" – meaning that the Korean central bank would slow its purchases of dollar-denominated securities in favor of higher-yielding assets and other currencies, including the euro. The news from Seoul sparked fears that other Asian central banks could follow suit.' As it turned out, the 'news' was a misinterpretation of a single paragraph in a document sent by the Bank of Korea to the government. Upon closer scrutiny, analysts saw that the paragraph contained the same language Bank of Korea officials had been using for more than a year. Early the following day, Japanese and South Korean monetary officials publicly denied having any plans to change the dollar portion of their reserves, and the dollar recovered on the news.[27]

Relief for the dollar: spring and summer 2005

After returning from Europe, Treasury Secretary Snow wisely avoided making public statements about the dollar. In January 2005, Treasury officials became proactive in a less conspicuous way by asking the Bond Market Association's treasury advisory committee to address the question of 'whether the high percentage of foreign ownership of Treasuries outstanding creates risks for future Treasury financing.' On 1 February 2005 the committee reported back to the US Treasury that 'if foreign buying stopped or went into reverse, domestic ownership could be increased sharply and quickly given US market liquidity, [so] foreign ownership does not present a risk to Treasury funding.' It concluded that because 'central banks are conservative by nature,' a 'decline in the role of the dollar, were it to occur, would likely be gradual... and thus does not present a risk of a sharp or destabilizing financial market event.'[28] This reassuring message was delivered to the Treasury and posted without ceremony on the Bond Market Association's website.

In May 2005, Mr Snow appointed a special envoy to China, who skillfully and quietly negotiated a switch in the Chinese exchange rate regime. In June, Snow and Alan Greenspan personally visited Capitol Hill to talk with protectionist senators who in April had sponsored an amendment to a spending bill that would have imposed stiff duties on all Chinese imports if Beijing didn't agree to revalue its currency. According to press reports, after the meeting with Greenspan and Snow, the senators announced they would delay a vote on the amendment. This allowed the Chinese authorities political room to change the exchange rate regime without appearing to have been pressured by Washington. In late July, the Chinese moved to a managed float of the yuan, which was tied to a market basket of currencies instead of being fixed to the dollar. The initial move resulted in a modest 2.2 per cent appreciation of the yuan against the dollar.[29]

By late spring 2005, earlier worries about the dollar had cooled off and negative attention turned to the euro, especially after referendums in France and Denmark rejected a proposed European Union constitution. Before the votes, the dollar had already strengthened from reports of strong foreign buying of US securities, stronger real economic growth in the US, and higher short-term interest rates in the US than in Europe, but after the negative votes on the European constitution the euro sank into a trading range around $1.20, where it remains. At the time of writing, the real economy of the US appears to continue in the healthy expansion that began in the second quarter of 2003, when it emerged from a two-year slump. Corporate profits are strong and real GDP continues to grow at annual rates exceeding 3.5 per cent. Job growth is brisk and unemployment rates have fall from a recent high of 6.3 per cent in June 2003 to 5 per cent of the labor force in June 2005. The US housing market is booming, with record existing home sales in April, May, and June and continued strong growth in residential construction. Median housing prices in June 2005 were almost 15 per cent higher than a year earlier, the fastest pace of housing price increases in twenty-five years, but overall inflation rates remained subdued at around 3 per cent growth in the Consumer Price Index including food and energy. The NASDAQ and S&P 500 stock indexes hit four-year highs in late July. In his final monetary policy report to Congress in July 2005, Alan Greenspan as usual pointed out areas of risk and uncertainty, but he concluded that 'our baseline outlook for the U.S. economy is one of sustained economic growth and contained inflation pressures.'[30]

With the US real economy in healthy shape and financial markets running smoothly, the loss of confidence in the dollar that occurred in the fall of 2004 and lasted into the spring of 2005 appears to have been overblown, and the pressure is off the president and Congress to rein in budget deficits. The president in July 2005 put in a request for a $0.5 trillion defense budget, a big highway spending bill passed through the Senate, the estate tax is up for complete repeal, and the US current account deficit has risen to 6.5 per cent of GDP. All of this has been enabled by continued strong buying of US securities by foreigners. The adjustment has been delayed by the foreign purchases of securities, but the magnitude of the adjustment problem has increased.

A smooth or turbulent adjustment: Greenspan vs. Volcker

The question is: when the adjustment process begins, will 'market forces restore, without crises, a sustainable U.S. balance of payments,' as Federal Reserve Chairman Alan Greenspan reassures us? In March 2005 at the Council on Foreign Relations, Greenspan reinforced his 'smooth adjustment' analysis with an additional Federal Reserve study just completed. Unlike the emerging market cases of Mexico (1994–95), South Asia (1997), Russia (1998), Argentina (2001), and Brazil (2002), which were occasioned by financial crises and economic hardship, the study of twenty-three industrialized-country cases found little evidence for a disorderly correction scenario, though some slowdown in economic activity was occasioned in the majority of the cases. Greenspan concluded that 'history suggests that current account imbalances will be defused with modest risk of disruption. Two Federal Reserve studies of large current account adjustments in developed countries, the results of which are presumably applicable to the United States, suggest that market forces are likely to restore a more long-term sustainable current account balance here without substantial disruption.'[31]

Former Federal Reserve Chairman Paul Volcker, who was brought in to halt the run on the dollar in the late 1970s, sees a different scenario. In April 2005, Volcker wrote in a *Washington Post* column:

> The difficulty is that this seemingly comfortable pattern can't go on indefinitely. I don't know of any country that has managed to consume and invest 6 per cent more than it produces for long. The United States is absorbing about 80 per cent of the net flow of international capital. And at some point, both central banks and private institutions will have their fill of dollars.
>
> I don't know whether change will come with a bang or a whimper, whether sooner or later. But as things stand, it is more likely than not that it will be financial crises rather than policy foresight that will force the change.
>
> There is a wide area of agreement among establishment economists about a textbook pretty picture: China and other continental Asian economies should permit and encourage a substantial exchange rate appreciation against the dollar. Japan and Europe should work promptly and aggressively toward domestic stimulus and deal more effectively and speedily with structural obstacles to growth. And the United States, by some combination of measures, should forcibly increase its rate of internal saving, thereby reducing its import demand.
>
> But can we, with any degree of confidence today, look forward to any one of these policies being put in place any time soon, much less a combination of all?
>
> The answer is no. So I think we are skating on increasingly thin ice. On the present trajectory, the deficits and imbalances will increase. At some point, the sense of confidence in capital markets that today so benignly supports the flow of funds to the United States and the growing world economy could fade. Then some event, or combination of events, could come along to disturb markets, with damaging volatility in both exchange markets and interest rates.

Recalling the turbulence he was brought in to tame, Volcker concludes with the comment, 'we had a taste of that in the 1970s.'[32]

The run on the dollar in the late 1970s

The period Paul Volcker is recalling was not included in the studies Alan Greenspan used in his analysis. What began in 1977 as an orderly depreciation of the dollar turned into a collapse of confidence in the fall of 1978 as foreign holders of dollar-denominated assets, including some foreign central banks, switched their dollar holdings into Swiss francs, German marks, and Japanese yen. From start to finish the dollar lost about 15 per cent of its value against a trade-weighted basket of currencies, 23 per cent against the German mark, and 34 per cent against the Swiss franc, depreciation roughly in line with recent weakening of the dollar against the euro. US banks operating abroad were able to adjust their balance sheets to a gradual shifting out of dollar holdings in 1977, but in the fall of 1978 foreigners shifted out of dollars so fast that each wave of panic selling and sudden drops in the dollar's value threatened the capital base of some major US banks operating abroad.[33] Market participants had already begun reacting negatively to anything President Carter or his Treasury Secretary said, and in October 1978, when Carter announced an anti-inflation policy, currency market participants interpreted it as ineffectual, and the dollar sell-off was so steep that major foreign exchange dealers dramatically widened their bid/offer spreads or withdrew bids to buy dollars altogether, a disorderly market situation that threatened a general liquidity crisis.[34] As one New York banker in the fall of 1978 put it, the nation was on the brink of 'a nineteenth-century style financial panic.'

As president of the Federal Reserve Bank of New York at that time, Paul Volcker relayed the urgency of an impending financial market crisis to the Carter administration. Before the Treasury and the Fed were at odds over monetary policy, but on 1 November 1978 they issued a joint communiqué that raised the discount rate to its highest level in the Fed's history (9.5 per cent) up until then, raised reserve requirements (a move very rarely used), and promised direct intervention in currency markets to halt the run on the dollar. Coordinating with other central banks, the Federal Reserve Bank of New York intervened massively to jolt the speculators; on the first day of intervention, the Swiss franc and German mark dropped more than 8 per cent in value against the dollar, and after two months of interventions orderly trading in currency markets was restored. In June 1979 another sell-off of dollar assets began, and gold, oil, and other commodity prices surged. This time around the Carter administration was forced to reshuffle its cabinet, replacing Treasury Secretary Michael Blumenthal with G. William Miller, who stepped down as chairman of the Fed to make way for Paul Volcker.

The run on the dollar continued into the fall of 1979. In early October 1979 Volcker, who had negotiated international monetary deals since the 1960s, flew to Belgrade to coordinate a strategy with his monetary authority colleagues at a joint meeting of the IMF and the World Bank. Upon returning from Belgrade on 6 October, bold new measures were introduced, which were publicly supported by central banks of the major industrialized countries. Harsh money medicine was introduced in the US to wring out inflationary expectations and restore confidence in the dollar. Interest rates would be allowed to soar to whatever levels they might reach in order to compensate foreigners for the perceived risk of holding dollar-denominated assets. Once the Fed adopted the new policy, interest rates fluctuated violently, and the prime rate zoomed upwards, peaking in late 1980 at 21.5 per cent, while conventional thirty-year mortgages climbed to 18.45 per cent. Between 1980 and 1981 the dollar recovered spectacularly against all major currencies, rising 40 per cent against most European currencies and 22 per cent against the pound sterling. However, the US economy suffered its worst contraction since the Great Depression, with US civilian unemployment rates exceeding 10 per cent of the labor force and remaining above 7 per cent for a period of five years. If there was ever a disorderly correction scenario it was the one Paul Volcker presided over from 1979 through 1985. Alan Greenspan wisely left this historical episode out of his analysis when he flew to Frankfurt to calm the waters in November 2004.

Among the many differences that set today's global financial order apart from two decades ago is that in the 1980s no other currency had anything close to the dollar's economic or financial market backing. The Swiss franc, the German mark, and the Japanese yen were certainly useful as temporary instruments of hoarding when the dollar was coming under fire, but after confidence was restored the dollar was far more liquid and convenient for foreigners to use for international transactions, managing cash balances, borrowing, lending, hedging, and storing long-term savings, considering US financial market breadth and depth. Today there *is* a currency with far more economic and financial backing than the German mark, the Swiss franc, or the Japanese yen had in the 1980s. It seems only logical that when the dollar suffers bouts of weakness, international actors who switch into the euro may continue to find it useful for making international payments and storing long-term savings, especially as euro financial markets are rapidly modernizing and becoming more deep and liquid. As corporate treasurers, fund managers, and central banks downsize their dollar holdings and increase their use of euros, the clout enjoyed for more than half a century by the US dollar will be permanently diminished. The situation of the dollar today more closely resembles the earlier decline of the pound sterling as an international currency.

The political economy of sterling's decline as global currency

Looking at the dollar's position in global finance today, British citizens might recall their own experiences when foreigners progressively switched from using sterling. Before World War I, there was no currency with the economic and financial backing enjoyed by the pound sterling, and sterling's wide use as an international currency made it easy to finance imperial expansion and British current account deficits without the British authorities having actively to defend the currency. The global payments system fragmented with the advent of World War I, and Britain's net wealth position suffered when approximately 20 per cent of its foreign assets were sold to finance the war. Furthermore, British trade channels were broken, and, after the war, newly industrialized economies successfully competed with British manufactures in formerly British dominated markets. By the mid-1920s the dollar had economic backing that rivaled that of sterling, and New York was fast catching up with London as an international financial center. Nevertheless, in 1925 the British successfully negotiated with the United States and five other industrial powers to restore the pound sterling to its position before World War I. It was believed by British authorities at the time that a strong pound, restored in status as an official reserve currency, would lower the costs of maintaining the empire, stimulate British overseas investment, and reactivate financial activity in the City of London. In 1925, Winston Churchill justified the move on imperial grounds, arguing 'If we had not taken this action the whole of the rest of the British Empire would have taken it without us, and it would have come to a gold standard, not on the basis of the pound sterling but a gold standard of the dollar.'[35]

In place between 1925 and 1931, the sterling exchange standard may have delayed the loss of empire, but the strong pound, set at the high prewar parity with gold, put British manufacturers at a competitive disadvantage in world markets, and British export industries suffered massive layoffs, wage cuts, and strikes. Furthermore, periodic runs on the pound forced British monetary authorities to defend the currency with interest-rate hikes at a time when the domestic economy was suffering. When interest-rate hikes alone were not enough to halt the speculation against sterling, the Bank of England would have to negotiate loans from other central banks. On several occasions, foreign creditors demanded that the British cut their budget deficits as a condition for loan approval. Emergency budgets typically consisted of slashing social programs, cutting wages of government employees, reducing unemployment benefits, and raising taxes. When foreign confidence in sterling returned, the government could relax on some of the harsher measures until another run on sterling ensued and the pattern repeated itself. Emergency budgets sparked civil strife and were followed by protests, strikes and accusations that the government was 'determined to attack the standard of living of workers in order to meet a situation caused by the policy pursued by private banking interests.' Unemployment rates soared, and Britain sank deeper into depression. Following austerity measures introduced in September 1931, British sailors struck over cuts in pay and the world press publicized the strike as a 'sailor's mutiny.' Doubts about the British government's ability to implement the austerity measures hampered foreign central bank coordination and led to a wave of speculation against sterling that no amount of help from central banks could stop. Within a week of the sailors' strike, Britain was forced to give up its defense of sterling and severed sterling's ties to gold.[36]

An almost identical pattern of sterling defense emerged in 1958–68, though by the 1960s Britain had lost most of its empire and the dollar had taken over sterling's former position as the hegemonic international currency. The agreement reached was for former colonies to continue to hold sterling reserves and use sterling for transactions between members of the British Commonwealth in what was called the 'overseas sterling area,' and the Bank of England promised to back up those sterling balances with dollars. Current account deficits in 1964, 1965, 1967, and 1968 were accompanied by runs on sterling. When runs occurred, the Bank of England first would try to reverse the outflow by increasing interest rates. If that action alone did not slow the sell-off of sterling assets, the Bank would be forced to draw on automatic lines of credit with the IMF and the Federal Reserve Bank of New York, and when those lines of credit were exhausted, the Bank of England would have to negotiate loans from a consortium of international creditors, who would demand that the British government reduce its deficit spending. Typically the creditor-induced emergency budgets would slash social programs, freeze wages, and increase taxes. If the implementation of an austerity package looked believable to financial market participants, confidence in sterling would be restored, dollars would flow back into the Bank of England, and the Bank could pay off the loan package with interest. When the pressure on sterling subsided, the government could relax on some of the harsher fiscal measures that had been introduced under the threat of a sterling crisis. This pattern of austerity–relaxation came to be known in the United Kingdom as 'stop–go' policy. Even when the Labour Party was in power, international creditors were able to force the Labour government to implement emergency budget measures, which included unpopular wage freezes and program cuts that were resisted by organized labor. In the fall of 1967, the run on sterling was so severe that international creditors were unable to coordinate a bail-out package.[37] On 18 November 1967 the Bank of England had no choice but to devalue the pound, punishing those who had held on to sterling assets. Following the devaluation, private holders of sterling were joined by central banks in the overseas sterling area, who 'in various styles and gaits ... began to shift their reserves out of sterling.'[38] The shrinkage of sterling's use as an international currency was painful for the British. Employment levels declined in 1967, 1968, and 1969. Only after what Harold Wilson in 1968 called the 'most punishing budget in Britain's peacetime history' was Britain's current account balance restored to a surplus in 1969. At the close of the period of shrinkage, the British public was left with a depleted and demoralized manufacturing sector and a large indebtedness to foreign central banks.[39]

Long-run lessons for the dollar's loss of hegemony

An orderly shrinkage of the dollar's use as a world currency is not a scenario to be feared. If foreign holders of dollar-denominated assets were gradually to diversify their portfolios toward the euro and other currencies, and if fresh savings were to be distributed more evenly across the globe, the dollar would decline gradually and so would the relative valuation of US securities. Surely this would increase real interest rates in the United States, dampen the growth of consumer spending, raise national savings relative to investment, and reduce US current account deficits to more sustainable levels. Because the relative economic backing for the dollar in today's world is healthier than it was for sterling in the 1920s and the 1960s, the shrinkage of the dollar's use would not be so severe, perhaps a reduction from 45 per cent of global foreign exchange market turnover (April 2004) to 35 per cent over a period of years with the euro rising from 19 per cent of turnover (April 2004) to, perhaps, 30 per cent over the same period. Likewise foreign central banks could slowly reduce their official foreign exchange reserves from 70 per cent in dollars (2004) down to 55 or 60 per cent over a period of years. Certain customary privileges of being the hegemonic currency would be reduced. It would be harder for the Federal Reserve to print up money and have it accepted and held on to by foreigners, it would be more difficult for the US Treasury to finance fiscal deficits, and it would be harder for corporations and government-sponsored agencies to sell debt abroad. It would mean a change in relative living standards for people in the United States, but it would not be the end of the world.

As Paul Volcker knows from personal experience, the problem arises when an orderly decline of the dollar turns into panic selling, so that foreign holders of dollar-denominated securities, who face currency risk in addition to normal risks associated with securities, begin selling their holdings en masse. Judging from the British experience, threats of an abrupt sell-off of dollar assets can be expected to force up US interest rates periodically, even at the risk of harming the US economy. In effect, the US will have lost its autonomy in setting monetary policy. If higher interest rates do not halt the speculation, the US Treasury and the Federal Reserve may need to seek help from foreign monetary authorities, who will be in a position to dictate deficit reduction on the president and Congress. In effect, the US will have lost autonomy in setting fiscal policy. Just as in the case of sterling, when foreigners have faith in the dollar it makes it appear easy for the US to finance deficits and exercise international sovereignty, but only at the cost of national sovereignty when dollar doubts surface.

The magnitude of the financial market threat can be roughly gauged by looking at the portion of US securities that foreigners hold. In the aggregate, the threat does not look formidable. From March 2000 to June 2004, foreigners increased their share of total marketable US securities from about 10 per cent to 14.3 per cent of the total value outstanding. With stocks, the problem looks even more manageable, because as of June 2004 foreigners held less than 10 per cent of the total market value of US equities, meaning a sell-off by foreigners could be adequately absorbed (at lower stock prices) by US fund managers, who report their performance in US dollars and therefore are not so exposed to currency risk. Even with government-sponsored agency securities, the problem of a sell-off by foreigners does not appear too severe, because as of June 2004 foreigners held only 10.5 per cent of the total value of these securities outstanding. Corporate bonds and other debt (which includes privately issued asset-backed securities) would be more vulnerable to a sell off by foreigners. As of June 2004, 17 per cent of corporate and other debt outstanding was owned by foreigners.

The Achilles heel of the orderly adjustment scenario is the concentration of US Treasury securities in the hands of foreigners. With more than half of the total marketable holdings of US Treasury securities, foreigners already control the fate of US long-term interest rates, because the market rates on ten-year Treasuries are used as the benchmark to set mortgage rates and other long-term interest rates. Considering the

15.4 / Foreign holdings of US long-term securities (% share of total outstanding)

	March 2000	June 2004
Equity	6.9	9.2
Corporate and other debt	12.3	17.0
US government agency debt	7.3	10.5
Marketable US Treasury debt	35.2	52.0
Total US long-term securities	9.7	14.3

Source: US Treasury, 'Report on Foreign Holdings of US Securities as of June 30, 2004,' June 2005.

special role of US Treasury securities in global financial markets, a sharp or destabilizing financial market event associated with these securities is so scary it is almost unthinkable. Next to the dollar itself, US Treasury securities have the highest daily turnover of any class of assets in the world. Every financial institution holds some Treasury securities, not just because they are considered safe and earn interest, but because they are so liquid they can be relied on for funding. As the shock of September 11th demonstrated, the secondary market in Treasury securities (and the treasury repo market) had to be jump-started first before the stock market, the corporate bond market, commodities trading, and foreign exchange could resume functioning smoothly, because all the institutions (other than US commercial banks that had direct access to the Federal Reserve) regularly relied on the Treasury securities market for access to funding needed to settle trades. A disruption in the Treasury securities market would disrupt settlement in all other financial markets, including foreign exchange.

The build-up of vulnerability was remarkably fast. In less than four years, foreigners picked up more than $1 trillion worth of US Treasury securities, 90 per cent of the new issues auctioned off to finance federal budget deficits run up during President Bush's first term in office. One-third of the foreign purchases went into private portfolios, which show up on the table in the sizeable increases in holdings in the United Kingdom and in offshore banking centers in the Caribbean. Pursuing their own peculiar national interests, foreign monetary authorities bought up two-thirds of the foreign purchases made over this period. Some of the smaller Asian central banks intentionally built up foreign exchange reserves as a way to protect against the wild swings in portfolio capital that had

15.5 / Major foreign holders of US Treasury securities (holdings at end of period, $ billion)

	June 2001	April 2005	Change 2001–05
Japan	300.8	685.2	384.4
Mainland China	72.7	230.4	157.7
United Kingdom	51.6	125.2	73.6
Caribbean banking centers	24.3	124.6	100.3
Taiwan	34.9	70.6	35.7
Germany	47.6	60.8	13.2
OPEC	43.4	60.6	17.2
Korea	27.3	55.9	28.6
Hong Kong	41.9	47.2	5.3
All Other	338.8	529.6	190.8
Total Treasury securities held by foreigners	983.3	1990.1	1006.8
Grand Total marketable Treasury securities	2722.6	3855.4	1132.8
(% marketable held by foreigners)	(36)	(52)	(16)
Federal Reserve Holdings	535.1	717.3	182.2

Source: US Treasury, 'Major Foreign Holders of US Treasury Securities,' 2001–05; Federal Reserve Bank of St Louis, Federal Reserve Holdings of US Government Debt, FREDII database.

caused the South Asian financial crisis of 1997–98; Taiwan and South Korea show up as the two most successful examples of this strategy (see Figure 15.5). The People's Bank of China purchased almost $160 billion Treasuries as a result of pegging their currency to the dollar; to prevent the yuan from rising above the 8.4 yuan per dollar peg, the central bank had to buy up dollars on the currency market, and it invested some of the proceeds in US Treasury securities. The largest buyer of Treasuries over the period was the Japanese Ministry of Finance, which bought them as a product of foreign exchange market interventions conducted on its behalf by the Bank of Japan. The Ministry of Finance ordered the Bank of Japan to sell yen and buy dollars to prevent the yen from rising against the dollar in an effort to help Japanese exporters; some of these dollar purchases were then invested in US Treasury securities. The Bank of Japan, however, used the injections of yen from foreign exchange interventions to boost the Japanese money supply in an effort to combat deflation in the Japanese economy at a time when interest rates were approaching zero.[40] None of these purchases by foreigners was intended to help the Bush administration pursue military expansionism and tax cuts, but they resulted in doing so.

Normally with fiscal deficits of this magnitude, the Treasury Department would have had difficulty auctioning off securities without driving up interest rates. Despite the heavy borrowing by the Treasury, interest rates the government had to pay on freshly issued securities *declined* by more than a full percentage point over the period, allowing the Treasury to refinance its previous high-interest-rate debts with lower-interest-rate obligations. Because of the favorable refinancing rates, annual interest payments on the federal debt declined from $223 billion a year in 2000 to $160 billion a year in 2004, despite a 30 per cent increase in the total debt owed. The favorable auctioning conditions and lower monthly installments gave the impression that deficit spending didn't matter any more.[41] The Bush administration could start a war, give two rounds of tax cuts, write a prescription drug benefit and other big spending bills for voters without calling for any sacrifice from American taxpayers.

Everyone seemed happy except those in the financial markets who saw the imbalance building. By June 2004, foreigners had acquired more than half of the marketable Treasury securities outstanding, and by September 2004 the Japanese Ministry of Finance reporting holdings of $698.9 billion in foreign securities,[42] approximately equal in value to the $700.3 billion in US Treasury securities owned by the US Federal Reserve system. Foreign official holdings became such 'large percentages of individual issues' that the Bond Market Association's Treasury Advisory Committee recommended that US officials engage 'with their foreign counterparts' to encourage 'lending of their securities' to 'alleviate potential shortages,'[43] a type of Treasury market intervention previously monopolized by the Federal Reserve Bank of New York.[44] Because of the concentration of foreign holdings of US Treasury securities, future runs on the dollar will trigger doubts about Treasury securities. The market story is already in currency traders' vocabulary. To prevent a disorderly market event, US officials may be put in the uncomfortable position of having to engage the Japanese and Chinese authorities to buy up US Treasuries that are being sold off. The Federal Reserve Bank of New York cannot aggressively buy up US Treasuries without inflating the US money supply, a move that would heighten speculation against the dollar. All the Japanese and Chinese authorities would have to do is sell some of their euro holdings and use the proceeds to buy dollars and US Treasuries, a set of transactions that would simultaneously prop up the dollar and the treasury bond market, without altering the Chinese and Japanese domestic money supplies. Perhaps the Chinese inventory of US Treasuries was the reason why the Group of Seven finance ministers and central bank governors of the largest industrialized countries invited China to sit at the table with them at their past two meetings. One of the lessons discovered by British authorities was that central bank coordination worked well to halt speculation against sterling when other central banks found it in their domestic interest to help the Bank of England. However, when the most powerful central banks were divided by conflicting domestic interests, speculators won. Who knows what negotiation contexts US Treasury and Federal Reserve officials will face during future runs on the dollar.

It is ironic that while foreign purchases of US Treasury securities supported an aggressive display of military sovereignty in the first Bush administration, their holdings could threaten US sovereignty later on. British political economist Susan Strange summarized her country's experiences of 1958–68 as a 'disastrous decade of periodic demand restraint,' occasioned by 'the recurrent need to go begging abroad for credit' and applying emergency budgets to stop runs on the currency. 'It seems as though by some 'Pavlovian process ... constantly repeated stimulus of short-term crises demanding instant crisis management and emergency action led to a total atrophy of the capacity for long-term policy planning and independent British policy initiatives.'[45] It appears that the US public has already witnessed a dress rehearsal of what may lie ahead when pressures on the dollar following the 2004 elections prompted President Bush to announce a sudden change of budget 'to convince foreigners to buy dollars.' President Bush's emergency budget did not touch the 2001 and 2003 tax cuts or look for ways to trim defense spending. Rather, it targeted

> health programs, subsidies to Amtrak, agricultural research and some federal education programs. Big cities received less federal aid to comply with anti-pollution laws and job training requirements, and the National Science Foundation saw its budget cut. Pell grants, the main source of federal funding for disadvantaged college students, [were] frozen at $4,050 for the third consecutive year.[46]

By July 2005, pressures on the dollar were off, and big spending bills were back on the President's agenda.

Alan Greenspan in Frankfurt and Paul Volcker, more recently, have both pointed to swift action now to reduce the fiscal deficit. As former Federal Chairman Volcker puts it, 'this is not a time for ideological intransigence and partisan posturing on the budget at the expense of the deficit rising still higher,' and he calls for action now, when 'everything seems so placid

15.6 / Legislation causing deficits to return (cost in 2005 of legislation enacted since January 2001 as proportion of cumulative deficits)

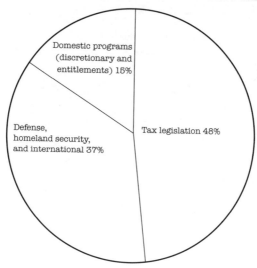

Domestic programs (discretionary and entitlements) 15%

Defense, homeland security, and international 37%

Tax legislation 48%

Source: CBO data; Carlitz & Kogan, Center on Budget and Policy Priorities, 31 January 2005, p. 1.

and favorable ... to ensure that there is time for orderly adjustment.'[47] If interest rates rise, the squeeze on the discretionary budget will be more severe than the benefit this budget enjoyed from lower interest payments during the first Bush administration. The total debt on which interest must be paid has risen 30 per cent since deficit spending began, and the duration of the federal debt has declined, giving the federal debt structure the characteristics of an adjustable rate mortgage.[48] Even now with easy financing terms, interest payments on the federal debt are equal to the combined federal spending on the environment and natural resources, community and regional development, education, and health. When interest payments balloon, it will be impossible to target these areas alone – as Bush's emergency budget did in late 2004 – and 'convince foreigners to buy dollars.'

The place to look for adjustment – without sacrificing the long-run health of the US economy – is simple: the recent changes in policy that caused the deficits to get out of hand.

Social security was certainly not the cause. In fact, if social security had not been running annual surpluses, the Treasury would have had to auction off $75 billion more in securities a year to finance the deficits.[49]

15.7 / Distribution of Bush administration tax cLuts, 2004

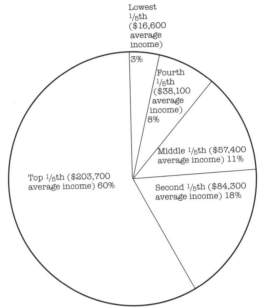

Lowest 1/5th ($16,600 average income) 3%

Fourth 1/5th ($38,100 average income) 8%

Middle 1/5th ($57,400 average income) 11%

Top 1/5th ($203,700 average income) 60%

Second 1/5th ($84,300 average income) 18%

Source: David Kamin and Isaac Shapiro, 'Studies Shed New Light on Effects of Administration's Tax Cuts,' Washington: Center on Budget and Policy Priorities, 13 September 2004, p. 5.

Using Congressional Budget Office data, a 2005 study found tax breaks were responsible for approximately half of the fiscal overruns since 2001, and increases in spending related to national security have been responsible for more than a third of the cumulative deficits.[50]

Taking the large item first, tax legislation passed in 2001 and 2003 altered a tax structure that had remained largely intact since a modest increase was imposed in 1993. The former tax code did not seem to lower US labor productivity, impede investment in new technology, or reduce overall rates of growth of the US economy. In fact, this code was active during the longest and strongest expansion in US economic history. A wholesale reversal to the pre-2001 tax code is unlikely to harm the real long-term growth potential of the United States.

However, if one examines who collected the benefits from the 2001 and 2003 tax breaks, it will be easy to see the political obstacles to an economically simple solution. A recent study shows that almost every American household got some tax relief from the two rounds of tax breaks, a fact that helped in election politics. However, the distribution was not evenly distributed amongst potential voters. The study shows that the richest 1 per cent of American households, with average incomes of $1,171,000, received one-quarter of the total benefit of the tax breaks, an amount larger than that received by the bottom 60 per cent of income earners. Those households in the top 20 per cent income bracket with average household incomes of approximately $200,000 got 60 per cent of the total largesse, though this underestimates their take because it does not include estate tax cuts and corporate tax cuts. Especially generous to the already wealthy were the dividend and capital gains tax cuts in 2003. Because stock ownership is so concentrated, these two tax breaks are mainly collected by the rich. In 2005, almost half (46 per cent) of the benefits from the capital gains and dividends tax cuts will accrue to the 0.2 per cent of the households with an annual income over $1 million, three-quarters of the benefits will accrue to those with incomes over $200,000, and 88 per cent of the benefits will go to households with incomes above $100,000.[51]

Every congressman and -woman and every senator falls in the category of the richest 20 per cent, and in 2003, the president and the first lady reported adjusted gross income of more than $800,000, and the vice-president and his wife more than $1.3 million, so they personally collected from the legislation they enacted and may not want to give that up. But, considering the broader issue of who exercises influence and power over elected officials while they are doing the regular work of government, the political obstacles to this simple solution to the deficit problem are clear. Between election campaigns, government officials are unlikely to see the average voter. In carrying out their daily tasks, government officials are more likely to engage with managers of enterprises – public, private, and non-profit – or with these enterprises' lawyers, lobbyists, and researchers, who are hired to represent their interests. The question is, how many of these high-level executives fall below the top 20 per cent of income earners, and how likely are they to approve of giving up this tax benefit? Most households with incomes of $200,000 can afford to pay for college, fund private retirement accounts, live in a home in a protected community, and self-insure for unexpected health problems. Between elections when the average person gets to vote, those who wield the greatest influence over government are more likely to favor cuts in spending on public education, health, and the problems of the inner city.

Turning to the second largest number, one can see a place to look for credible deficit reduction. Prime military contractors saw their fortunes escalate from $133 billion in fiscal year 2000 to $231 billion in fiscal year 2004, a 74 per cent increase in four years. Certainly some of the

15.8 / Prime beneficiaries of the Bush administration's war (top twelve military contractors in FY 2004, US$ billion)

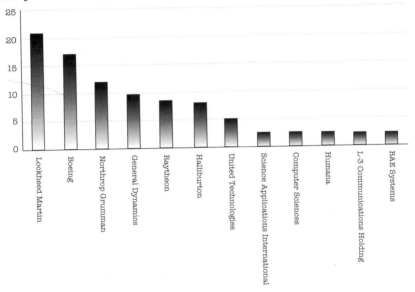

Note: contractors with more than $2 billion in government contracts represent 40% of $230 billion total prime contracts.

Source: Department of Defense, *Top 100 Companies FY 2004*, Table 2.

additional procurement was necessary to guard against future terrorist attacks, and once the decision was made to send US troops into harm's way, it would have been morally wrong not to provide them with the best armor. The urgency surrounding appropriation decisions did not allow sufficient time to ask which of the pre-9/11 and pre-Iraq defense orders could be terminated to make more budget room for the new strategic challenges. In the haste of emergency appropriations, many contractors were able just to add on to customary deliveries they had successfully marketed to Congress during the 1990s. In fiscal year 2000 there were thirteen defense contractors that received more than $1 billion from the government; by 2004 this number had swollen to twenty-five. With some strategic priority-setting, the entire defense procurement budget could be streamlined and reduced 40 per cent without sacrificing national security. The currently acting secretary of defense, Donald Rumsfeld, is fully capable of doing this. Such a move would send a message to the world that the US is serious about fiscal responsibility, and it would set a precedent for streamlining domestic programs that could stand improvements in efficiency.

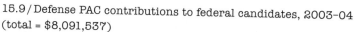

15.9 / Defense PAC contributions to federal candidates, 2003-04
(total = $8,091,537)

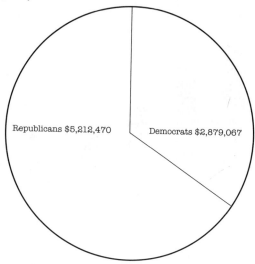

Unfortunately, the political machinery to block such a move is far more entrenched, well funded, and organized than the 20 per cent of the scattered households who got 60 per cent of the 2001 and 2003 tax breaks. In 2004, half the value of prime contracts awarded by the Department of Defense was channeled into thirty companies; and twelve companies, each receiving more than $2 billion in contracts, collected 40 per cent of the award money.

Take a modest fraction, say 5 per cent of $2 billion, and you have a promotional budget of $100 million, a healthy amount to make a convincing case that one's wares are essential for national security. Take 5 per cent of Lockheed Martin's $20,690,912,000 contract revenues and you have a 2004 sales promotional fund of $1,034,546,000, or a billion dollars and change. Of course, there is intense competition for such a lucrative market, and all sorts of creative methods are used to capture market share. The most successful contractor between 2000 and 2004 in terms of total increases in sales revenue was Northrop Grumman Corporation, which saw an $8.8 billion surge in prime contract awards, almost three times the amount it received from the government in fiscal year 2000. Lockheed Martin, General Dynamics, and Boeing, each successfully increased sales to the government by more than $5 billion between fiscal year 2000 and fiscal year 2004. The most spectacular increase in market share, however, was

15.10 / Federal election cycle PAC contributions by top contractors, 2003–04 ($ million)

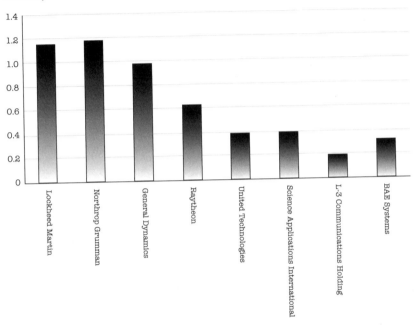

Source: Center for Responsive Politics, *Political Action Committees*, Washington DC: CRP, July 2005.

achieved by Halliburton, which rose from 22nd place in the FY 2000 Department of Defense ranking of contractors to 6th place in FY 2004, with an absolute increase of $7.4 billion in awards, the second largest sales increase and more than twelve times the contract money it was getting before Richard Cheney, CEO of Halliburton from 1995 through August 2000, became vice-president of the United States. This should be a marketing lesson to the competition that it makes sense to have someone in place to help design the type of war that one's company is particularly capable of supplying.[52]

Some contractors were less successful in placing former executives into government decision-making posts, and they relied on some tried and true marketing techniques. Only the tiniest fraction of defense contractors' marketing budgets gets earmarked for visible campaign contributions, but goodwill passed along for election campaigns is smart business. During the 2003–04 federal election campaign, candidates from both major political parties received some $8 million in campaign contributions through forty-six defense industry Political Action Committees (PACs).

Eight of the top twelve 2004 contractors had Political Action Committees with their names visible on the committee. Halliburton does not appear on this list, but Northrop Grumman – the corporation with the largest sales increase – appears as the largest contributor behind Lockheed Martin, the largest contractor.

A hopeful conclusion

Hopefully, some strong leadership will rise above the political forces standing in the way of fiscal responsibility. Hopefully, no rogue event will shock financial markets. Hopefully, President Bush's appointment to chair the Federal Reserve will have Alan Greenspan's abilities to analyze financial market instability and calm markets in times of stress. Hopefully, the new Federal Reserve chairman will have a favorable debut in currency markets and will be viewed as someone who is not pushed around by presidents. Hopefully, there will be skillful collaboration, preferably behind the scenes, with the Chinese and Japanese monetary authorities. Hopefully, Alan Greenspan's smooth adjustment scenario without the risk of a financial crisis will play out, and the US and the world will not suffer a repeat of the British experience.

Glossary

Aussies Currency trading slang for Australian dollars.

Bank for International Settlements (BIS) International organization headquartered in Basel, Switzerland, that acts as a bank for central banks and fosters international financial cooperation in pursuit of monetary and financial stability. The BIS coordinates the triennial survey of foreign exchange and derivatives activity.

Base currency First or primary currency quoted in a currency pair. In the example EUR=1.22USD (also written EUR/USD and euro–US dollar) the euro is the 'base' currency and the dollar is the pricing or '**terms currency**'; in this case one euro is worth $1.22. In the example, USD=107JPY (also written USD/JPY or dollar–yen), the US dollar is the base currency and the Japanese yen is the 'terms' currency, whereby one dollar is worth 107 yen.

Bid [buy] price The price quoted that a dealer stands willing to buy a currency for.

Bond Type of security that promises the owner a stream of interest payments from the issuer and a repayment of principal a certain number of years from the date of issue.

Brokerage house A securities **broker** connects buyers and sellers of securities, often through brokerage accounts where individuals or institutions deposit funds, hold securities, and place securities orders, which the broker handles for a commission. Frequently brokerage houses are also securities **dealers** that hold inventories of securities and stand ready to buy or sell the securities to customers. **Investment banks** distribute freshly created securities through connections with large institutional investors and with **broker/dealers**, who then distribute the securities to retail and institutional customers. Financial investment houses have for many decades effectively combined investment banking with brokerage and dealing functions, but only recently (the late 1990s in the US) have **financial holding companies** formed that combine investment banks, brokerage houses, securities dealers, insurance companies, and commercial banks under a single corporate umbrella (example: Citigroup). Eight of the top ten foreign exchange dealers (in 2005) were part of financial holding companies that combined commercial banking with investment banking and broker/dealer businesses.

Cable (sterling) Currency trading term used for British pounds. 'One cable' is slang use by traders to mean a contract for £1 million.

CHAPS-euro the London-based euro payments facility that uses euro-denominated accounts at the Bank of England to accomplish Real Time Gross Settlement for its members.

CHIPS (Clearing House Interbank Payments System) The largest international dollar delivery system in the 1990s. Used a deferred net settlement system to process payments flows between banks, but switched to a real time net settlement system in 2001. Advantage: accomplishes large volumes of payments with extremely efficient use of liquid reserves, thereby saving money for participants. Disadvantage (relative to Continuous Linked Settlement Bank): CHIPS settles only the dollar side of foreign exchange transactions.

Commercial bank (creator of bank account money) Financial institution that issues 'demand deposit accounts' that are immediately redeemable for currency and serve as a convenient substitute for currency. This money-creating feature of commercial banks requires the commercial bank to hold adequate sums of vault cash to cover withdrawals and to hold liquid deposits at settlement facilities (e.g. reserve deposits at the Federal Reserve) that will support the movement of demand deposits to other commercial banks.

Complexity (chaos) models of currency markets Computer simulation models that contain non-linear reaction functions for groups of traders with different trading strategies, some based on fundamental factors, others following technical trading strategies. Simulations are run to compare the sensitivity of price changes to initial conditions, reaction functions, and shocks introduced in midstream. Even the simplest of these models generate complex, sometimes chaotic, price movements in which it is difficult to tell whether the price changes were induced by a fundamental shock or were the result of interactions between traders with different trading strategies.

Contagion effect How a collapse of confidence in one financial market quickly spreads to other financial markets through the actions of fund managers who must adjust their portfolios and global exposures in response to losses initially suffered in the first area. Example: South Asian financial crisis of 1997: the collapse of financial market confidence in Thailand quickly spread to Malaysia, Indonesia, South Korea, the Philippines, and other 'emerging market' economies.

Continuous Linked Settlement (CLS) Bank Achieves settlement finality for both sides of a currency transaction at the same instant in real time Advantage: eliminates Herstatt risk (settlement risk) from foreign exchange deliveries. Disadvantage (relative to CHIPS): requires larger liquid reserve balances to process payments flows.

Currency futures Exchange-traded contracts agreeing to deliver (or take delivery of) a standardized amount of currency at a future date at a predetermined exchange rate; prior to the delivery date, the holder of a futures contract may remove the obligation to deliver the currency by selling the contract on the exchange and collecting a profit or taking a loss depending on the performance of the underlying exchange rate.

Currency options Foreign exchange contracts that give buyers the option (but not the obligation) to buy or sell a certain amount of currency for an agreed-upon time period at an agreed-upon rate, in exchange for the payment of a premium to the writer of the option. There are over-the-counter and exchange-traded currency options. Currency options provide buyers flexible insurance coverage against adverse exchange rate movements.

Current account balance The measure of the change in a country's net wealth position vis-à-vis the rest of the world due to saving or dissaving out of current income; the current account measures a country's current income from all sources from abroad and subtracts all of its current expenditures. If the balance of these two is positive the country's net wealth position vis-à-vis the rest of the world has been improved by the amount of the current account surplus; if negative, its net wealth position has declined due to the current account deficit.

Customized forward contracts   A foreign exchange contract a currency dealer may tailor for a customer usually involving an irregular value (delivery) date or an amount not regularly traded in the inter-dealer market.

Deferred Net Settlement System   Settlement agreement whereby payments between member financial institutions are netted first, and final payments for the smaller, net amounts owed are deferred until the end of a batch. Example: CHIPS in the 1990s. Advantage: much smaller liquid balances are required than in gross settlement systems. Disadvantage: final, secure payments are delayed, thereby introducing an element of settlement risk.

Efficient markets hypothesis   A financial market is said to be 'efficient' when there are large numbers of rational, profit-maximizing traders actively competing, each trying to predict future market values of assets using current information that is readily available to all. In this situation, competition between knowledgeable traders is thought to lead to financial asset prices (exchange rates) that reflect all information about past valuations and factors that may affect future valuations, making the current price an accurate measure of the asset's intrinsic worth. The value of the asset will change as relevant news is quickly and efficiently incorporated into the price. In the 'weak' form of efficiency, all past market prices and data are fully 'priced in' to the current price, so technical forecasting does not provide any trading advantage. In the 'semi-strong' form of efficiency, all past data and publicly available news on fundamental variables are already fully contained in the current price, so fundamental forecasting provides no trading advantage. In the 'strong' form of efficiency, insider information not available to the public is so quickly absorbed into the current price that acting on insider information gives fleeting advantage only for the first traders who act on the information.

Federal Reserve System (The 'Fed')   The system of twelve district reserve banks governed by the Federal Reserve Board of Governors, located in Washington DC. The Federal Open Market Committee of the Federal Reserve System meets approximately once a month to decide upon the direction of US monetary policy, which currently (2006) consists of setting targets for the federal funds rate, the interest rate banks charge each other for overnight access to reserve deposits at the Fed.

Foreign exchange derivatives Foreign exchange contracts derived from the performance of an underlying asset, usually the spot exchange rate for a currency pair. Frequently traded over-the-counter foreign exchange derivatives include outright forward contracts and foreign exchange swaps. Currency options are standardized foreign exchange derivatives traded on organized exchanges; currency futures are foreign exchange derivatives sold in a variety of forms in the over-the-counter market and in standardized amounts on organized exchanges.

Foreign exchange swap Swapping of currencies for an agreed-upon time period at agreed-upon exchange rates; a foreign exchange swap combines into a single contract a 'short-leg' exchange of currencies and a 'long-leg' reversal of the flow. A foreign exchange swap is basically borrowing one currency and lending another for an agreed-upon time period. Financial institutions and corporate treasurers frequently use foreign exchange swaps in global cash management.

Fundamental forecasting Forecasts based on the view that fundamental economic forces move exchange rates. One example of a fundamental exchange rate model looks at changes in relative interest rates; if interest rates rise in one country relative to another, that country's currency will be expected to appreciate as investors seek higher returns. Purchasing power parity is another example of a fundamental forecasting model.

Group of Seven (the 'G7') Comprising Canada, France, Germany, Italy, Japan, the United Kingdom and the United States, which together account for about two-thirds of the world's economic output. G7 finance ministers meet four times a year to review developments in their economies and the world economy. The G7 Central Bank governors join the finance ministers at three of these meetings, usually issuing a joint statement that is closely watched by financial market participants.

Herstatt risk (foreign exchange settlement risk) The risk arising from foreign exchange deliveries not arriving at the same instant in real time. If one currency is delivered with finality and the other is not, the bank due to receive currency will suffer a loss of the entire amount of the transaction. Because currency transactions can be large, a single failure to deliver could obliterate the entire capital of a bank and lead to a string of payments systems problems. Alarmed after Bankhaus Herstatt in 1974 failed to deliver dollars after it had received German mark deliveries, bank regulators and the international banking community sought ways to reduce settlement risk, a thrust that shaped the evolution of currency delivery systems for twenty years, culminating in the creation of the Continuous Linked Settlement Bank in 2002.

Institutional investors (holders of securities) Own portfolios of securities that they manage (on behalf of savers) usually employing the services of broker/dealers, who act as agents on their behalf. Examples of institutional investors include (in order of assets under management for US households and nonprofits in Q1 2005) **pension funds** ($9.4 trillion), **mutual funds** ($3.6 trillion), **insurance companies** ($1.1 trillion), and **hedge funds** (approximately $950 billion). Global exposures of institutional investors and sometimes-high portfolio turnover yield large demands for services of foreign exchange dealers.

Interbank settlement The way banks pay (settle with) each other when account money moves between banks. Example: If a check is drawn on an account at one bank and the check is deposited in an account at a second bank, the first bank must 'settle' (pay) the second bank for the amount of the draft in order for the funds to transfer, at which time the deposited check is said to 'clear.'

International Monetary Fund (IMF) One of the international financial institutions originating in the Bretton Woods Conference of 1944, with its main purpose being to regulate the international monetary exchange system to promote international monetary stability. The IMF is located across the street from the World Bank in Washington DC.

Investment bank (developer of securities) Financial institution that has the capacity to raise money for a client (issuer) by creating securities (stocks, bonds, and money market instruments) to be offered for sale on financial markets. Corporations or other entities wishing to raise money without borrowing from commercial banks may engage an investment bank to undertake an initial public offering of stock (equities) or bonds; the investment bank collects underwriting fees, often including a portion of the offering itself.

Investment currency A currency that has deep and liquid financial markets attached to it; the US dollar (in 2006) was the world's premier investment currency because of the wide array of highly liquid financial assets denominated in US dollars, an attribute that makes the currency attractive to fund managers.

Invoicing currency A currency in which international invoices are denominated.

Liquidity (of a financial asset) How easily a financial asset can be exchanged for money, usually depending on how active trading is in the secondary market for the asset. For a highly liquid asset, large amounts of it can be sold without greatly affecting its price because many buyers and sellers are actively trading it. Example: US dollars (on foreign exchange markets) and US Treasury securities are examples of extremely liquid assets that under most circumstances can be exchanged in a matter of seconds; a house, however, is not so liquid because it may take several months to find a buyer.

Liquidity preference theory of financial markets Keynes's theory of financial markets. This perspective views the current price of an asset as reflecting the balance of diverse opinions about the future of those actively participating in the market at the time. Because future events are uncertain in the sense of being unknowable, market participants play a guessing game about what the balance of other market participants' opinions on asset valuation will be as new information arises or as sentiments change. Because of the radical uncertainty market participants face, a liquidity premium is placed on assets that can be readily and reliably exchanged for money, the ultimate safe harbor in unsettled times. Because of the comfort of knowing an asset can be exchanged for money, market participants pay most attention to current spot prices, and the spot price of the most liquid asset in an asset class usually becomes the conventional benchmark off of which other assets are priced. According to this perspective, rapidly changing prices are no cause for alarm so long as two-way trading continues, but when liquidity suddenly dries up in one market, panic can spread to others.

New York Fed The Federal Reserve Bank of New York (FRBNY). The most powerful of the twelve Federal Reserve district banks. Located in the financial district of Lower Manhattan, the New York Fed is responsible for: US Treasury security auctions, keeping the secondary market for US Treasury securities flowing smoothly, conducting monetary policy by keeping overnight borrowing rates (federal funds rate) close to the target rate set by the Federal Open Market Committee, intervening in the foreign exchange market (on behalf of the US Treasury) during times of extreme stress, and intervening when financial market (or other) shocks pose a threat to the payments system.

Offer (ask) [sell] price The price quoted that a dealer stands willing to sell a currency for.

Outright forward contract A foreign exchange transaction with an exchange rate and amount agreed upon on the trade date for settlement (delivery) on a specific value date in the future, normally between three business days up to one year after the trade date. A convenient hedge against currency risk when future foreign currency payments or receipts are known in advance.

Overshooting model A fundamental model that attempts to explain why exchange rates are so much more volatile than fundamental variables like relative money supplies and rates of inflation. Even without destabilizing speculators, the model shows how a shift in a fundamental variable requires the exchange rate to at first overshoot the new long-run equilibrium before it adjusts to the new equilibrium.

Payments (transactions) currency A currency in which international contracts specifying payment for delivery are denominated. Example: the US dollar (2006) is the world's most important payments currency; most firms engaged in international commerce hold dollar accounts to meet obligations arising from contracts specifying the dollar as the payments currency.

Pip Minimum fluctuation or smallest increment of exchange rate movement used by dealers in quoting exchange rates, usually the fourth decimal place of an exchange rate. For example, a EUR=USD (EUR/USD) quote of 1.2200/1.2206 means there is a 6 pip spread between the bid price ($1.2200) and offer price ($1.2206) for euro.

Purchasing Power Parity Theory that exchange rates will adjust so that currencies will have equivalent purchasing power over real goods and services. If the currency of one area has greater purchasing power over goods and services than the currency of another area, the currency of the first area will be bought up to buy the less expensive goods from the first area. This action will drive up the price of the first currency in terms of the second, and this appreciation of the first currency (depreciation of the second) will continue until the two currencies have equivalent purchasing power over goods and services.

Random walk hypothesis The view that a currency's price (or the price of any other financial asset) is just as likely to rise as to fall from its current, known position. From this perspective, exchange rate movements will not follow any patterns or trends, so technical models cannot be used to forecast exchange rate movements effectively. The most basic random walk begins with a known starting point and takes successive steps of equal distance, each in a random direction. The future path of a random walk cannot be forecast based on past steps taken.

Rational expectations theory   A view that forecasters rationally adjust their forecasting methods based on past forecasting errors. The fine-tuning of forecasting models leads to the same result as the efficient markets theory, that the current price incorporates an accurate assessment of the future value of an asset based on all available information. As random shocks occur, forecasters revise their views of the future, and traders quickly incorporate these views producing random walk behavior.

Reserve currency   a foreign currency held by central banks as a reserve or buffer against external shocks.

RTGS (Real Time Gross Settlement Systems)   Final settlements between financial institutions that are made for total (gross) amounts, one payment at a time. Example: FEDWIRE. Advantages: safety and finality in real time; Disadvantage: requires financial institutions to hold large liquid balances (earning no interest) to cover large payments.

Securities   Financial assets that specify future claims on an issuer; once issued, securities may be exchanged on secondary markets.

Securitization   The process (usually carried out by investment banks) of taking a group of assets, bundling them, dividing the bundle into fractional amounts with legally specified claims for each fraction, and selling these fractional amounts (securities) to investors. Advantages: the bundling of assets carries a lower risk than holding any one of the individual assets taken alone, the distribution of claims on the bundle to many investors distributes the risk of the bundle, and, with many holders of the securities issue, secondary markets develop allowing investors to exchange their holdings for money, providing liquidity that may not have been feasible for the original assets.

Settlement   Process of finalizing an exchange.

Settlement system   System that financial institutions use for handling large volumes of exchanges between each other.

Speculative bubble model   An exchange rate model that contains groups of traders acting on different trading strategies, some based on fundamental factors and others following technical trends. As an exchange rate begins forming an upward trend, a larger proportion of traders shift to a technical trading strategy, thus reinforcing the trend and creating conditions for a bubble to form. In the bubble phase, the exchange rate gets absurdly out of line with fundamentals, making it ever more vulnerable to being popped.

Spot contract The basic foreign exchange contract, usually specifying settlement (delivery) within two business days of when the trade takes place, a convention set to allow time for settlement between banks and delivery to the appropriate accounts to be accomplished across two different banking systems.

Spread (bid/offer spread) [bid/ask spread] The gap between the buying (bid) price and the selling (offer) [ask] price a currency dealer quotes simultaneously. When markets become more volatile, less liquid, or less competitive, bid/offer spreads widen. Spreads are a major source of earnings for foreign exchange dealers, who typically do not charge sales commissions or transaction fees.

Stock (equity) A type of security that gives the owner a specified share or fractional claim on the capital or net worth of an enterprise; stockholders are sometimes paid dividends from the net income of a corporation.

Straight dates Value (delivery) dates for foreign exchange contracts that are regularly traded in the inter-dealer market (e.g. 1 week, 2 weeks, 1, 2, 3, 6 and 12 months); a three month forward contract for EUR/USD trades would be considered a straight date contract because of the large turnover volume, but a 51-day forward contract is not regularly traded and would be called a 'broken-date' or 'odd date' contract. Because of increased liquidity and competition in straight-dated contracts, trades can be accomplished more quickly and the available bid/offer spreads are typically thinner than on broken-dated contracts.

SWIFT (Society for Worldwide Interbank Financial Telecommunication) The largest message-carrying system for global payments. SWIFT is a financial industry member-owned cooperative that sets standards for payments messages, and supplies interface software, secure networks and other messaging services to financial institutions.

Swissies Currency trading slang for Swiss francs; one Swissie is sometimes used to mean a contract for 1 million Swiss francs.

TARGET The official payments system for cross-border funds transfers in euro; Europe's version of Fedwire.

Technical forecasting Forecasts based on past exchange rate behavior. Technical forecasters, also called **chartists**, look for patterns of past exchange rate behavior in charts and base their forecasts and currency strategies on these observed patterns under the assumption that patterns tend to repeat themselves.

Terms currency The second currency quoted in a currency pair. In the example GBP=1.81USD (GBP/USD) the US dollar is the 'terms' or pricing currency and the British pound is the 'base' currency. In this case £1 is worth $1.81.

US Department of Treasury Department of the executive branch of the United States federal government. The Treasury Department collects revenues and disburses expenditures. When federal revenues from taxes and other sources are insufficient to cover spending, the US Treasury sells securities to cover for the shortfall, thereby increasing the federal debt by the amount of the federal deficit.

Value date The date a foreign exchange contract settles and the currencies are due to be delivered to the appropriate bank accounts.

Vehicle currency A currency in foreign exchange markets that, because of its liquidity, is used as a vehicle to move between less liquid currency pairs. The US dollar is frequently used as the vehicle for moving between non-commonly traded currency pairs. For example to sell Mexican pesos to buy South Korean won, it is faster and less expensive to first sell Mexican pesos for US dollars (for which there is active trading) and then to sell the US dollars for South Korean won (for which there is also active trading) than to wait for the chance that someone has South Korean won who wishes to buy Mexican pesos (an avenue through which there is little or no active trading).

World Bank (IBRD International Bank for Reconstruction and Development) One of the international financial institutions originating in the Bretton Woods Conference of 1944, its main purposes being to provide development funds and technical assistance for infrastructure, agriculture, industry, education, health and other development projects in developing countries. The World Bank Group, headquartered in Washington DC, includes five development assistance organizations including the IBRD (the largest of the five), the International Development Agency, the International Finance Corporation, the Multilateral Investment Guarantee Agency, and the International Center for the Settlement of Investment Disputes.

Notes

acknowledgments

1. Paul Davidson, *Financial Markets, Money, and the Real World,* Northampton MA: Edward Elgar, 2002.
2. John Maynard Keynes, *The General Theory of Employment, Interest and Income,* New York: Harcourt, Brace, 1936; *A Treatise on Money: The Pure Theory of Money,* London: Macmillan, 1930; *A Treatise on Money: The Applied Theory of Money,* London: Macmillan, 1930.

preface

1. The *Triennial Central Bank Survey of Foreign Exchange and Derivatives Market Activity* provides the most reliable picture of the structure of foreign exchange markets. These surveys can be downloaded from the Bank for International Settlement's website at www.bis.org/publ/. Early in the survey year, central banks around the world distribute the survey to the major foreign exchange dealers operating within their borders. These middlemen, who hold currency inventories and continuously offer to buy and sell currencies to their customers, keep track of the volume of trades they do in which currency, by type of counter party and type of contract for the entire month of April, at the end of which time they send the information to their central bank, which publishes its version and sends the standardized data along to the Bank for International Settlements for tabulation and distribution. Because of the seriousness attached to the survey by the monetary authorities, dealers pay attention to it, though it means considerable staff time allocated to the project for one month every three years. The portion of the market covered by the survey has increased as more central banks have taken on this duty. From four central banks participating in the first survey in 1986, the number has risen

to fifty-two in 2004, increasing survey coverage to an estimated 94 per cent of the world currency market. These snapshots of money-changing activity taken from the vantage point of the money changers themselves provides us with benchmark information on the size of the market, the geographical location of trading, the currencies and contracts traded, the concentration of the market in the hands of major middlemen, who the middlemen trade with, and other information useful for watching the evolution of the system over time. Also helpful are the national results of the survey published by and posted on the websites of the Federal Reserve Bank of New York, the Bank of England, the Bank of Japan, and other central banks. The national survey results often contain more evidence on concentration in the business and technological features of trading.

Far less representative than the central bank survey, but useful for visualizing the changing structure of the market, is an annual poll taken by *Euromoney* magazine that surveys the corporate treasurers, institutional fund managers, hedge fund managers, and other clients who deploy the services of the major foreign exchange dealers. Essentially this poll takes a picture of the money changers from the vantage point of the customers. While the statistical coverage varies widely from one poll to the next and compliance is voluntary, the *Euromoney FX Survey* published every May reveals the names of the major currency dealers and their market shares as derived from information supplied by their clients, features left out of the confidential central bank survey. If results are read with a critical eye, one can compare surveys from one year to the next and get a glimpse of the changing face of competition as major players merge and jockey for position at the top. Also one can see changes in the client base and the technologies clients use to place orders with the currency dealers.

2. From my perspective as a heterodox economist, the great contribution of orthodox economics is in the realm of deductive modeling. From some simplifying assumptions, results can be logically derived that allow one to simulate how an admittedly artificial system responds to shocks, and one can test how sensitive a system is to changes in behavioral parameters. By estimating behavioral parameters statistically and then introducing plausible shocks, these models are useful in making forecasts. When interpreted with proper judgment, deductive models yield critical insights into the working of a more complex world. As I see it, a problem arises when a practitioner becomes so attached to a model that he or she mistakes it for the real world. In such instances the model is being used as a blinder instead of a lens.

3. The inductive method used here could be called strategic ethnography, whereby close attention is paid to the strategic position of the organization being observed or the person being interviewed. For example, in order to interpret what I am observing in a trading room I need to know the strategic position of the trading room within the enterprise and in connection with the larger market. A short interview with the chief economist or someone else higher up in the enterprise can help establish a strategic overview of the trading room's position. Also helpful is to go into the fieldwork setting with a structural mapping of the overall system taken from comprehensive survey data. With this preparation, I can more quickly sort out the division of labor, information flows, counter parties to deals, client connections, and other relations observed in the trading room, and I am in a better frame of mind to pick up cues on market power of the enterprise in relation to clients and to major currency dealers at the center of the market. From all this, I try

to arrive at an understanding of the strategic logic of that enterprise's participation in the currency market. I then attempt to arrange visits to enterprises that occupy very different positions in the system to illuminate the market from alternative vantage points. Frequently my working hypotheses turn out wrong in some way, or I observe a market channel or convention I was unaware of or did not understand. Occasionally, I luck out and meet an expert whose wealth of direct experience sheds bright light on system dynamics. The ethnographic fieldwork allows me to return with fresh eyes to analyze survey data, read financial news reports, and interpret results of economic studies.

4. Readers familiar with my previous research in Central America will recognize the multidisciplinary approach used to uncover the social relations of production, finance, and exchange of a key economic activity. The Central America studies examined product chains of real physical commodities, cotton and beef in the first book, and coffee in the second. See Robert G. Williams, *Export Agriculture and the Crisis in Central America*, Chapel Hill: University of North Carolina Press, 1986; and *States and Social Evolution: Coffee and the Rise of National Governments in Central America*, Chapel Hill: University of North Carolina Press, 1994. *The Money Changers* examines the phases of exchange and delivery in an industry that supplies a service: the global transfer of purchasing power.

5. For college students interested in pursuing topics covered in this book, I highly recommend taking courses in macroeconomics and international finance.

introduction

1. On its website, Visa allows you to estimate the rate your account will be charged for cash advances in twenty-four currencies. You put in your home currency, the foreign currency you are buying, and the markup (0 per cent to 5 per cent) your bank charges, and the currency converter calculates the exchange rate you may receive if your purchase is posted that day. The rates Visa charges your bank are very close to wholesale foreign exchange rates. Merchants are increasingly offering to convert into your home currency when they bill you, but there may be implicit charges you should ask about, www.corporate.visa.com/pd/consumer_ex_rates.jsp?src=sitemap.

2. Visa instituted the 1 per cent 'international service assessment' on 1 April 2005 for all cross-border payments and suspended its 'multi-currency conversion fee.' For example, if you travel to Ecuador, where the US dollar is the currency, you will have no exchange rate, but Visa will collect the 1 per cent international service assessment anyway. Almost 30 per cent of Visa's revenue in 2004 came from 'multi-currency conversion fees,' and the annual report cited strong growth in cross-border payments as one of the reasons. Visa International, *Annual Report 2004*. Card companies have various ways of handling currency conversions and their methods and charges change periodically, so it is a good idea before traveling to check with your card-issuing bank for up-to-date billing details.

3. US Commerce Department, Bureau of Economic Analysis, 'National Income and Product Accounts,' 'Nominal GDP and its Components 2004,' 26 May 2005.

4. WTO, International Trade Statistics Database, 1 June 2005. Comparing 1984 and 2004, world trade in current prices rose almost fivefold (4.8 times 1984 levels), but when deflated by price level increases, real world trade in goods and services

expanded 2.9 times 1984 levels.

5. Bank for International Settlements, *Triennial Central Bank Survey Foreign Exchange and Derivatives Market Activity in 2004*, 17 March 2005.

6. US Department of Commerce, Bureau of Economic Analysis, 'National Income and Product Accounts,' revised 26 May 2005 (www.bea.gov/bea/) estimates total GDP in 2004 for the United States at $11.7 trillion. World Trade Organization, 'Statistical Data, World Trade in Goods and Services,' 31 May 2005, http://stat.wto.org. Trade in services for 2004 was estimated at $2.09 trillion and world trade in merchandise was estimated at $9.3 trillion, giving a total trade value for goods and services of $11.4 trillion. Because total world exports and imports should be identical, exports and imports were added and the sum divided by two to even out the statistical discrepancy in measurement.

7. World development indicators database, World Bank, April 2005, estimates 2003 world GDP at $36.5 trillion and estimates a 2.8 per cent growth rate in 2004, yielding a $37.5 trillion preliminary estimate of world GDP in 2004.

8. New York Stock Exchange, Statistics Archive, 'Daily Share Volume,' 31 May 2005.

9. Federal Reserve Bank of St Louis, 'Federal Debt Statistics,' 31 May 2005. The $3.5 trillion figure does not include debt held by the Federal Reserve. 'Federal Debt Held by Private Investors' includes foreign official and non-official holders but does not include debt held by Federal Reserve Banks. 'Federal Debt Held by Foreign & International Investors' includes foreign central bank and private holdings.

10. Bond Market Association, Research–Statistical Data, 'Average Daily Trading Volume – US Treasury Securities – Monthly,' 2 June 2005.

chapter 2

1. Mr Roberts is referring to the Bretton Woods System set up after World War II, when most currencies were pegged at fixed rates to the dollar, and the dollar was pegged at a fixed rate to gold. Currency fluctuations were minor, except at rare moments when a currency under pressure would be revalued or devalued. In 1968, the US quit exchanging gold with private holders of dollars, and in 1972 closed the gold window to foreign monetary authorities. What emerged was a mixed exchange rate system, and the dollar floated against other currencies.

2. The key connecting place between the lakes is the City of London, where banks from all over the world borrow and lend major currencies without having to hold reserves or pay taxes. The borrowing and lending rates in this unfettered offshore money market are used to price forward contracts, swaps, and other foreign exchange derivatives in the major currencies.

3. Fifty-three central banks participated in the April 2004 survey, and forty-three dealers in the United States participated in it.

4. He also mentions that electronic brokerage has reduced the number of inter-dealer trades. He says his dealers used to have to make trades with some of the big banks just to find out what the real going rates were in the market. With electronic brokerage, his dealers can find out immediately what the others in the market will trade with his bank for, and they don't have to enter a trade to find out. He thinks this has reduced the volume of inter-dealer trades.

5. Gabriele Galati and Michael Melvin, 'Why Has FX Trading Surged? Explaining

the 2004 Triennial Survey,' *BIS Quarterly Review*, December 2004.

6. Mr Roberts said that 'spot-next' and 'tomorrow-next' swaps are frequently used by financial houses when they are temporarily short of a currency but are due to receive payments in that currency soon; he describes this use of the FX swap as rolling over settlement dates to balance currency positions. Swap points are calculated from interest rate differentials between currencies, so portfolio managers use swaps to hedge against or bet on changes in interest rate differentials. Banks can use swaps as an alternative to borrowing in a currency where one doesn't have established credit relations. For example, a US bank that needs foreign currency for a period but would have a difficult time getting a loan in that currency can use a swap. It could borrow in dollars where credit is best, swap for foreign currency for the period the currency is needed, when a reverse back into dollars would occur. The swap is equivalent to getting a collateralized loan in the foreign currency. A very clear exposition of how to calculate forward premium/discount points, swap points, and options pricing is in Sam Cross, *All About the Foreign Exchange Market in the United States*, Federal Reserve Bank of New York, 1998, chs 5 and 6.

chapter 4

1. For full details of the Barings crisis, see: Bank of England, *Report of the Board of Banking Supervision Inquiry into the Circumstances of the Collapse of Barings*, London: Bank of England, 18 July 1995.

2. Mr Roberts is referring to Federal Reserve Bank of New York, 'The Foreign Exchange and Interest Rate Derivatives Markets Survey: Turnover in the United States,' April 2004 Survey, p. 7. US survey results show the market share of the five largest dealers rose from a third of the spot market activity in 1998 to 41 per cent of the FX spot market in 2001 to 47 per cent of spot turnover in 2004. Similar increases in concentration were found in the outright forwards (the top ten accounted for 77 per cent of this segment of the market in 2004, up from 69 per cent in 2001) and FX swap markets (top ten accounted for 76 per cent in 2004 up from 68 per cent in 2001).

3. The central bank survey of the US foreign exchange market during the 1990s confirms jockeying for position at the top more closely followed by the *Euromoney* surveys. For example, in the US market, only three of the firms that were in the top five in 1995 remained there in 1998, and only six of the top ten firms in 1995 stayed in the top ten in 1998. Among those six that remained, only one rose in rank and the other five fell. Bank for International Settlements, *Central Bank Survey of Foreign Exchange and Derivatives Market Activity in April 1998*, Basle, 1999.

4. Financial innovations and the formation of financial holding companies have blurred the traditional distinctions between commercial banking and other types of banking, but a key distinction is that commercial banks accept deposits that are guaranteed to be usable on demand and that are thoroughly interchangeable with currency. This account money function requires a commercial bank to hold reserves of vault cash to support currency withdrawals and to hold highly liquid reserve deposits (at the Federal Reserve, for example) to support net outflows of account money to other commercial banks. When commercial banks make loans they credit the borrower's account with the funds; in this way they are said to be 'issuing' account money. Also when a customer places currency on deposit,

the commercial bank 'issues' account money to the customer in exchange for the currency. Account money at commercial banks is the ultimate settlement for most financial market transactions, including foreign exchange. Traditionally investment banks and brokerage houses were by law separated from commercial banks, and they held account money deposits at commercial banks to settle financial market transactions. Now financial holding companies have commercial banks, investment banks, brokerage houses, and insurance companies all under the same ownership structure. The commercial banking arm still does the account money function for the other arms, so when Salomon/Smith Barney (investment bank/brokerage business) delivers final payments it does so through its commercial bank, Citibank.

chapter 5

1. The number of branches and subsidiaries of foreign banks in March 2004 were 287 in London, 235 in New York, 129 in Frankfurt, 157 in Paris, and 74 in Tokyo. IFSL, 'International Financial Markets in the U.K.', London: International Financial Services in London, May 2005, p. 6, Table 7.
2. Ibid., p. 2, Table 3. Statistics are for 2004.
3. New York has about twice the number of hedge fund managers as the second largest center, London, and the US has (end of 2004) about 70 per cent of the world's hedge fund assets under management. Ibid., p. 13.
4. Bank for International Settlements, *April 2004 Triennial Central Bank Survey of Foreign Exchange and Derivatives Market Activity*, Basle, March 2005.
5. For the year 2003, it was estimated that the City of London (the 'square mile') employed 311,000 people, 145,000 of whom were in financial services. IFSL, 'International Financial Markets in the U.K.', p. 2, Table 2.
6. This description of the world trading day is taken from a chart on euro/dollar and dollar/yen average one-minute volumes calculated from Electronic Brokerage Service data from 1999–2003 taken for the summer session trading days when North America and Europe are observing daylight savings time. Tokyo and other major Asian financial centers stay on standard time throughout the year, thereby removing one hour of overlapping bankers' hours between Asia and Europe. The charts for this data set are presented in a working paper by A. Chaboud, Sergey Chernenko, Edward Howorka, Raj Krishnasami Iyer, David Liu, and Jonathan Wright, 'The High-Frequency Effects of U.S. Macroeconomic Data Releases on Prices and Trading Activity in the Global Interdealer Foreign Exchange Market,' International Finance Discussion Papers No. 823, Board of Governors Federal Reserve System, November 2004, Figure 1a. Also see Sam Cross, *All About the Foreign Exchange Market in the United States*, New York: Federal Reserve Bank of New York, p. 17.
7. Raymond de Roover, *The Rise and Decline of the Medici Bank*, Cambridge MA: Harvard University Press, 1963, pp. 128–9.
8. *Euromoney*, May 2005, Foreign Exchange Poll.
9. Edward Seidensticker, *Low City, High City*, New York: Alfred Knopf, 1983, pp. 190–91.
10. Takeo Yazaki, *Social Change and the City in Japan*, Tokyo: Japan Publications, 1968, p. 348.
11. Ibid., pp. 426–29.

12. De Roover, *The Rise and Decline of the Medici Bank*, p. 3.
13. Ibid., p. 80.
14. Seven Bardis from three generations were partners, branch managers, and employees of Medici branches at different times, and two, Ilarione Bardi and Benedetto Bardi, served terms as general manager of the entire Medici bank in Florence. Contessina di Bardi married Cosimo de Medici in 1413. Ibid., pp. 386–7.
15. Raymond de Roover attributes the failure of the Peruzzi enterprise in 1343 to excessive lending to Edward III, 'who owed them the value of a realm.' The houses of Bardi and Acciaiuoli failed shortly before the Black Death (1348) due to similar reasons, according to de Roover, ibid., p. 2.
16. In essence if the Church had more deposits than withdrawals, it meant the bank in question had interest-free access to the capital, but if a pope was an excessive spender it meant the bank was forced to lend to the Vatican at zero interest. The Medici Bank gave up the Rome account for this reason in the late fifteenth century during a portion of the reign of Pope Sixtus IV. Ibid., ch. 9, pp. 194–224.
17. William Clarke, *How the City of London Works*, 5th edn, September 1999, p. 121.
18. Personal interview with William Clarke, London, 2 July 1999.
19. Brian Groom, 'UK to Target Offshore Tax Havens,' *Financial Times*, 20 March 2000.
20. Tony Dawe, 'City Remains the Capital of Euroland,' *The Times*, Tuesday 23 November 1999, p. 5.

chapter 6

1. Federal Reserve Chairman, Alan Greenspan, 'The Euro as an International Currency,' Presentation to the Euro 50 Group Roundtable, Washington DC, 30 November 2001.

chapter 7

1. Also the portfolio balance approach watches money supply growth, but the mechanism of adjustment is through capital flows. Very simply put, excess money growth in one area will spill abroad as portfolio managers expect higher returns elsewhere. This capital flow will drive down the value of the currency of the high money growth area, though there may be a lag before the flow gets going.
2. The original table has thirty-one currencies listed. Big Mac Purchasing Power Parity Exchange Rate is found by dividing the cost of a Big Mac in local currency (incl. taxes) by the average cost of a Big Mac (incl. taxes) in four US cities ($2.54). For each country it gives the exchange rate that would make a Big Mac cost the same as in the US. Source: 'Big Mac Currencies,' *The Economist*, 21 April 2001, p. 74.
3. 'Big Mac Currencies: Can Hamburgers Provide Hot Tips about Exchange Rates?', *The Economist*, 12 April 1997.

chapter 8

1. Rudiger Dornbusch, 'Expectations and Exchange Rate Dynamics,' *Journal of Political Economy*, vol. 84, no. 6, 1976, 1161–76. Dornbusch, 'Exchange Rate Economics: 1986,' *Economic Journal* 97, March 1987, 1–18.
2. It is thought that the term 'random walk' was first used in a 1905 article in *Nature*.

The discussion was on how optimally to search for a drunk who'd been left in a field. The best way would be to go to the precise place where he was left. K. Pearson and Lord Rayleigh, 'The Problem of the Random Walk,' *Nature* 72, 1905, pp. 294–342. Burton Malkiel applied the concept along with the efficient markets hypothesis to the stock market in his celebrated book *A Random Walk down Wall Street*, New York: W.W. Norton, 1973, which has been revised and updated at least seven times.

3. Richard Meese, 'Currency Fluctuations in the Post Bretton Woods Era,' *Journal of Economic Perspectives*, vol. 4, no. 1, Winter 1990, pp. 117–34; Richard Meese and Kenneth Rogoff, 'Empirical Exchange Rate Models of the Seventies: Do They Fit Out of Sample?' *Journal of International Economics*, vol. 14, no. 3024, 1983. Economists in the 1970s used data from past exchange rate changes to test for which fundamental variables best explained the behavior of exchange rates. Meese and Rogoff took a comprehensive range of the best explanatory models from the 1970s and tested them against 1980s' data. They also took a range of private-sector forecasting firms and compared forecasts with what actually happened to exchange rates. Their findings were that neither the best fundamental models nor the professional forecasters beat a pure random walk. The study provoked a huge controversy in the economics profession.

4. In a pure random walk previous movements from spot rates would not be correlated with later movements from spot rates. Studies have found that there is serial auto-correlation in the movements of rates, so some trending is taking place. Christina Liu and Jia He, 'A Variance-Ratio Test of Random Walks in Foreign Exchange Rates,' *Journal of Finance*, vol. 46, no. 2, June 1991, p. 773.

5. Jeffrey A. Frankel and Kenneth A. Froot, 'Understanding the U.S. Dollar in the Eighties: Expectations of the Chartists and the Fundamentalists,' *Economic Record* 62, Supplementary Issue, 1986, pp. 24–38.

6. Paul De Grauwe, 'Exchange Rates in Search of Fundamental Variables,' Centre for Economic Policy Research, Discussion Paper No. 1073, December 1994.

7. Paul De Grauwe, H. De Wachter, and M. Embrechts, *Exchange Rate Theory: Chaotic Models of the Foreign Exchange Markets*, Oxford: Basil Blackwell, 1993.

8. For microstructure tests of the treasury market see Michael Fleming and Eli Remolona, 'Price Formation and Liquidity in the US Treasury Market: The Response to Public Information,' *Journal of Finance*, vol. 54, no. 5, October 1999, and more recently Pierluigi Balduzzi, Edwin Elton, and T. Clifton Green, 'Economic News and Bond Prices: Evidence from the US Treasury Market,' *Journal of Financial and Quantitative Analysis*, vol. 36, no. 4, December 2001.

9. Reuters saved the electronic dealing conversations to settle potential trading disputes, and Richard Lyons and Martin Evans used four months of foreign exchange dealer conversations (through the Reuters 2000–1 direct dealing system in 1996) to test the role of net order flow (buying or selling pressure) on German mark–dollar and dollar–yen prices. Martin Evans and Richard Lyons, 'Order Flow and Exchange Rate Dynamics,' *Journal of Political Economy*, vol. 110, no. 1, February 2002, pp. 170–80. More recently, another team used Reuter's bid–ask quotes to construct a 5-minute interval price series from January 1992 to January 1998 which allowed them to test the currency price effects of macroeconomic announcements for seven currency pairs. Torben Andersen, Tim Bollerslev, Francis Diebold, and Clara Vega, 'Micro Effects of Macro Announcements: Real-Time Price Discovery in Foreign

Exchange,' *American Economic Review* 93, 1998, pp. 38–62.

10. The Bank of England April 2004 foreign exchange survey found that 48 per cent of total foreign exchange turnover was going through electronic platforms and 66 per cent of spot market activity was going through inter-dealer electronic platforms. Electronic brokerage systems were capturing two-thirds of inter-dealer spot trades in the UK in 2001 and 2004. The proportions were about half that in the US market. Peter Williams, 'The Foreign Exchange and Over-the-Counter Derivatives Market in the United Kingdom,' *Bank of England Quarterly Bulletin*, Winter 2004, p. 474, Table C. EBS (Electronic Brokerage Service) gets the lion's share of euro–US dollar and US dollar–yen spot market, while Reuters electronic brokerage service takes the lion's share of sterling–US dollar trades. One group of researchers from the Fed is now working with a five-year long time series (January 1999 to January 2004) of second-by-second dealable prices and minute-by-minute actual trade volumes that were entered through Electronic Brokerage Service, the largest broker for euro–dollar and dollar–yen currency pairs. Alain Chaboud, Sergey Chernenko, Edward Howorka, Raj Iyer, David Liu, and Jonathan Wright, 'The High-Frequency Effects of Macroeconomic Data Releases on Prices and Trading Activity in the Global Interdealer Foreign Exchange Market,' International Financial Discussion Papers No. 823, Federal Reserve Board of Governors, November 2004; and David Berger, Alain Chaboud, Sergey Chernenko, Edward Howorka, Raj Iyer, David Liu, and Jonathan Wright, 'Order Flow and Exchange Rate Dynamics in Electronic Brokerage System Data,' International Financial Discussion Papers No. 823, Federal Reserve Board of Governors, April 2005.

11. Kathryn Dominguez, 'The Market Microstructure of Central Bank Intervention,' NBER Working Paper 7337, September 1999.

12. The speech she was referring to was: Alan Greenspan, Remarks at the European Banking Congress, Frankfurt, 19 November 2004.

13. Ito studied forecasts of 44 Japanese companies, including 15 banks and brokerage houses, 4 securities companies, 6 trading companies, 9 export-oriented firms, 5 import-oriented companies, and 5 life insurance companies. Takatoshi Ito, 'Foreign Exchange Rate Expectations: Micro Survey Data,' *American Economic Review*, vol. 80, no. 3, June 1990, pp. 434–49.

14. There is controversy over whether the largest currency dealers can use their favorable private information vantage point to enhance their own trading profits. Alan Greenspan doesn't seem to think so when he says, 'The seeming ability of a number of banking organizations to make consistent profits from foreign exchange trading likely derives not from their insight into exchange determination but from the revenues they derive from making markets.' On the other hand, microstructure studies have shown that signed net order flow, at least over short periods, explains a high portion of exchange rate changes, e.g. when there are more buy orders than sell orders, the price of that currency rises. Evans and Lyons, 'Order Flow and Exchange Rate Dynamics.' This result implies that large dealers with a market share larger than say 5 per cent of the entire market have a sample size that allows them to gauge the whole market through the order flow going through their trading rooms than a dealer with less than 1 per cent of the market. An even larger sample size like Deutsche Bank's reported 16 per cent of the market in a 2005 survey would give Deutsche Bank an edge if the management were able to channel this information effectively to the firm's proprietary traders, those who

make bets on currency moves with the bank's own capital. Others would reply that the order flow advantage is very fleeting (which it may be). But Genevieve would probably reply that even if order flow doesn't give an advantage for long, the close connections the research departments of the major dealers have with important foreign exchange customers gives good researchers an edge in anticipating how the customers are likely to act in different scenarios, allowing them to anticipate changes in order flow with greater lead time than analysts from smaller outfits.

15. In 2001 Genevieve's organization signed on to FXall, the multi-bank portal set up by Bank of America, Goldman Sachs, and some of the other big players. FXall became the leading multi-bank portal in April 2002, when Citibank, Deutsche Bank, and JPMorgan Chase abandoned their multi-bank portal (ATRIAX) and integrated their systems into FXall. With a single logon and password entry, Genevieve says she can go to the research screen and select from all the research products of the dealers her company has credit with. She can go to the calendar screen and see when important data will be released, and she can click to get access to released data. She can go to the forecast window and see consensus forecasts on almost thirty currencies, and then she can click on the currency and obtain individual forecasts. Without having to log on again, she can launch trading, obtain price quotes from several dealers at once, execute orders, and have the orders processed straight through. In addition to FXall, FX Connect, and Currenex provide multi-bank access at a single site. User access to many research departments at once has added clout to the story-generating power of the best analytical teams. In the 2005 *Euromoney* survey, approximately half of the group of respondents who were using multi-bank access portals were using FXall and approximately a quarter reported using FX Connect. Deborah Kimbell, Andrew Newby, David Skalinder, 'The Big Get Bigger – But is it for the Best?' *Euromoney* 2005 FX Poll, *Euromoney*, vol. 36, issue 433, May 2005.

16. In the *Euromoney* customer survey in May 2005, four of the top five dealers in overall market share were ranked in the top five with respect to quality of research in all categories (fundamental analysis, technical analysis, quantitative, short-term, long-term, options and volatility, flow research, risk advisory and hedging and tailor-made research. Those ranked best in research were Deutsche Bank, Citibank, UBS, HSBC, and JPMorgan; JPMorgan was the only one not ranked in the top five in market share. *Euromoney* 2005 FX Poll, Research Tables.

chapter 9

1. CLS Corporate Communication, 'CLS Bank Settles New Record Value,' *CLS News*, 15 December 2004, www.cls-group.com; CHIPS Annual Statistics, 28 February 2005, www.chips.org.

2. See CLS Bank, 'Q&A for Banks and Brokers,' 'Q&A for Corporates,' and 'Q&A for Funds,' 2005, www.cls-group.com.

3. Passacantando is referring to the largest international carrier of money messages, SWIFT, the Society for Worldwide Interbank Financial Telecommunication. SWIFT transports a larger value of payment instructions in an ordinary working day than VisaNet, the biggest retail network, carries in an entire year. In addition, SWIFT is the largest messenger service for international securities transfers. SWIFT was started by a group of private banks in 1973 in response to the surge in orders for international money payments and securities transfers. Things were getting

confusing, and these banks saw it in their collective interest to set up an electronic communications network that they could all safely use instead of having to rely on a hodgepodge of bilateral communications networks with no industry-wide standards. Since then, SWIFT has set the standards for international bank message formats and bank identifier codes, which other networks make sure they are compatible with. SWIFT accepts messages from participants, validates them, matches orders, stores them, and delivers messages to other participants in the network. In Canada, France, and England SWIFT handles more than one-quarter of their domestic banking systems' message traffic.

4. To keep payments flowing smoothly, many RTGS systems allow intraday credits, usually collateralized, to participants. But this is costly, too, in that large blocks of collateral are tied up to secure intraday credit, or the central bank charges for overdrafts.

5. The unwind would have occurred despite the fact that only 1 per cent of the ECU payments that day had anything to do with Barings. See Bank for International Settlements, *Settlement Risk in Foreign Exchange Transactions*, Basle, March 1996, pp. 6–8.

6. The Group of 10 central banks initiated efforts to reduce cross-currency settlement risk, and a special committee on payments systems was set up at the Bank for International Settlements to deal with cross-currency settlement risk and securities settlement risk. Among the reports available at www.bis.org on foreign exchange settlement risk are: 'A Glossary of Terms Used in Payments and Settlement Systems,' January/July 2001; 'Core Principles for Systemically Important Payment Systems,' no. 43, January 2001; 'The Contribution of Payment Systems to Financial Stability,' no. 41, May 2000; 'Core Principles for Systemically Important Payment Systems,' no. 34, July 2000; 'Reducing Foreign Exchange Settlement Risk: A Progress Report,' no. 26, July 1998; 'Real-time Gross Settlement Systems,' no. 22, March 1997; 'Settlement Risk in Foreign Exchange Transactions,' no. 17, March 1996 (Allsopp Report); 'Central Bank Payment and Settlement Services with Respect to Cross-border and Multi-currency Transactions,' no. 7, September 1993 (Noël Report); 'Report of the Committee on Interbank Netting Schemes of the Central Banks of the Group of Ten Countries,' no. 4, November 1990 (Lamfalussy Report); 'Report on Netting Schemes,' no. 2, February 1989 (Angell Report).

7. All of the efforts of central bankers and private industry groups to find solutions to foreign exchange settlement risk led to the creation of the Continuous Linked Settlement Services in 1997. By 2000, the Continuous Linked Settlement Bank was created, and by 2001 more than sixty commercial and investment bank shareholders had invested in excess of $300 million to make continuous linked settlement of currency transactions a reality. In 2002, settlement members tested the new system, and, following Federal Reserve Board approval in October 2002, the system began operating in seven currencies (US dollar, euro, Japanese yen, pound sterling, Swiss franc, Canadian dollar, Australian dollar). For more details, see the appendix to Chapter 11.

8. The primary interview for material in this chapter was in July 1997. Subsequent discussions with Passacantando and more recent updates by the BIS suggest that central banks and private netting systems have worked together to lower settlement risk. But, despite these efforts, cross-currency settlement risk remains a threat to domestic payments systems.

9. In the earlier hypothetical example of three banks, the bilateral amounts owed were many times larger than the net–net amounts. So the chances of a participant running into a liquidity bind, being unable to settle, is much larger for bilateral netting arrangements between banks than in multilateral netting with many banks. The study encouraged multilateral netting to reduce exposures, and it suggested best practices of multilateral netting arrangements.

10. For example, computer programs have been developed that allow much smoother payments processing and message transmission, so payments can be timed or re-ordered in such a way that they are kept moving. Real time gross settlements systems, deferred netting systems, and hybrid systems have all benefited from information technology of this sort. See BIS, Report No. 43, 'Core Principles for Systemically Important Payment Systems,' Box 8: Hybrid Systems, January 2001.

11. Since this first interview with Passacantando on payments systems the eleven national payments systems of Europe were merged when the euro formed (January 1999). All of the national RTGS systems of the euro area are integrated into the TARGET system, so simultaneous settlements denominated in euros can be made across Europe, just as the final payments between banks in California and Maine can be made at the same moment through the Fedwire system.

12. For a description of the funds transfer system see New York Clearing House Association, CHIPS, 'The Transfer of Funds Yesterday,' p.5.

13. On 22 January 2001, CHIPS went online with a hybrid system that nets payments bilaterally and multilaterally in flexible batches using a complex algorithm. This system allows for real-time settlement but very low funding balances need to be held at the Fed. This recent improvement is discussed in the appendix to Chapter 11.

14. Mergers and acquisitions have reduced the number of CHIPS participants. By August 2001, there were fifty-nine participants in CHIPS. Smaller foreign banks without offices in New York frequently use correspondent services of a CHIPS participant to deliver dollar payments for them, www.chips.org.

15. Three years after this interview, CHIPS made the major processing breakthrough that achieves real-time finality while maintaining the cost efficiencies of netting. This best-of-both-worlds system will be discussed in the update appendix to Chapter 11 along with Continuous Linked Settlement, which provides a settlement path that eliminates foreign exchange settlement risk.

chapter 10

1. Since the interview with George Thomas in July 1997, the New York Automated Clearing House (NYACH) facility, which at the time was processing automated payments for the greater New York banking region, went national to become the Electronic Payments Network (EpayNet), the largest of three private ACH systems: EpayNetwork, VisaNet ACH Services, and American Clearing House Association. Its innovations and cost efficiencies have made it the main competitor with the Federal Reserve's automated clearing house service, which has consistently lost market share to EpayNetwork. George Thomas was made president of EpayNetwork. For recent innovations at CHIPS and EPayNetwork see appendix to Chapter 11.

2. Three years after this interview, George Thomas's team of experts brought online a new netting and settlement procedure that allows continuous, final settlements all

day long across pre-funded accounts at Fedwire. Put into operation on 22 January 2001, the new procedure eliminates settlement risk on the dollar leg of foreign exchange deliveries while maintaining the cost efficiencies of netting. What made this breakthrough possible was the invention of the balanced release engine, a payments processing algorithm that George Thomas, Robert Cotton, and Joseph Pawelczyk got patented (United States Patent 6,076,074 Cotton et al., 13 June 2000). For a summary of the more recent evolution of the CHIPS/Fedwire dollar delivery system, see the appendix to Chapter 11.

3. By 2002, EpayNetwork, the smaller value domestic payments system that Thomas now runs, regularly handles 8 million payments a day, but the average payment is $4–5,000 at EPayNetwork compared to average payment size of about $5 million at CHIPS, which handles about 240,000 payments a day.

4. Thomas is referring to 21 January 1997, when 418,743 payments were processed totaling over $2.178 trillion (www.chips.com, 27 August 1997). This record has since been broken.

5. The provision George refers to is contained in the 1991 Federal Deposit Insurance Corporation Improvement Act.

6. The recommendations are in Bank for International Settlements, 'Report of the Committee on Interbank Netting Schemes,' Basle: BIS, November 1990 (Lamfalussy Report).

7. At the time of the interview, 23 July 1997, the following banks owned CHIPS: Bank of New York, Chase Manhattan, Citibank, Morgan Guaranty Trust Company, Bankers Trust Company, Marine Midland Bank, United States Trust Company of New York, National Westminster Bank USA, European American Bank, and Republic National Bank of New York. In 2005, CHIPS had 50 participants that settled continuously with prefunded balances at the Fed. In 2005, the Clearing House was owned by the US commercial banking affiliates of: ABN AMRO, Bank of America, The Bank of New York, Citigroup, Deutsche Bank, Fleet National Bank, HSBC, JPMorgan Chase, US Bank, Wachovia and Wells Fargo. www.chips. org, 30 March 2005.

chapter 11

1. Bank for International Settlements, *Supervisory Guidance for Managing Settlement Risk in Foreign Exchange Transactions*, September 2000; Bank for International Settlements, *Settlement Risk in Foreign Exchange Transactions*, March 1996.

2. The CLS bank's website reported 170,000 average daily transactions for a gross average daily value of $1.9 trillion in late 2004. The gross amount counts both sides of each trade. In the April 2004 Foreign Exchange Survey, the average *net* daily turnover in the world currency market was approximately $1.9 trillion, so CLS was settling approximately half that value. The CLS website reports a record gross value day of $3.684 trillion set on 15 December 2004. CLS News, 'CLS Bank Settles New Record Value,' 15 December 2004, www.cls-group.com.

3. For a more detailed description of the 'balanced release engine' and the simulated test runs, see Cotton et al., 'System and Method for Intraday Netting Payment Finality,' U.S. Patent #6076074, at www.uspto.gov/.

4. For final settlement, multilateral net positions of the banks involved in the residual batch of payments are calculated and the banks with a net-debit position exceeding

the remaining funds in its settling account will be notified and given 30 minutes (until 5:30 p.m.) to come up with the additional funding, which will be sent over Fedwire to add to their settling account balance. After all the banks in the net-debit position have deposited any extra cover needed, the funds are sent to the CHIPS settlement account, which in turn distributes these funds to the banks in the net-credit position. At this moment the engine discharges with finality all the payments in the residual batch. If a bank in a net-debit position is unwilling or unable to provide additional cover, the payments that can be made with that bank's existing funding balance are included in the batch and the payments that cannot be settled without additional cover from the dropout bank are removed. The multilateral net positions of the banks with payments remaining in the smaller residual batch are calculated.

5. CLS Services was created by the merger of ECHO and Multinet in 1997. The initial currencies CLS Bank International offered delivery services for in 2002 were: US dollar, euro, Japanese yen, pound sterling, Swiss franc, Canadian dollar, and Australian dollar. In 2005, CLS had added eight more currencies to its settlement services including the Swedish krona, Danish krone, Norwegian krone, Singapore dollar, South African rand, Korean won, Hong Kong dollar, and the New Zealand dollar.

6. Of the thirty top currency dealers according to the *Euromoney* May 2004 survey, the two CLS shareholders that were not also listed as members (those that have settlement accounts) of CLS were Merrill Lynch and AIG. In April 2005, there were 69 shareholders of CLS, 55 of which were members who had settlement accounts at CLS. *Euromoney* FX poll, May 2004. CHIPS customer list at www.chips.org, and CLS lists of shareholders and members at www.cls-group.com.

7. CLS operates as a private limited holding company headquartered in London with CLS Bank based in New York as a special purpose bank under the supervision of the New York Fed. There is a representative office in Tokyo. The central computer system is located in Coventry, UK.

8. CLS Bank uses risk-control algorithms to calculate the net position for each member across all currencies. If volatility of a particular currency is high, and a member has a net long position in that currency, the net overall position is discounted, or as they say, given a 'haircut.'

9. See 'Enhanced FundFX Product Profile,' 'Q&A for Banks and Brokers,' 'Q&A for Funds,' 'Q&A for Corporates,' and 'CLS: How it Works,' at www.cls-group.com.

10. In December 2004, live third-party users of CLS numbered 238. By April 2005, live third-party users reached 400, 165 of which were investment funds. 'CLS Third Party Participants List – 400 Now Live,' 4 April 2005.

11. CHIPS, 'Annual Statistics,' www.chips.org, and CLS, 'CLS Netting Efficiency,' Slide 19 in 'CLS Product Overview,' 2004.

12. See, for example: Payments Risk Committee, 'Managing Payment Liquidity in Global Markets: Risk Issues and Solutions,' New York Federal Reserve, March 2003, and Gabrieli Galati, 'Settlement Risk in Foreign Exchange Markets and CLS Bank,' *BIS Quarterly Review*, December 2002, pp. 55–66.

13. Government Accounting Office (GAO), 'Potential Terrorist Attacks: Additional Actions Needed to Prepare Critical Financial Market Participants,' GAO 03–251 Highlights, February 2003, p. 49.

14. Interview with former student, Midtown Manhattan, 19 May 2004.

15. GAO, 'Potential Terrorist Attacks,' p. 46.
16. Ibid., p. 39.
17. Ibid., p. 49.
18. 'Repo' is short for a repurchase agreement. A firm that wants account money at a bank to make payments coming due that day will enter a repurchase agreement before other markets open with another firm that has excess account money and wants to earn interest on it. The one that wants money will sell the security to the other party and agree to buy it back the next day (or at a later date) at a pre-specified higher price, the difference in the price being an implicit interest payment for borrowing the bank account money for the time period. In a repo transaction, the Treasury security serves as collateral for an implicit loan. The repo market is very active, very efficient, and very well organized, and it is the most reliable source of funding for many participants in the stock, bond, and commodity markets. Looked at as a system, the repo market recycles account money at commercial banks, keeping it in active circulation in the financial markets.
19. GAO, 'Potential Terrorist Attacks,' p. 50.
20. Correspondence with former student, 27 April 2005.
21. GAO, 'Potential Terrorist Attacks,' p. 52.
22. Jeffrey M. Lacker, 'Payment Systems Disruptions and the Federal Reserve Following September 11, 2001,' *Journal of Monetary Economics* 51, 2004, p. 946, Table 1.
23. Stacy Coleman, 'The Evolution of the Federal Reserve's Intraday Credit Policies,' *Federal Reserve Bulletin*, February 2002, p. 81.
24. Under normal circumstances banks are reluctant to borrow overnight from the Fed through the discount window, and to do so they must pledge Treasury securities as collateral and explain their circumstances.
25. The most thorough account of the Fed's actions following the attacks is by Jeffrey Lacker, the current president of the Richmond Fed. Lacker, 'Payment Systems Disruptions,' pp. 944–54. Table 1 on page 946 shows the numerical amounts of each type of action.
26. Ironically the action of lending Treasuries to the dealers reduces the reserves banks have available at the Fed. By Friday the 14th, the cumulative effect of these security loans amounted to a $24 billion drainage of reserves from the system, an amount more than compensated for by the short-term lending by the Fed into the overnight Treasury repo market. The problem of lack of the right type of issues available in the market continued into October. The Fed continued to support the increased needs of certain issues by dealers, and early in October the Treasury had an unscheduled auction of 10-year notes, a maturity highly sought after in secondary markets.
27. Overall the Fed's actions increased reserve levels on Wednesday, Thursday, and Friday by approximately $100 billion over pre-attack levels of only $12 to $13 billion.
28. On Wednesday 12 September, $5 billion was drawn through these central bank swap lines, on Thursday $20 billion was drawn, and on Friday $9 billion. Lacker, 'Payment Systems Disruptions,' p. 946, Table 1.
29. Payments Risk Committee, p. 32.
30. The 'critical financial markets' identified are: foreign exchange, federal funds, commercial paper, government securities, and corporate debt and equity markets. 'Firms that play significant roles' are those that if they were unable to clear and

settle pending transactions by the end of the business day could present systemic risk. As a rule of thumb, the interagency paper gives 5 per cent of a particular market as representing a 'significant role.' Federal Reserve System (Docket No. R-1128) , Office of Comptroller of the Currency (Docket No. 03–05), Securities and Exchange Commission (Release No. 34–47638; File No. S7–32–02), 'Interagency Paper on Sound Practices to Strengthen the Resilience of the U.S. Financial System,' 7 April 2003.

31. The deadlines were set for the end of 2004 for core clearing and settlement organizations, and April 2006 for private firms playing a significant role in a particular critical financial market.

32. Interview with former student, 19 May 2004.

33. The so-called 'inside–outside swaps' at CLS bank allow participating banks to swap currencies with each other inside the system to cover short positions in particular currencies during settlement hours, but these exchanges are reversed after CLS closes the day, when banks rely on the normal foreign exchange swap market to fund the reverse payments.

34. Payments Risk Committee, March 2003, p. 34.

chapter 12

1. The charts Paul prepared for me looked like hourly averages of best bid/ask rates, so they showed greater volatility and they showed a dramatic widening of spreads around the time the particular storms hit. These charts show average daily mid-rates, so the spread information is left out, but they support most of the discussion I had with Paul.

2. Guillermo Calvo, 'Capital Flows and Macroeconomic Management: Tequila Lessons,' *International Journal of Financial Economics* 1, 1996; Guillermo Calvo with E. Mendoza, 'Reflections of Mexico's Balance of Payments Crisis: A Chronicle of a Death Foretold,' *Journal of International Economics*, September 1996; more recently, 'Contagion, Globalization and Volatility of Capital Flows,' in Sebastian Edwards (ed.), *Capital Flows and the Emerging Economies*, Chicago: University of Chicago Press, 2000.

3. In 1999, Persaud left JPMorgan to become managing director and global head of research for Global Markets Group of State Street Bank and Trust, the third largest financial custodian in the world with $6.3 trillion under custody (March 2002). In March 2002 State Street, the number one investment manager for US pension plans and mutual funds, had approximately $808 billion in assets under management. In 2000/01 Persaud was Visiting Scholar at the International Monetary Fund. Some of his recent publications include: 'The Knowledge Gap: A Penny for Your Thoughts?' *Foreign Affairs*, March/April 2001; 'The Puzzling Decline in Financial Market Liquidity,' BIS Papers no. 2, 2001; 'Sending the Herd off the Cliff,' First Prize Essay on Global Finance for the year 2000 in the Institute of International Finance competition in honour of Jacques de Larosière, 27 March 2001; 'Liquidity Black Holes: Why Modern Financial Regulation in Developed Countries is Making Short-term Capital Flows to Developing Countries Even More Volatile,' Discussion Paper no. 2002/31, World Development Institute, March 2002.

4. In 2001 Persaid and a colleague developed a much more sophisticated risk-appetite indicator. See Manmohan Kumar and Avinash Persaud, 'Pure Contagion and

Investors' Shifting Risk Appetite: Analytical Issues and Empirical Evidence,' *IMF Working Paper*, August 2001.

chapter 13

1. The original euro-11 consisted of: Belgium, Germany, Spain, France, Ireland, Italy, Luxembourg, Netherlands, Austria, Portugal, and Finland. Greece joined the European Monetary Union (common currency) in January 2001. Sweden, Denmark, and the United Kingdom are members of the European Union (the common market) but have kept their own currencies. Financial markets converted to the euro on 1 January 1999, but euro notes and coins were not introduced for another three years, beginning in January 2002.

2. According to the first survey of foreign exchange activity following the birth of the euro, in April 2001, the United Kingdom accounted for about $\frac{1}{3}$ of the global foreign exchange turnover in euro, 30 per cent more daily turnover than in all of the euro area combined. This trading was concentrated in London. Similarly in April 2001, the UK captured 35 per cent of the euro-denominated over-the-counter single-currency interest-rate derivatives market, 60 per cent higher turnover than in Germany, the home of the European Central Bank. BIS, April 2001 FX survey, pp. 62, 110. In April 2004, the UK captured 35 per cent of global foreign exchange market turnover in euro and a 54 per cent share of over-the-counter interest-rate derivative contracts in euro. BIS April 2004 FX Survey, pp. 56, 108. In 2004, 60 per cent of the primary trading in eurobonds and 70 per cent of the secondary market trading in eurobonds took place in London. Half of the investment banking business for Europe in 2004 went through London, and London-led teams of experts were managing the structure and distribution of underwriting deals taking place in Italy, the Netherlands, and Spain. 'International Financial Markets in the U.K.,' May 2005, London: International Financial Services, pp. 5, 6.

3. Romano Prodi was quoted in English as saying 'Italy had very low inflation in 1998 but above our European partners. If we continue to have costs which diverge from other European countries it will be more difficult to remain in the Euro... If Italy continues to lose a percentage point of competitiveness per year, as is happening, and if the trend continues in the long term, it will be a tragedy for us. It could be difficult to remain within the Euro.' Stephen Castle, 'Italy told lira cannot withdraw from Euro,' *Independent*, 23 June 1999. Ironically in New York, the Prodi incident was buried in Section C in the tenth paragraph of the Foreign Exchange column of the *Wall Street Journal*. Dagmar Aalund and Marianne Sullivan, 'Dashed Hopes May Hurt Euro,' *Wall Street Journal*, 23 June 1999, p. C15.

4. I have taken data from Johnson's table and made graphics for easier reading.

5. Johnson uses 1998 estimates of GDP and 1990 purchasing power parity exchange rates to make these comparisons.

6. Johnson bases this on 1997 estimates of percentage shares of world trade, which show the euro-11 at 17 per cent of the total, the US at 14 per cent, and Japan at 4 per cent.

7. Johnson estimates that in 1998, the dollar constituted 70 per cent of foreign exchange reserve holdings, the euro-11 11 per cent (most of which was in German marks), and the yen 5 per cent.

8. Bishop uses the Salomon/Smith Barney definition of 'bond' as having a fixed rate

with one year or more left to maturity, and he is counting bonds held outside of the federal governments that issued them.

9. See Bishop, 'Securitising European Savings,' pp. 6–13.
10. Bishop now has a website with coverage of economic and political developments in the European Union. See grahambishop.com.
11. Even with higher local costs, a lower exchange rate allows businesses to continue to compete with lower cost producers elsewhere.
12. At the time of this interview (July 1999) the bull market in the tech sector had entered a bubble phase.
13. EMU: European Monetary Union.
14. The mass conversion to euro of corporate and individual bank accounts did not take place until the final six months of 2001.
15. Translation from Italian mine.

chapter 14

1. Since July 1999, the European Central Bank has been tested repeatedly by the financial markets. A summary of the episodes is included in the update appendix to this chapter.
2. The four 'out' central banks Signor Marini refers to are: Bank of Sweden, Bank of Denmark, Bank of England and Bank of Greece. In January 2001, Greece joined the monetary union, raising the number of euro participants from eleven to twelve.
3. The five private-sector euro payments systems he refers to are EAF in Germany, PNS in France, POPS in Finland, SEPI in Spain, and the EBA (EURO1) pan-European.
4. The ECB responded to problems by updating and distributing the *User's Guide to TARGET.*
5. Bank of England, *Practical Issues Arising from the Euro*, London: Bank of England, June 1999, p. 52.
6. Since the interview with Lewis, CHIPS introduced a real-time net settlement facility that continuously achieves final settlement using pre-funded balances at Fedwire. See appendix to Chapter 11 for a description of the way the new system works.
7. The largest of the private-sector cross-border payments in euro is EURO1, which was set up by the European Bankers Association (EBA), a group that has 118 members with 65 clearing members who include 16 of the 18 member banks of CHAPS-euro. Euro1(EBA) is a pan-European system that has daily multilateral netting cycles with final settlements at the end of the day at the European Central Bank. The second largest is EAF (Euro Access Frankfurt), which has several batch settlements during the day using member accounts at the Bundesbank for final settlements. Euro Access Frankfurt has a total membership of 68 banks, 33 of which are German-based and 35 foreign-based. Eight of the 18 members of CHAPS-euro are also clearing members of EBA and EAF. The overlapping members include: ABN–AMRO, Bank of America, Bank of Tokyo–Mitsubishi, Barclays Bank, Chase Manhattan, Citibank, Deutsche Bank, National Westminster Bank. The third largest is the French one, Paris Net Settlement, which is similar to EAF but has more batches run per day. There are much smaller private netting systems in Spain (SEPI) and Finland (POPS).
8. In June 1999, cross-border TARGET (including CHAPS-euro) payments were

approximately 370 billion euros per day, of which CHAPS-euro (the second-largest RTGS system) processed €62.3 billion per day, or about 15 per cent of the total, and the German-RTGS(ELS) system (the largest) processed 99 billion per day in cross-border payments. The four largest private netting schemes were processing €428 billion per day, of which EURO1(EBA) processed €169 billion, EAF processed €154 billion, PNS processed €100 billion, and SEPI processes €4 billion per day. www.ecb.int/target/stats/table2.htm, 16 August 1999.

9. In March 1999 Robert Pringle and Benedict Weller sent surveys to 100 of the world's 173 central banks. By the 30 April 1999 deadline 48 had responded; 42 per cent of these listed 'lack of a track record on monetary policy' and 'lack of unified capital markets' as obstacles faced by the monetary union. Pringle and Weller (eds), *Reserve Management*, p. 26.

10. When the Maastricht Treaty was signed in 1992 the Executive Board and the national central banks were balanced with six members each on the Governing Council. Now twelve national central bank governors vote in the Governing Council, in contrast with six votes by the members of the Executive Board. As other countries join the monetary union, the imbalance will grow and the Executive Board's relative voting power will be diminished. Relative staffing exaggerates the imbalance.

11. Weller noted a paradox in the survey results. While they were full of doubts about monetary union, most reserve managers said their holdings of euros would rise from current levels, which averaged about one-fifth of their total holdings in April 1999. He said Eastern European central banks responding to the survey averaged more than half their reserves in euro. In our discussion, we concurred that as countries' imports and loan payments became denominated in euro, central bank reserve managers would be inclined to build up their euro balances even if they had doubts about the European Central Bank.

12. The krone has remained closely pegged to the euro within a plus or minus 2.25 per cent band supported by Danish Central Bank euro reserves and an open and credible credit line with the ECB.

13. See, for example: 'Zip It, Wim,' *The Economist*, 21 October 2000, p. 87; 'Intervention: The Euro and Oil,' *The Economist*, 30 September 2000, p. 23, 2p, 1 graph.

14. Banks worked closely, one-on-one, with corporate customers in the switch-over to the euro. Many companies had the euro programming systems ready, but waited to switch because customers and suppliers continued to use legacy currencies. National and local governments were generally slower than the private sector in converting bank account money to euro.

15. For details of bank account conversions, see Bank of England, *Practical Issues Arising from the Euro*, December 2001. For details of the distribution of notes and coins and withdrawal of legacy currencies, see Bank of England, *Practical Issues Arising from the Euro*, May 2002.

16. In 2001, US investment banks had a 32 per cent share of the euro-denominated bond underwriting business. European Commission, *Financial Integration Monitor 2004*, p. 14. By March of 2002 the value of euro-denominated international bonds was two-thirds as large as dollar-denominated international bonds, and by September of 2003, euro-denominated international bonds surpassed dollar-denominated in total amounts outstanding. BIS, *Quarterly Review*, March 2004, p. 34.

17. As a percentage of total outstanding value, the BBB segment of the European bond market went from 2 per cent in 1998 before the euro to 27 per cent in 2003.

Lieven Baele, Annalisa Ferrando, Peter Hordahl, Elizaveta Krylova, and Cyril Monnet, 'Measuring Financial Integration in the Euro Area,' European Central Bank Occasional Paper Series, no. 14, April 2004, p. 46.

18. James McAndrews and Chris Stefanadis, 'The Consolidation of European Stock Exchanges,' Federal Reserve Bank of New York, *Current Issues*, vol. 8, no. 6, June 2002.

19. The German mark accounted for 19.8 per cent of average daily turnover in 1992, 18 per cent in 1995, and 15 per cent in 1998, while the euro accounted for 18.8 per cent of average daily turnover in 2001 and 18.6 per cent in 2004. BIS, *Triennial Central Bank Survey of Foreign Exchange and Derivatives Market Activity in April 2004*, Preliminary Global Results, September 2005, Table 3.

chapter 15

1. Current earnings include export earnings from sales of goods and services, income from accumulated wealth holdings abroad (profits, dividends, rent, royalties, and interest collected from foreigners), gifts from foreigners and foreign government transfers to the US. Current expenditures include payments to foreigners for US imports of goods and services, earnings paid to foreigners on assets they own in the US, foreign aid distributions, and payments for US military bases abroad.

2. Approximately half the dollars in the hands of the public in 2004 were being held abroad by foreigners, an uncollected interest-free loan to Uncle Sam.

3. Government-sponsored agency securities are primarily mortgage-backed securities issued by the Federal National Mortgage Association (Fannie Mae), Federal Home Loan Mortgage Corporation (Freddie Mac), the Government National Mortgage Association (Ginnie Mae), and the Federal Agricultural Mortgage Corporation (Farmer Mac). These agencies buy mortgages from banks, pool and bundle the mortgages, and sell to fund managers and individual investors securities with backing of the bundled mortgages. These securities issues are then traded on secondary markets, making them highly liquid and therefore attractive to fund managers. In the first quarter of 2005 there were approximately $3.55 trillion in mortgage-backed agency securities outstanding and an additional $2.7 trillion in other types of government-sponsored agency securities, compared with $4 trillion in marketable US Treasury securities. Bond Market Association, 'Outstanding Level of Public and Private Bond Market Debt,' July 2005.

4. Michael R. Sesit, 'Going Global: Snow's Remarks Jolt Dollar,' *Wall Street Journal*, 18 November 2004, p. C20.

5. In early March 2002, the Securities and Exchange Commission began an inquiry into questionable accounting procedures at WorldCom, an investigation that led to the admission in late June by WorldCom executives that earnings had been overstated by $3.8 billion, a figure that later turned out to be on the order of $9 billion. This overstatement of earnings had allowed major investment banks to sell some $17 billion in WorldCom bonds to investors between May 2001 and May 2002.

6. Grainne McCarthy, 'Currency Trading: Dollar Falls Against Key Rivals, Amid Fallout from WorldCom,' *Wall Street Journal*, 27 June 2002, p. C13.

7. Grainne McCarthy, 'Currency Trading: Foreign Central Banks' Holdings in Dollars Are Closely Watched,' *Wall Street Journal*, 15 July 2002, p. C11.

8. Michael Phillips, 'Currency Trading: Global Investors Prepare for War,' *Wall Street Journal*, 31 January 2003, p. C10.

9. Agnes Crane, 'Currency Trading: Dollar Declines Against Rivals after Treasury Chief's Comments,' *Wall Street Journal*, 6 March 2003, p. C14.

10. Before joining the Clinton team, Robert Rubin had worked for twenty-six years at Goldman Sachs, one of Wall Street's top investment banks.

11. Michael Phillips, 'Chief Snow Puts Emphasis on Confidence rather than Market Value,' *Wall Street Journal*, 19 May 2003, p. A1.

12. 'Playing with Fire,' *Wall Street Journal*, 20 May 2003, p. A18.

13. Michael Phillips, 'The Economy: U.S. Sways G-7 on Exchange Rates; Endorsement of Flexibility is Jab at Japan and China and a Signal to Voters,' *Wall Street Journal*, 22 September 2003, p. A2.

14. Agnes Crane, 'Treasurys Slide on Demand Fears; Call by G-7 for Flexibility on Foreign Exchange Rates Helps to Spark Steep Selloff,' *Wall Street Journal*, 23 September 2003, p. C15.

15. 'Snow's Currency Job,' *Wall Street Journal*, 23 September 2003, p. A24.

16. Tom Barkley and Jamie McGeever, 'Dollar Hits Low on Euro,' *Wall Street Journal*, 19 November 2003, p. C12.

17. See John D. McKinnon, 'Bush's Big Domestic Agenda May Crimp Plans to Curb Deficit,' *Wall Street Journal*, 9 September 2004, p. A2, Craig Karmin in New York, Andrew Morse in Tokyo and Sara Calian in London, 'Dollar Bears Growl, End Hibernation of 2004,' *Wall Street Journal*, 28 October 2004. p. C.1.

18. Greg Ip, 'Bush Policy: Talk a Strong Dollar but Let it Slide; Tacitly Approved, Decline in Currency Aids Trade Gap while U.S. Works on Yuan,' *Wall Street Journal*, 10 November 2004, p. A1.

19. World Watch, *Wall Street Journal,* November 17, 2004, p. A14.

20. Laurence Norman, 'Dollar's Drop Will Continue, Traders Predict,' *Wall Street Journal*, 22 November 2004, C4; Michael Sesit, 'Going Global: Snow's Remarks Jolt Dollar; Currency's Woes Persist while Markets Sharpen Focus on Yuan,' *Wall Street Journal*, 18 November 2004, p. C20.

21. Federal Reserve Board, 'Remarks by Chairman Alan Greenspan at the European Banking Congress 2004, Frankfurt, Germany,' 19 November 2004.

22. Aaron Lucchetti, 'Bond Market Finally Flinches,' *Wall Street Journal*, 30 November 2004, C1.

23. It wasn't until 9 December 2004 that President Bush squelched the rumors by reappointing Mr Snow for another term.

24. European Central Bank, *Financial Stability Review*, 15 December 2004, pp. 9–10.

25. Greg Ip in Washington, G. Thomas Sims in Frankfurt and Andrew Morse in Tokyo, 'For Dollar Fears, Bush Prescribes Lower Deficit and Higher Rates; President Tells Berlusconi that It's up to Markets to Set Currency's Value,' *Wall Street Journal*, 17 December 2004, p. A2.

26. Robert Pringle and Nick Carver, *Reserve Management Trends 2005*, London: Central Banking Publications, January 2005, pp. 1–2.

27. Craig Karmin, 'Dollar Selloff Sends Shocks Through Markets; Stocks Plunge as Gold, Oil Surge Amid Concerns on Shift in Foreign Reserves,' *Wall Street Journal*, 23 February 2005, p. A1.

28. Report to the Secretary of the Treasury from the Treasury Borrowing Advisory Committee of the Bond Market Association, February 1, 2005, posted 2 February

2005 at www.bondmarkets.com.

29. James Areddy, Neil King, Jr., Mary Kissel, and Jason Dean, 'Behind Yuan Move, Open Debate and Closed Doors,' *Wall Street Journal*, 25 July 2005, p. A1.

30. Testimony of Chairman Alan Greenspan, Federal Reserve Board's Semiannual Monetary Policy Report to the Congress, Before the Committee on Financial Services, U.S. House of Representatives, 20 July 2005.

31. Remarks by Chairman Alan Greenspan, 'Globalization,' at the Council on Foreign Relations, New York, 10 March 2005. The two studies Mr Greenspan used for his smooth adjustment scenario were Caroline Freund, 'Current Account Adjustment in Industrialized Countries,' Board of Governors of the Federal Reserve System, International Finance Discussion Paper 692, December 2000; and Hilary Croke, Steven B. Kamin, and Sylvain Leduc, 'Financial Market Developments and Economic Activity during Current Account Adjustments in Industrial Economies,' Board of Governors of the Federal Reserve System, International Finance Discussion Paper 827, February 2005.

32. Paul A. Volcker, 'An Economy on Thin Ice,' *Washington Post*, 10 April 2005, p. B07.

33. Central banks of major oil exporting countries' Eurodollar deposits dropped from a valuation of 25.8 billion (SDR's) in 1977 to 14.9 billion SDR's in 1978, and in February 1978 these central banks became net sellers of US Treasury securities. IMF, *Annual Report*, 1979. From January 1977 to October 1978, US banks operating abroad reported the per cent of their assets denominated in dollars decline from 78 per cent to 73.6 per cent, while the per cent of their liabilities in dollars declined from 77 per cent to 72 per cent. Federal Reserve System, *Annual Statistical Digest*, 1974–78, Table 56.

34. As of July 2005, the last time the Federal Reserve Bank of New York intervened in currency markets to combat disorderly market conditions was March 1995 in the midst of the turbulence following the Mexican peso crisis.

35. Stephen Clarke, *Central Bank Cooperation 1924–31*, New York: Federal Reserve Bank of New York, 1967, p. 81.

36. Ibid. Robert G. Williams, 'The Political Economy of Hub Currency Defense: Sterling and the Dollar,' *Review of Radical Political Economy*, vol. 13, no. 3, Fall 1981.

37. Charles Coombs, *The Arena of International Finance*, New York: John Wiley, 1976, pp. 137–9.

38. Susan Strange, *Sterling and British Policy: A Political Study of an International Currency in Decline,* London: Oxford University Press, 1971, p. 75.

39. Williams, 'The Political Economy of Hub Currency Defense,' pp. 1–20.

40. About half the yen injected through foreign exchange interventions on behalf of the Ministry of Finance over this period was not 'sterilized' by the Bank of Japan but left in the banking system to prop up the Japanese money supply. For analysis of the monetary policy of quantitative easing when interest rates cannot be pushed below zero, see Ben Bernanke, Vincent Reinhart, and Brian Sack, 'Monetary Policy Alternatives at the Zero Bound: An Empirical Assessment,' Board of Governors of the Federal Reserve, Finance and Economics Discussion Series 2004–48, September 2004.

41. Because each month government securities mature and the treasury refinances them by issuing new securities, the whole debt structure of the government works like an adjustable-rate mortgage. The average interest rate paid on total government debt to the public declined from 7.6 per cent in 2000 to 4.4 per cent in 2004, allowing

for monthly payments to decline despite total debt levels increasing dramatically. In June 2001 10-year treasury notes yielded 5.27 per cent and by December 2004 they had fallen to 4.23 per cent. Interest rates on 3-year notes and 3-month bills fell even more dramatically. In tandem, conventional fixed-rate mortgages fell from 7.13 per cent in June 2001 to 5.75 per cent in December 2004, and the prime rate fell from 7.34 per cent to 5.15 per cent. Federal Reserve Bank of St. Louis, *Monetary Trends*, 18 July 2005 and 17 November 2003.

42. Japanese Ministry of Finance, *International Reserves/Foreign Currency Liquidity*, end of previous month statistics reported in the second week of each month. Yen-denominated security holdings converted into dollars at inter-bank exchange rates.

43. Report to the Secretary of the Treasury from the Treasury Borrowing Advisory Committee of the Bond Market Association, 1 February 2005.

44. The Federal Reserve Bank of New York, which has traditionally held the largest single portfolio of Treasury securities, will lend special issues to private broker/dealers when there is a shortage of a particular issue needed in the markets to settle certain contracts. This type of intervention keeps bottlenecks from forming that would sacrifice the liquidity reputation of US Treasuries, one of the key reasons the US Treasury has such an easy time auctioning securities.

45. Susan Strange, 'Sterling and British Policy: A Political View,' *International Affairs*, vol. 47, no. 2, April 2001, p. 311.

46. Jackie Calmes, 'Sharpening the Knife: As Bush Vows to Halve Deficit, Targets Already Feel Squeezed; Less Budget Funding for Aid, Education, Cities, Science; Bracing for the Boomers; Republican Governors Resist,' *Wall Street Journal*, 21 December 2004, p. A1.

47. Volcker, 'An Economy on Thin Ice,' p. B07.

48. The average duration on the federal debt has fallen from almost 6 years in 2000 to 4.4 years in 2005, meaning when interest rates rise the quickly retiring notes will have to be refinanced at higher rates, making total interest payments balloon. Greg Ip and Mark Whitehouse, 'The 30-year Tresury Bond Could Return, *Wall Street Journal*, 5 May 2005, p. C1.

49. Another way to look at it is that Social Security surpluses have financed the emergency supplemental defense measures of the past few years. Medicare and Civil Service Retirement entitlements erase budgetary benefits of Social Security's surpluses. See Congressional Budget Office, *Social Security FY 2003*.

50. Ruth Carlitz and Richard Kogan, 'CBO Data Show Tax Cuts Have Played Much Larger Role than Domestic Spending Increases in Fueling the Deficit,' Washington: Center on Budget and Policy Priorities, 31 January 2005.

51. Joel Friedman, 'Dividend and Capital Gains Tax Cuts Unlikely to Yield Touted Economic Gains,' Washington: Center on Budget and Policy Priorities, 10 March 2005, p. 6.

52. Department of Defense, *Top 100 Companies FY 2004*, Table 2, comparison with Department of Defense, *Top 100 Companies FY 2000*, Table 2.

Index